21099925.

WINGS
OF
FURY

Other Books by Robert K. Wilcox

Shroud
The Mysterious Deaths at Ann Arbor
Fatal Glimpse
Japan's Secret War
Scream of Eagles*
Wings of Fury*

*Published by POCKET BOOKS

WINGS
— OF —
FURY

From Vietnam to the Gulf War—The Astonishing
True Stories of America's Elite Fighter Pilots

ROBERT K. WILCOX

POCKET BOOKS
New York London Toronto Sydney Tokyo Singapore

POCKET BOOKS, a division of Simon & Schuster Inc.
1230 Avenue of the Americas, New York, NY 10020

Library of Congress Cataloging-in-Publication Data

Wilcox, Robert K.
  Wings of fury / Robert K. Wilcox.
    p.   cm.
  ISBN 0-671-74793-2
    1. Fighter plane combat—United States—History.   I. Title.
UG703.W55   1997
358.43´4´0973—dc20

                                             96-42256
                                             CIP

First Pocket Books hardcover printing May 1997

10   9   8   7   6   5   4   3   2   1

To my mother,
Agnes Kalleen Wilcox

Acknowledgments

THIS BOOK WAS harder to write than I thought it would be, but it was a lot of fun, primarily because of the subject and the people I was dealing with. In addition to those written about or mentioned in the text, I would like to thank the following:

My longtime agents and good friends, Jim and Liz Trupin, of Jet Literary Associates Inc. They sold the concept with only a one-page letter from me and for enough money to get the job done.

Ralph Platt, my able transcriber and air advisor. Ralph, a former air force pilot, always came through when I asked him to help, regardless of the difficulties of my requests.

Colonel Tom Hornung and Major Tony Cherney of the air force's Western Region Office of Public Affairs in Los Angeles helped me get started with the air force. Jim Ruliffson, Captain Rich Potter, and Commander Skip Sayers did the same for me with the navy. Once started, things pretty much open up.

There were many I interviewed, mostly fighter pilots, who did not make it into the story. But what they told me certainly helped shape it. These men include: Guy Brubaker, Ted Carson, Ron Dorn, Chris Greene, Colonel Lawrence W. Green, Jr., who gave me an excellent Red Flag briefing, Jon Hults, Brian Neeves, Jim

Papageorge, Colonel Rick Parsons, Bill Rudy, Kyle Skalisky, J. D. Smidt, Jon Snyder, Dave Stillings, Mike Wallace, John Wilcox, and Ted Winters.

Lieutenant Don Collins, a public information officer, helped me at Langley Air Force Base.

Midway through the writing, when I realized I needed help in getting information through the Freedom of Information Act, Gary Stern, of the American Civil Liberties Union in Washington, and Paul Hoffman, of the organization's Los Angeles office, put me in touch with Penelope Glass, a skillful and gracious attorney, who, with ACLU backing, instituted a suit on my behalf.

Although we are still in the midst of that lengthy process, and probably will not be able to utilize the results in this book, I want to thank each of them and stress that without such help, authors such as myself are basically wanna-be Davids against a much more powerful and skillful Goliath than the Bible portrays.

Bego, my wife, deserves mention here. She's always been supportive and when I'm in doubt I count on her reading of my pages to set me straight.

Finally, I'd like to thank my editor, Paul McCarthy. Paul appreciates fighter aviation as I do. He gave me the time I needed. His editing was insightful and helped shape the work for the better.

Onward and upward.

Contents

INTRODUCTION

I'M NOT A FLYER, but I always wanted to be. I can't remember why I failed the aviator's written test the air force sergeant gave me back in 1967, right after I'd graduated from the University of Florida. I thought I'd done well. So I became an air force information officer instead. That was during the Vietnam War.

But I always kept my interest, eventually getting to write a book about fighter pilots in Vietnam, *Scream of Eagles*, which came out in 1990—just before the Gulf War.

A lot had happened in fighter aviation since the late 1960s and early 1970s, the period I had concentrated on in the book. I knew our fighter pilots were well trained as the Gulf War heated up, but I'll never forget that day (early morning in Saudi) when co-workers came running into my office and said, "They've started!"

No one really knew what was going to happen.

I turned on the television and began a vigil that wouldn't end for days, whether I was in the office or at home. Being fighter interested, I marveled at the crab-looking F-117 Stealth's early performance. But I also couldn't figure out why they were calling it a fighter. It was a bomber and was bombing.

The fighters were elsewhere—nimble, ferocious gun-and-

1

missile platforms hunting for kills or patrolling the skies, making sure enemy fighters didn't interfere with the bombers. At least that's the way it appeared on television.

But there was a much bigger fighter story.

By the end of the war, these American fighters had posted an astounding kill ratio of something like thirty-five to zero, although there were later rumors that one U.S. fighter might have been shot down by an Iraqi pilot. Presumably, the enemy had not beaten a single U.S. pilot in air-to-air combat, while it appeared the American fighter pilots had downed every Iraqi jet they had tangled with (a presumption I later found to be wrong).

The interesting thing was that the fighter pilots were not usually identified—and if they were, only by call sign. "Disco" and "Vegas" come to mind. Fearful of retaliation on their families by terrorists, they were shunning publicity. Depictions showed them handsome, confident, articulate. Who were these new lions? I wondered. How had they gotten where they were? Were they the same as the rare breed I'd encountered in writing *Scream of Eagles*, which was the story of the founding of Topgun during the Vietnam War.

The way to find out was to find the pilots, interview them, get to know them—if I could. But most were away in the war. Even if I could find them, there was no guarantee they would talk to me. And there was always the formidable obstacle of the military's office of "public information," a misnomer for the officers and noncoms whose express job it is to keep in-depth information on military affairs away from the public.

I understand the need to keep the public at bay, but dealing with information officers' requirements, forms, shallow press releases, and interminable bureaucratic delays is a sure road to failure—which, of course, is the point. The military has little use for or understanding of nonfiction book writing, which is the highest form of journalism because it goes the deepest.

So a hard problem was getting access. And once I got that—by calling friends I'd made while writing *Scream*—the hardest part of all was finding the best fighter pilots, whom the book was going to be about; not all the best, which was impossible, but a good sampling of them. There's an unofficial pecking order, not throughout the services but within each, usually pinpointed geographically; that is, by base or region (although some of the pilots you'll read about beginning in Chapter 1, like Dale Snod-grass, are known service wide). The pecking order is generally known on the bases, and you can learn about it if you ask at the right places, like the officers' club.

Fighter pilots are notoriously egotistical—especially about their own fighting abilities—so you have to use some judgment there, too. But eventually you hear the same names enough times, or go to the places where only the best are serving—like Topgun for the navy and Fighter Weapons School for the air force—and you can come up with a pretty good selection.

Both schools were visited and are written about in this book.

Eventually, I was able to get a pretty good sampling of some of the best, a good number of whom are profiled in the first half of this book, as well as to zero in on an air force squadron with the most kills in the Gulf War. The 58th "Gorillas" from Eglin Air Force Base, Florida, was a ringer squadron with some of the best fighter pilots in the United States. As you will read in the second half of the book, the job they did was as responsible for America's spectacular victory in the Gulf as any segment of the military that has been credited.

But back to the task.

Not only did I want to find out about and profile some of our best fighter pilots—taking them through the Gulf War—but I also wanted to put their stories into the proper context—which, to me, from what I already knew, was the continuum that had started with the Vietnam War and moved through the last two decades to the present.

As you'll read in the main text, the Vietnam War was the crucible that forged the Gulf War victory. Fighter pilots were not trained well for the Vietnam War, and the mistakes made there—including the shootdowns, deaths, and imprisonments of U.S. fighter pilots—were the rallying cry for fighter pilots—air force, navy, and Marine—who emerged from that conflict and were given the task of training the country's future fighter drivers.

These veterans—and in some cases their students, who, as time went on, became teachers as well—were determined not to repeat the fighter training mistakes of pre-Vietnam. They re-solved to make sure that future U.S. fighter pilots knew how to dogfight, a skill that had been neglected in training after the Ko-rean War because the predominant opinion among "experts" at that time was that missiles were going to eliminate dogfighting from the air arena forever.

So this story, while mostly concentrating on the hearts, skills, and minds of today's fighter pilots, actually starts in the late 1960s in Vietnam, alludes to that war's legacy in the 1970s, and then begins in earnest in 1981 with a never-before-seen look at the first shootdown of enemy planes by U.S. fighters since Vietnam. That shootdown, seen through the eyes of Dale Snodgrass, serves as a prelude to the rest of the decade—with its conflicts and fighter innovations—as we follow some of our best fighter pilots as they grow, learn, and, finally, test themselves in the Gulf War.

To personalize the Vietnam legacy, I've early on told the story of Joe Satrapa, a gutsball navy fighter pilot legend whose fighter pilot life started in Vietnam and ended right after the Gulf War, thus spanning the time period this book is concerned with. Satrapa, like all other good fighter pilots, lived a personal quest to shoot down enemy planes—"bag a MiG," in the current parlance—as a way of validating all he'd been and lived for professionally.

Certainly, the quest to get a MiG is a major theme of this book. Some pilots do and some don't. Often success or failure is simply a matter of being in the right place at the right time, for the chances are not what they were in World War II or Korea. But proving oneself in mortal combat—skillwise; heartwise; often in subliminal ways, good and bad, that even the pilots themselves don't always appear to be aware of—is a continuing theme through the book because it is a theme in the lives of most fighter pilots.

From Snodgrass and Satrapa, whom, like all the rest, I try to follow through the decade to the Gulf War, we will meet other top fighter pilots in the air force and navy as they go through some of the most exciting and meaningful episodes in their professional lives. These include bouts with deadly "vertigo," the disorientation in bad weather or at night that is a chief noncombat killer of fighter pilots, and launches from and recoveries to carriers under dangerous and scary conditions.

We fly with young Rob Graeter, who will later get two kills in the Gulf War, on his first real combat mission, protecting search planes looking for survivors of the 1983 Russian shootdown of a

Korean Air Lines passenger plane; and experience near death in separate mishaps with naval fighter pilots Brian Fitzpatrick and Mark Fox, both of whom go on to play prominent roles in the Gulf War.

In the middle of the decade, we see a major change in fighter tactics that affected all fighter pilots and dogfighting itself. Shooting missiles beyond visual range with good chance of success became a reality for both sides—the United States and the Soviet Union—and thus caused our fighter pilots to change the way they approached the arena.

We fly with them in the preliminaries to the Gulf War, see how the 58th is readied for such a conflict, and then fly with them into harm's way—the first few days of the Gulf War, when no one really knew what was going to happen and the dangers and fears were palpable.

I've tried to personalize the story by going beyond the fighter pilots' jobs and machines to show who they are on a human level. What their lives are like. What they care most about; their ups, their downs. Who they really are.

While the air force and navy are amply covered, the Marines, possessing the smallest group of fighter pilots of the three, are not. Early on, I heard how good Marine fighter pilots were and wanted to include them, but after spending literally three years hunting down, traveling to, and interviewing air force and navy pilots—amassing over two hundred hours of taped interviews—there just wasn't enough time or money left to go further.

However, one Marine, Chuck Magill, was flying with the 58th when it forged its great record—a near-moment-by-moment account of which occupies the last 40 percent of the book—and he and his exploits are covered. I hope that suffices, because the Marines have always had a great fighter tradition, and now—flying the F/A-18 Hornet and AV-8 Harrier, the jet that can lift off and hover like a helicopter—they are certainly continuing that tradition.

However, no Marines, other than Magill, got air-to-air kills during the Gulf War, as their planes concentrated mostly on bombing, and my focus was on "getting MiGs."

Most of all, I think this story, especially as it moves through the 1980s, shows how important the pilot—as opposed to the plane or branch of service—is in air-to-air combat. One fighter pilot told me that at the top—that is, among the best of the best of them—you could put any pilot in any one of the jets and, with a little orientation (including carrier landing for the air force pilots) he'd do just as well as he had in his own jet.

At the top, the skill and spirit are what counts—not the uniform.

The men written about here are a rare, elite breed. They are like professional all-star athletes but, on the average, are more mature—mainly, I would guess, because of the more dangerous nature of the "sport" they are in. As they like to say, in their league there are no points for second place.

So, at its essence, this is a behind-the-scenes story of the best of those little-known men who fly and fight our fastest, most deadly jet fighters—the F-14 Tomcat, F-15 Eagle, F-16 Viper, and F/A-18 Hornet. It's timely, for these men are in our aircraft carriers now, or on alert fields waiting to scramble. Some have assumed higher positions of authority for the air wars of the future, or have gotten out and now fly in the Reserves or National Guard because they didn't want to end their flying with a desk job or, at best, reduced flying hours.

They all love flying fighters, which is not to say just flying.

They are men of action more than words. So buckle your chin strap and hold on. Like the lawmen who built and tamed the early Wild West, these fighter pilots should make Americans— and all lovers of individualism and courage—proud. The horses are now mighty jets spewing fire, and the six-guns have given way to missiles and 20-millimeter cannons.

But the tradition lives.

BOOK I

TO FLY AND FIGHT

1

DALE "SNORT" SNODGRASS was pumped. He felt the way he had before his college swim meets. Even more. Anxiety and anticipation. Hard to describe really. This might be it, what he'd been hoping and training for, the fighter pilot's Super Bowl and Olympics all rolled into one.

It was just before dawn, August 19, 1981, in the hazy, daybreak skies off Libya, and the thirty-two-year-old veteran F-14 pilot, waiting to launch above the warming Gulf of Sidra, had a real chance of bagging a MiG.

Although he'd looked cool going through the prelaunch ritual of checking his plane and then taxiing the big fighter onto the catapult, Snodgrass was excited—excited beyond the normal apprehension of being hurled off the carrier's deck by a steam engine that routinely launched multiton warplanes like they were made of paper.

Being a "MiG killer" was what fighter piloting was really all about. There weren't many MiG killers around anymore. It didn't matter how much you'd flown, how many times you'd chalked up victories in the practice arena, or worn the reputation with silent pride as others stared at you, knowing you were the one to

beat. Fighting for real was the ultimate test, the validation pilots like Snodgrass craved.

His most terrifying moments would come a decade later leading a squadron into "Desert Storm," America's Gulf War with Iraq. But right now he knew nothing of that. Today's mission promised to take him as close to combat as he'd ever been.

Yesterday had been one of the tensest days for navy fighter pilots since the end of the Vietnam War. As many as thirty-six times, fighter crews from the *Nimitz* and *Forrestal* had intercepted sections (pairs) of Libyan MiG, Sukhoi, and Mirage jet fighters from bases near the Libyan coast. Not since the Iranian hostage crisis had things been so tense. Bengházi had Russian-built MiG-23s. Tripoli had the French Mirages and the newer MiG-25s. Hostile intercepts were nothing new, but in yesterday's numbers, they had been record.

The F-14 Tomcats were under strict rules of engagement (ROE). They could not fire unless fired upon. And that had not happened—at least officially. So most of the engagements had been brief jousting duels—the Libyans, holding the cards, trying fruitlessly to get an advantage; the Americans, better trained and flying deadlier jets, keeping them at bay with itchy trigger fingers.

The year 1981 was the twilight of a heyday. Because of lessons learned in the Vietnam War, American fighter pilots in all U.S. services were among the best trained, best equipped, and most deadly in the world. Their radar-guided and heat-seeking missiles could be shot from greater distances and at more target aspects (including head-on, or "face," shots) than enemy missiles, which were generally reliable only when shot at the "rear quarter" (or "six o'clock") of the adversary. This meant navy flyers could often toy with adversaries like a mongoose with a cobra—at least that had been the case through much of the 1970s.

But that superiority was waning. Some of the Libyan Mirages they'd been sparring with were believed to be carrying the new French-built Matra Magic 550, a heat-seeker that was nearing "all-aspect" capability, meaning it wasn't restricted to the traditional stern shot. It could be fired at almost any aspect of a target and home in on it. The Americans had to be on their guard. And, in fact, Snodgrass later wrote to his father that Naval Intelligence, probably interpreting E-2 radar plane data, believed that

during one of the previous afternoon's engagements a MiG-25 might have fired a missile head-on from eighteen miles out, although neither of the F-14 crews in the area had seen it.

But the possible shot was one of the reasons today promised more.

There had been tensions between the United States and Libya almost since Libyan leader Colonel Muammar Gadhafi had come to power following a revolutionary coup in 1969. In 1973, Libyan Mirages had shot at a U.S. Air Force plane Gadhafi said was spying. Angered by continued American surveillance of Libya and support of Israel, Gadhafi, himself an American-trained pilot, had allowed the destruction of the U.S. Embassy in Tripoli in 1979, following the Iranian revolution. But President Jimmy Carter, preoccupied with American hostages in Iran, had not responded.

Most recently Gadhafi had warned U.S. ships and planes to stay out of the Gulf of Sidra and drawn a much-publicized "Line of Death" across the Gulf's entrance. The line stretched roughly from Benghazi to Tripoli. Any U.S. ships or planes crossing it would be attacked, he'd warned.

The warning was all new American President Ronald Reagan had needed. In early August 1981, he had given the Libyan leader public notice that the U.S. Sixth Fleet would be conducting missile practice in the Gulf. The operation was code-named "Guns of August." It just as well could have been named "High Noon." Reagan wanted Gadhafi to "know we had no intention of honoring his territorial water claims," Snodgrass later wrote to his father.

Snodgrass, watching the signaling deck crew position his big Tomcat, had been in the thick of the jousting.

Returning from an early morning combat air patrol (CAP) station over the Gulf two days prior, he and Commander Hank Kleeman, commanding officer of VF-41, one of the *Nimitz*'s two fighter squadrons, had almost been sneak-shot by two fast-moving MiG-23s. After orbiting the CAP for over an hour that morning, they'd decided nothing was going to happen and had started back for the *Nimitz*. To conserve fuel, they'd exited slow.

That had been a mistake.

With their backs turned, the Libyans, seeing a chance for a hit, had come out after them—and at a much faster speed. It was a smart tactic. The distinctly swing-winged "Floggers," as NATO designates the MiG-23s, had heat-seekers, and the Tomcats were showing red-hot exhaust.

Luckily, the relief CAP, two F-14s from VF-84, the *Nimitz*'s other fighter squadron, spotted the trailing MiGs on radar before they (the MiGs) were in shooting range, and gave warning. After initial confusion because, at first, Kleeman thought the relief CAP was mistakenly tracking the F-14s, Snodgrass and the CO had broken back hard into the MiGs and the Libyans had fled.

"Not a great spot to see your first MiG," later wrote Snodgrass, "3 miles in trail at 6 o'clock." But he and Kleeman had relearned a lesson: Never relax until you're safely back on ship.

The next afternoon, Snodgrass and another Tomcat from VF-41 had engaged two more Libyans. They were in nimble, delta-winged Mirage 5s—with the Magic 550s—and chose to dogfight after being spotted.

Merging with the intercepting Tomcats, the lead Mirage had darted high; his wingman, low. "For Ragheads, they maneuvered quite well," wrote Snodgrass. But he and his wingman, Stocky Smith, had quickly gotten behind them, pulled to within guns range, which was about as close as you can get, and stayed on their tails.

Snodgrass's young backseater, RIO (Radar Intercept Officer) Dan Cannan, call sign "Vegas," had had the composure during the wild ride to snap a picture of one of the Mirages.

That fight had really gotten Snodgrass's adrenaline flowing. Even though the Mirages were covered, Smith's "bogey," as they commonly called hostile aircraft, had aimed its weapons at Snodgrass several times as it flashed by, trying to shake Smith. Snodgrass was sure the Libyan would have fired had he not been covered by Smith. He hadn't liked having to hold his shots while being so vulnerable.

But that was past. He had no real fear of combat, just of making a mistake, botching his chance today. The Libyans, he believed, were, as a group, mediocre pilots, with maybe a few good ones sprinkled in. It was rumored they had some Syrian and North Korean combat veterans flying for them, but so far, he'd seen nothing to compare with some of the better U.S. pilots he'd routinely beaten in training fights back in the States.

But training fights didn't include the shooting of live ammunition.

Snodgrass was now positioned on the catapult, the first step in the actual launch. With a finger, he flicked a cockpit switch, making the Tomcat's nosegear compress, or "kneel," as they called it. The spring housing over the strut descended approximately fourteen inches, crouching the plane like a cat ready to pounce. This would give it a leap at the end of the three-hundred-foot, two-and-a-half-second launch when the sudden steam thrust abruptly halted at the end of the deck and the housing sprang back up to lift the nose into the air.

Lift was critical at that millisecond. The Tomcat would need all the help it could get. Otherwise it might plummet into the sea, just thirty-five or so feet below, leaving only seconds in terms of reaction time.

Few survived such crashes.

This launch was a real fighter show, the decks cleared of most all other aircraft except the Tomcats, the tanker-configured A-6s and A-7s, and the radar-laden E-2 Hawkeyes. There was nothing for the attack pilots to do but watch, which pleased Snodgrass as he sat high in his cockpit, waiting, because there was always a rivalry between the bomber and fighter crews.

He felt a familiar jolt as the scrambling, green-shirted "hookup man," wearing mouse-eared noise protectors and large, bug-eyed goggles, clamped the thirty-two-ton, heavily loaded fighter to the "shuttle," the relatively small, visible part of the catapult barrel, which, like a giant shotgun beneath the track on the deck, would "shoot" the Tomcat into dark dawn sky.

The lack of light meant that this would be a night shot, the hardest kind. The darkness would hamper Snodgrass's ability to gauge depth and speed with his eyes, and put even more emphasis on instruments, which were always hard to read in the critical milliseconds after the violent, body-quaking shot.

On the side of the darkened deck, perhaps thirty feet away and shielded, the catapult officer figured the exact blast of steam the Tomcat would require. With the push of a button he would signal release of the awesome steam bullet that would come rushing into the barrel. Each aircraft was different—as was each launch, because of the immediate environment. The Tomcat's gross weight, which was approximately 62,000 pounds with a full load of missiles, bullets, and gas; the wind over the deck, which was about twenty knots; and the temperature, a balmy cool, all figured into the calculation.

When he had it, and all figures were confirmed with Snodgrass, the officer signaled with an amber deck light for Snodgrass to cycle up his engines to full military power (the highest setting they could reach without afterburner). As he did that, Snodgrass also rotated the control stick in his lap to all sides in order to move all outside flying surfaces so the scampering, crouching deck crew could hurriedly check all around the straining airplane for fuel and hydraulic leaks, malfunctioning parts, breaks, cracks, bad engine noise, or any other problem.

It wouldn't be long now, he knew.

Signaled that everything was thumbs-up outside, Snodgrass "staged up" to full afterburner. He needed as much power as possible on the launch in case one of his engines quit. The F-14 quivered in harness—a massive sprinter at the block, a monster arrow arcing the bow—its screaming engines firing heat waves and flame trails onto a large metal blast deflector raised at an angle behind it.

On deck, the noise was deafening. Thundering. It roared and vibrated throughout the nuclear carrier and out over the Mediterranean dawn. But Snodgrass only dimly perceived it, feeling more than hearing it; his bright red helmet, dark in the burgeoning light, admitting only the incessant deep *whooooosh* of the encapsulating cockpit's air conditioning.

Everything was ready. Actually quiet to his ears. In a few seconds, he would hunch slightly forward, tensing his body for the negative "push" that would thrust nearly a ton of force against him and Cannan, who was doing the same thing in the backseat. So powerful was the thrust, or "pull," of the shuttle—to contrast it with the "push" in its wake—that it would actually dent their eyeballs, if ever so minutely, and had been calculated to measure approximately eighty tons.

In daylight, he would have saluted, touching his hand to his helmet as a signal that he was ready. But in the vanishing darkness, he turned on the Tomcat's outside lights.

They tweaked like tiny beacons of the mayhem to come.

There was no stopping it now.

14

The catapult officer made one final check and pushed the button.

They were off—the chance Snodgrass had so long been waiting for.

Nearing his prime, a graduate of the navy's Fighter Weapons School—Topgun, for short—Snodgrass was one of the chosen, the best of the best. Not every navy fighter pilot got to go to Topgun. The idea was to send the squadron's best young pilots and RIOs so they could return and teach the rest. Snodgrass, a "natural," had been sent as soon as he had been eligible. Individualistic, athletic, fiercely competitive in the air, he resembled a tall Robert Redford, even to his longer-than-average hair. He had loved the thrill of flying as long as he could remember.

The son of a Long Island aviation executive and former Marine Corsair and test pilot, he'd been a nationally ranked surfer and all-American swimmer in New Jersey, where he'd gone to prep school. His father had taken him up in private planes when he was a youngster and taught him to hunt and shoot, including with a bow and arrow, which he preferred because of the challenge.

"A fighter pilot is a hunter," he says. "You've got to be patient. I tried [skeet] shooting competitively and found it came naturally. . . . It's a hand-eye-timing-depth-perception-type problem . . . good fighter pilots normally have great visual acuity . . . the hunting also relates to flying. You have to be sensually aware of a lot of different things going on . . . be able to pick them up and react to them."

He went to the University of Minnesota on complementary Navy ROTC and swimming scholarships. He competed against champion swimmers like Olympic gold medalist Mark Spitz, made it to the NCAA finals several times, and graduated in 1973, too late to fly in the Vietnam War, which he'd hoped to do.

Basic flight school at Pensacola—the course depicted in the movie *An Officer and a Gentleman*—wasn't "overly rigorous" but "very competitive," he recalls. The navy was gearing down after the war and had only one F-14 pilot's seat to offer per class of roughly ninety students. He got sick briefly, but based on grades and overall ranking, he got the second set of F-14 orders offered. "That was probably my biggest success in life up to that date. . . . All through flight school, I remember, I wanted the fastest plane we had, the fastest fighter we had."

At that time, early in 1974, the Tomcat was just being introduced

15

to the fleet. It was a long-awaited answer to all the Vietnam-era problems fighter pilots had encountered. Sleek, bubble-canopied for better sight, able to carry as much firepower, in its new Phoenix missiles, as a six-plane World War II fighter squadron, the F-14's innovative, movable swing wings gave it both speed (swept back) and maneuverability (extended).

Along with the air force's F-15, it was one of the world's hot new air machines.

It had been during his F-14 training at NAS (Naval Air Station) Miramar, California, that he had first been introduced to ACM (air combat maneuvering), what the layman calls "dogfighting." Performing maneuvers under the tutelage of an instructor, he found he had an aptitude. "I remember it was just something that came naturally to me."

Good dogfighting takes more than desire, courage, and flying skills. Gifted pilots have a rare talent that enables them to make sense out of a huge, three-dimensional chunk of sky in which other jets, trying to best them, are wildly maneuvering at speeds sometimes approximating those of fired bullets. Somehow, in the millisecond-long glimpses of almost imperceptible targets afforded them, and despite crushing G forces, fear (hopefully controlled), and confusion, the really talented can deduce enough hair-trigger information to project their opponent's travel in the next fifteen to thirty seconds and make the appropriate countermoves.

Fighter pilots call this ability "situational awareness," or "SA." Snodgrass had it, although at the time he didn't have enough experience to really know it.

"I went out against instructors . . . TOPGUN pilots in F-5s and T-38s. . . . I didn't really know exactly what I did, but it worked. . . . It was kind of like I was bred or born to do it."

He had been the first student to land a Tomcat on a carrier, one of the most precise and steely-nerved skills in piloting in the world. Up until his class, only carrier-seasoned pilots had been allowed to "trap" (referring to the arresting cables they must hook with almost pinpoint accuracy) the new fighters. And while he thinks landing skills are paramount for a navy fighter pilot, as a young JO (junior officer) reporting to his first squadron, the VF-142 "Ghostriders," he chiefly remembers concentrating on ACM.

"I always had my ears open, listening for some little technique or something that worked or didn't work. . . . If somebody I knew was a good driver was saying something, even if I wasn't involved in the conversation, I'd try and pick up as much as I could."

But he worked on his landing skills, too. "You can't fight again if you can't land," he says. And a year and a half into his first tour, after a cruise in the Mediterranean, he had the best landing grades in the squadron, competing against pilots with much greater experience. Early on, he'd volunteered to learn to be a squadron LSO (landing signal officer), one of the pilots who directed the "recoveries at the back of the boat," as they called carrier landings. He'd qualified faster than any of the others.

His fighting skills advanced rapidly, too. Whereas they were usually handed down piecemeal from lead to wingman in a long process of trial and error usually spanning several cruises of hands-on training, he was routinely beating his seniors on his first cruise. They'd awarded him flight lead during his first cruise. Like the LSO qualification, it wasn't normally done that fast.

"Dale was every bit as good as any of the older guys," recalls Navy Captain Dave Walker, then Snodgrass's flight lead and now an astronaut. "He had better judgment in the air than most people of his age . . . was real strong and athletic . . . the size Tom Cruise would have liked to have been during that silly movie [Paramount's 1986 *Top Gun*]. . . . He was nice looking, well spoken. . . . In another era, I'm sure he would have been a knight, or cavalryman, if it were medieval or Indian wars we were fighting."

Snodgrass wasn't cocky, he just had "honest arrogance," as Walker called it, "which I liked. . . . I don't have much use for false modesty. . . . But he could back up what he said. I'd never call him a braggart. . . . It was self-confidence. . . . He didn't make mistakes twice." He was a voracious learner because he loved what he was doing. "You've got to love it," said Walker, "because it's so hard on you. . . . [ACM] is the toughest game really there is. I mean it's like aerial chess. You can go a long way on plain old natural ability . . . but unless you're a real student, you're not going to be the best."

Snodgrass was building a reputation, a "bag of tricks," both of which stemmed from his situational awareness.

"Snort had an uncanny ability to know everything that had

17

happened in a fight and re-create it in the debrief," recalls Cannan, who later became a pilot and practiced against Snodgrass after leaving his backseat. "He knew more about what you'd done
than you did, and you'd been flying the airplane. . . . He didn't
rub it in either. A lot of guys made enemies that way. But Snort
was very diplomatic and soft in telling others what they did
wrong. He didn't have to impress people with how good he was.
They knew it."

There were a myriad of variables to recognize in a dogfight:
type of threat; speed or "energy" of the adversary; weapons available; and attitude and projected position of an opponent, which
indicate where he is headed and whether he is about to take a
shot. For instance, if a plane were zooming up against gravity, it
was losing energy and would be less able to maneuver and thus
be more vulnerable. But coming down, it would gain the energy
back.

All these variables were flashed to the pilot in milliseconds,
often at distances hard to see, and were often disguised by the
opponent in order to deceive.

And you also had to know everything about your own jet in order to take advantage of what you saw.

Snodgrass: "I'd pass the guy, and the next time I'd see him, I
could tell with a glance how fast he was going. . . . It's a relative
motion thing. You know what his airplane is capable of doing.
You know what he did to get to that point. You've seen it before.
So you say, okay . . . that was a six-G turn. . . . He did it level,
therefore he lost 150 knots. . . . Of course, I know what I did and
what is available to me, so I can work him [a few more turns]. . . .
I'd wind up with a slight to significant energy advantage."

Victory was probably just a matter of seconds.

But if the opponent was good, and he was able to evade the
distant missile shots, the two planes would fly closer and that
probably meant a "slow fight": two jets swirling, entwining, so
close they could almost touch each other, each looking to "spit"
the other out in order to take a shot.

The one-versus-one fight, especially slow fighting, made reputations. Airplane advantages tended to dissipate; pilot skills pre-
vailed. Since jets are harder to turn at slow speeds, the chances
of dangerous stall, spin, or departure (going out of control) increased. Stick and rudder skills were paramount. The good

fighter pilot was furiously working his hands and feet, performing unbelievable controlling moves, staying close, waiting for the other to make the mistake.

They'd come to call Snodgrass a "Golden Arm," a name that made reference to those skills.

Snodgrass: "If I'm going against a very good guy in a very good airplane, generally I'd try and get the fight slow as soon as tactically possible . . . take out a lot of the other airplane's potential advantages and get it down into what we call a 'phone booth'. . . . I'm full flaps, 150 to 225 knots . . . my turn radius is a lot smaller . . . [the full flaps are] a semiprohibited maneuver [in the F-14] . . . but I do it [against a more maneuverable jet] in order to force it into a guns versus guns arena . . . outradius him . . ."

Against a lesser airplane or driver, where he felt he didn't have to worry about nullifying advantages, he might opt for "a little more sustained-energy-type fight"—turn at high speeds with the bandit, eating angles, conserving his own energy, while making the bogey expend his. Then, once he knew he had the advantage, he'd "extend up into the vertical and force the slow fight from above."

Meat on the table.

Going into his second cruise, with five-hundred hours in the Tomcat and the mounting accolades, he "pretty much" felt "king of the hill," which was "probably the most dangerous time in my career . . . because you feel experienced enough and you're confident enough, but maybe not as mature as you should be. . . . I felt invincible. . . . I could do anything in an F-14."

He remembers roaring into the landing break (turning down toward the runway) above NAS (Naval Air Station) Oceana, Virginia, at 600-plus knots, which was wildly faster than allowed. "The RIO passed out from the G and I wound up very tight at the 180 and basically did a split-S [snapped the plane's nose from up to down] to land [a dangerous maneuver at that low altitude]."

The landing was perfect, but reaction to it from senior officers wasn't. He got ten days confined to quarters, which was two weeks less than he got at Rota, Spain, for a more devious stunt.

Rota, a U.S. naval base in the south, near Gibraltar, had a 10,000-foot runway that dipped at its end. He took off and, instead of going upward, did a "low transition," hugging the runway.

"I'm about five to ten feet off the deck . . . they can't see me at all . . . I pass the end of the runway, raging out across this field." It's dry, red clay. "All they see in the tower is this giant cloud of red dust." There was a low undercast. "I pitched straight up into the clouds and they thought I'd crashed . . . all the trucks and crash crews came roaring out . . ."

Unfortunately, the base CO had been in the "hold short" behind him, waiting to take off.

He'd gotten away with other stunts: flying so close to the ocean he'd been able to drag his tailhook in it; using sonic boom to shatter windows in Sigonella, Italy; and almost totally destroying a Tomcat engine while setting a personal altitude and speed record on a postmaintenance check flight.

"They were always trying to keep me under control. . . . I was a 'shit hot JO' flying a 'shit hot' machine. . . . I'd say at that point my ego was probably as high as it ever got."

But he'd "always known when to pull it back, toe the line, so to speak, when I had to."

He still got picked for Topgun, and following his second cruise, when it was time for his first shore duty, he'd been assigned as LSO training officer and, later, tactics phase leader at Oceana's VF-101, the Atlantic Fleet's replacement squadron. The squadron furnished new F-14 pilots and backseaters to the fleet.

"All of a sudden I'm an instructor, taking brand-new pilots out to the boat and getting them carrier qualified. Then I became tactics phase leader, indoctrinating them into fighting the airplane. . . . It was a fairly big responsibility. . . . I couldn't afford to be a knucklehead anymore."

LSO and tactics leader were real plums. But the jobs meant he had to start thinking of safety and the cost of losing one of those $30 million jets. Married, with one young daughter and a second child on the way, he'd given up his motorcycle and bought a more family-oriented BMW.

In late 1980, as proof of his transformation, he'd been made Air Wing 8 LSO aboard the nuclear carrier *Nimitz*, the world's largest warship. CAG (carrier air group commander) LSO was the ranking landing signal officer on the flight deck, a position normally given to senior lieutenant commanders (he was still a junior lieutenant commander). It meant he'd be recommending to the air wing commander, carrier CO, even the admiral at times, whether the ship should launch, for instance, in stormy seas. He was barely thirty-one.

To fulfill his flying requirements, he'd taken a slot with Kleeman's VF-41, nicknamed "The Black Aces," which, along with VF-84, had been part of the *Nimitz* force that had launched the aborted helicopter attempt to rescue U.S. hostages from Iran in April 1980. The squadrons were to fly cover. In that sense, as Snodgrass streaked up to "tank" (take airborne fuel) before going on to their CAP station, they had a score to settle with Gadhafi, whom they regarded as part of a growing but minimal Arab threat (the Soviets were still the main enemy).

Despite his charmed rise, Snodgrass had had an experience every LSO dreads.

Working backup on the stern during night exercises four months prior to arriving off Libya, he'd watched helplessly as a Marine EA-6B Prowler, packed with equipment for its radar-jamming mission, came screaming toward the 600-foot deck and made a sudden nervous correction that put it high and off centerline.

Day carrier landing was hard enough, the margin for error being only a few feet. At night it was likened to hurtling through space, a few stars (deck lights) the only reference.

By the time the controlling LSO was radioing "Power," the Prowler, its three crewmen bracing, was already hitting a row of A-7s with its wing and spinning at 145 miles per hour toward fueling Tomcats at the other end of the deck. It crashed into one, which exploded and dominoed into the others.

"Fuel tanks became incendiary bombs, ejector seats blasted from burning planes," missiles triggered, and "a superheated machine gun opened fire spontaneously," reported *Time* magazine in its June 8, 1981, issue. The Prowler crew died sometime between the first crash and explosion, and eleven deck personnel, including three VF-41 sailors, burned to death in the ensuing battle against the fire and explosions. When the holocaust was finally extinguished, nearly fifty others were injured.

It was the worst carrier disaster since the *Forrestal* fire in 1967.

Snodgrass and Cannan neared their CAP. Mark Wheeler, "Wheels," with Jim McMinn in his backseat, was their wingman. They had originally briefed to be Kleeman's wingman, but their tanker had malfunctioned and they hadn't been gassed when the ship radioed that it needed someone at CAP 4, the farthest station south.

CAP 4, out in the middle of the gulf, was the most isolated station, and therefore the easiest for the Libyans to sneak by. Carrier defense was the primary job of the fighters. *Nimitz*, getting nervous about the growing daylight, wanted F-14s out there pronto.

Kleeman had jumped at the call, taking Larry Muczynski, an already tanked pilot, with him, leaving Wheeler to accompany Snodgrass to CAP 5, one of the two western stations near Tripoli.

VF-84 and *Forrestal* F-4s were manning the other CAPs.

The streaking silver Tomcats bristled in the dawn, their tails flashing the squadron's emblem, a black ace of spades playing card. They carried two long-range Phoenix radar missiles, two shorter-range Sparrow radar missiles, and two Sidewinder infrared heat-seekers. The heat-seekers, attracted primarily to tailpipes, were the main dogfight missiles. In addition, each had a full Gatling gun of 20-millimeter high-explosive bullets.

The section arrived on station and began an orbiting "racetrack" pattern, a roughly ten-mile-long oval from which they projected their cone-shaped radar swaths, searching for bandits. While one Tomcat cruised up one leg of the oval, the other came down. In that way, since the radar projected forward, they could simultaneously cover their front and rear.

"We hadn't been there very long, about 10 to 15 minutes, when we got the first call from the E-2 [radar plane]," wrote Snodgrass: Two bogeys out of Tripoli. They were climbing fast through 17,000 feet.

The Tomcats turned their radars to the vectors and immediately found the bogeys. "It's rough to explain what it was like . . . odds were this was the big one."

The bogeys weren't too far away.

The Tomcats joined in "combat spread" battle formation; the two planes a mile or two apart, roughly abreast. The formation was designed for optimum flexibility. Either fighter could take the lead, depending on the circumstances. "The adrenaline was definitely flowing . . . we were 'breathing fire and seeing blood' . . . all the years of training and thinking. . . . Now it was for real."

They sped toward their targets.

Tripoli, they knew, had the better-piloted Mirages and new MiG-25 Foxbats. While the Foxbat had a "forward-quarter" radar missile, meaning it could target fronts of aircraft, the missile's radar lock, which had to be maintained by the attacking aircraft, was thought to be easily broken by maneuvering.

Most radar missiles worked by keeping the airplane-housed radar beaming at the target. That meant the shooting pilot had to keep the target illuminated with a conical beam. Fly out of that beam with a fast "beaming" maneuver and the lock could be broken.

Their main threat, according to Navy Intelligence, was the Soviet-supplied Atoll, a pretty good rear-quarter heat-seeker that, once shot, could guide with its own heat-sensitive seeker. And it could maneuver pretty well.

But it wasn't that good. Keep the Libyans off their tails, the Americans believed, and, barring a sneak attack or lucky "face" shot, they'd prevail.

They spotted the bogeys before the bogeys spotted them: two twin-tailed gray Foxbats with green Libyan "meatballs" below the cockpits. They had descended and were streaking together unaware at 10,000 feet, going about 700 knots. Snodgrass went high and turned toward them from out of the rising sun. Wheeler went low and zoomed up from the sea. It was an encircling pincer. By the time the MiGs saw them, the Tomcats were already curling behind them, getting position.

The Libyans stoked their afterburners and broke opposite ways, the leader going vertical and reversing back; the wingman diving low.

"Wheels was in a better position to follow the leader so I jumped on the wingman," wrote Snodgrass. "He reversed into a hard [left] turn," a good move. But Snodgrass, already with an advantage, and in a better turning airplane, was able to make the same turn more quickly and thereby close some of the distance.

"The MiG-25 is super fast but doesn't turn worth a damn," wrote Snodgrass. It was easy for him to stay behind the MiG. The fight was supersonic, at about 1.0 to 1.2 Mach (700-plus miles per hour), Snodgrass cutting angles at every turn, getting closer.

The Foxbat couldn't lose him.

At about half a mile, and closing to the range for his 20-millimeter Vulcan cannon, he switched from a Sidewinder lock on the Foxbat's exhausts to "guns," which started his "gun camera," the film used for recording kills in training.

"There's not a fighter pilot around who doesn't dream of having a MiG-25 in his [gun sights] . . . full A/B [afterburner] 1,500 [feet away, which was optimum] with the 'Pipper On' [the bull's-eye of his gunsight on the target]. . . . The Foxbat has giant engines, and in full afterburner it's a hell of an experience. . . . If they'd only tried to shoot something . . ."

But they hadn't. Wheeler had his Foxbat in roughly the same predicament, but because of the rules of engagement, neither could take a shot.

At least Snodgrass had his pictures.

Unable to shake the Tomcats, the MiGs turned back. Snodgrass and Wheeler, although visually separated, chased them to the Libyan SAM (surface-to-air missile) line (the point at which they were threatened by them), which was about twelve to fifteen miles from the coast, then decided to return and tank. SAMs could be maneuvered against, too, but the Tomcats were getting low on gas.

It was approximately 7:15 A.M., local time. They'd been in the air a little over an hour.

They'd just reversed and were executing a high-speed "bug-out" (exit) when they heard Kleeman over their radios: "Tallyho—two Fitters." "Fitter" was the NATO (North Atlantic Treaty Organization) nickname for the Soviet-built Sukhoi-22, Su-22 for short. It carried heat-seeking Atolls but was an attack jet (bomber), so Snodgrass didn't think much was going to happen. Then he heard a screamed, "They're shooting! They're shooting!"

"Well, I'll tell you," he wrote his father, "my blood was already boiling, but we almost went crazy when we learned that."

Snodgrass and Wheeler turned back, thinking that, with the other fight starting, they too might get a chance to shoot some missiles. But the Foxbats they had been chasing were not returning.

Back at CAP 4, Kleeman and Muczynski had been listening to Snodgrass and Wheeler grunt and groan through the turns with the Mirages. Then Kleeman's RIO, Lieutenant Dave Venlet, had picked up two bogeys coming toward them at high speed from the south. Determining intention, they'd sped out, loose deuce (a side-by-side formation allowing maximum flexibility), to intercept.

Meeting the Sukhois almost head-on at a combined closure rate of a thousand knots, they'd been surprised to see the lead, at only a thousand yards in front of them and slightly below, fire an Atoll.

"Absolute insanity," Snodgrass wrote about the shot. The Sukhoi wasn't even directly in front of the Tomcat for the slight possibility of a straight-line ballistic hit. And the Atoll, having limited capability, couldn't possibly home in on the Tomcat's exhausts from head-on.

But the fight was on.

Kleeman and Musczynski pulled hard up as the missile shot below them, then curled back down after the Libyans, who split beneath them and tried to run.

The lead who had shot the Atoll continued relatively straight out to sea, while his wingman turned east, giving Kleeman his exhaust. Kleeman jumped on him.

For a few seconds, the Libyan wingman flew into the low morning sun, so Kleeman, right behind him, had to hold his Sidewinder shot. But once the sun's heat was no longer a problem, he fired. The heat-seeker exploded in the Sukhoi's tailpipe area, sending the plane out of control. The pilot ejected, eventually opening a parachute.

Kleeman (who died several years later in an aircraft accident) had just become the first U.S. pilot to shoot down an enemy plane since the Vietnam War (although rumors persisted that Americans had recorded kills in the 1973 Israeli war), and the first ever to do so in a Tomcat. But he'd lost sight of Musczynski.

Musczynski, with Lieutenant Junior Grade Jim Andersen in his backseat, had rolled back down behind the leader and taken a fixed position from which he could follow the Fitter's every move. He was in a blind spot, slightly below and directly to the rear of the bandit. Unaware of him, the leader, for thirty to forty seconds, tried no evasive movement, not even a turn.

Musczynski was holding a gun barrel to the Libyan's head but he was mindful of the ROE and didn't want to go against them.

Snodgrass: "Music came up [on the radio] and asked whether he was cleared to fire. We all shouted, 'Shoot! Shoot!' How could you ask such a question?" One of those joining Snodgrass in the shout was Kleeman, who, streaking from his kill, had lost sight of both Musczynski and the other Fitter and was afraid it might be targeting him.

Musczynski fired. His Sidewinder went right up the Sukhoi's tailpipe, blowing the entire rear section off in a fiery explosion. The pilot ejected.

Back at the tanker, Snodgrass, along with the *Nimitz*, which had announced the fight over its public address system, was still going crazy. "I was scheduled to be there!" he wrote his father about the last-minute switch in CAP stations.

But he hadn't been. It was a great disappointment.

"Only after we'd topped off and Wheels and I were back to CAP Station 5 did I ever get a little scared." The reality of the situation was sinking in. "It was now a real shooting proposition and I was forced to live with a 'they've got to shoot first' environment. They'd just fired at some of my pals. . . . But the [Libyans] on my side of the Gulf were their best [Mirages and superior missiles]." What if this was just the beginning of some kind of coordinated attack?

There was still hope.

Instinctively, he pulled his lap belt another notch tighter.

"I remember doing that after we'd gotten established back out on the CAP station. It's like buckling your football helmet. You know, 'Okay, let's go' kind of thing. You do it when you're about to fight so you won't flop around in the seat when you load or unload [slow down or speed up] the jet during an engagement."

They'd been back on station only about fifteen minutes when the E-2 radioed that it was picking up an occasional "paint" at 280 degrees, eighteen nautical miles away. Snodgrass and Wheeler sped to the point but didn't see anything with their eyes, nor could their RIOs find any blips on their radars.

"We did a few hard 360s and the only thing we saw was a ship underneath us," wrote Snodgrass. But as they turned one more circle, Snodgrass suddenly spotted two MiG-25s at his two o'clock high. "[They were] about 3–5 miles away, noses on us [meaning they were in perfect position to shoot]. . . . If we'd continued our turn back to station, we would have rolled out right in front of them," giving the Foxbats excellent targets for their Atolls.

He alerted Wheeler, and both of them turned hard into the MiGs, throttling in afterburners. "As soon as we turned on them, they went full burner and hauled ass. The closest we got was $2\frac{1}{2}$ miles in a brief tail chase. I'm absolutely positive if I hadn't picked them up we would have been shot at—not to mention that it would have been a very good shot!

"Thanks for the good eyes!" he told his father.

It was approximately nine A.M. They'd been flying for three hours, been involved in some lively dogfights, but not been able to take any shots. It was frustrating. But that was the job. Snodgrass was getting used to it. They went back to CAP 5 and started orbiting again. After about fifteen minutes they asked for relief so they could tank.

"About that time they gave us another vector, 265 degrees at 75 nautical miles." This was the wrong time for an engagement. They didn't have enough fuel, Snodgrass told the Hawkeye. So the E-2 vectored VF-84 Tomcats on CAP 6, the westernmost station, where there had been no activity. They reluctantly would have to start home.

But a problem dawned on Snodgrass. The bogeys, according to the vector, were between them and CAP 6 and speeding at over 600 knots per hour. Because they were low on fuel and needed to conserve, he and Wheeler would normally exit at a relatively slow 230 knots. They were already down to seven thousand pounds of fuel apiece, "which was not a lot if you have to engage somebody and then fly back 120 nautical miles to the ship."

The bogeys were closing. Snodgrass finally decided that the relieving Tomcats, which should be there any minute, would give them such superiority that the fight would be easy. Four against two. He swung back and got the bandits on radar. They were twenty-three nautical miles away and closing fast.

Without using their afterburners, he and Wheeler turned into the bogeys. Then his radar went down. Now he was not only low on fuel but without his best intercept tool.

Wheeler and McMinn still had their radar. He relinquished lead to Wheeler, dropping two to three miles in trail so Wheeler's radar could sweep for both of them.

Wheeler finally sighted one of the bogeys. It was a Mirage 5. But where was the other?

The Mirage did a hard turn on Wheeler, passing close around and behind him.

Wheeler countered, turning into him, diving.

Looking for the second Mirage, Snodgrass lost sight of Wheeler and the first. Now, for a blink or two, he lost everybody, a dreaded position. If you can't see them, he knew, they can surprise you—usually with a missile.

The VF-84 relief, in radio contact, was still twenty nautical miles away. He began to think that his decision to turn and fight had been "a real bad idea."

Then he suddenly saw the Mirage Wheeler was fighting, its delta wings glinting in the sun. It was zooming up vertically, Wheeler right behind.

Wheeler had position, but what sent a chill up Snodgrass's spine was that he also saw the second Mirage. It was below Wheeler, gaining, drawing a bead.

"I screamed at Wheels to reverse, nose low," which he did. The attacking Mirage overshot. Snodgrass zoomed after it. Wheeler's Mirage split-S'ed below them, Wheeler chasing.

The two Tomcats now had the offensive and would keep it. But they were gulping already precious fuel in amounts they could ill afford, and could neither shoot nor retreat because of the ROE and the fact that if they tried to run, they'd give their exhausts to the Libyans.

If they didn't do something fast, they really would be in trouble.

Snodgrass was about to radio the admiral and say the only way out was to shoot down the Libyans when the VF-84 Tomcats finally arrived. The Mirages "went into easy turns" and exited.

Snodgrass and Wheeler tanked and returned to station. But no more Libyans came out. Snodgrass figures that once word traveled about the shootdowns, they decided to stand down. "There was still a lot of adrenaline and at the same time, some disappointment. My section didn't get to shoot. No ordnance expended." But there wasn't that sense of finality. "We didn't know the game was over."

As they orbited, he said, they heard one of the downed Libyans calling for help in his lifeboat. "If anybody hears me, please radio for help," Snodgrass says the Libyan radioed in broken English. But there was only silence. Then the Libyan asked for clicks, an international sign of recognition. "You heard all these clicks from everywhere."

The Libyan eventually got picked up.

Snodgrass and Wheeler returned to ship thinking there was "a distinct possibility" they would launch again. But then word filtered down that "we weren't going to press it." Operation "Guns of August" was over.

While the score was a very satisfying United States 2, Libya 0, all Snodgrass had to show for it was his gun camera film. He'd wanted more, but that was the luck of the draw. "Frankly," he'd say a decade later, "if I had it to do over again, I would have shot first and begged forgiveness later. The ROE were bullshit. . . . The system [should you violate it] has no option but to make you a hero."

But in the heat of battle, he'd done what he was supposed to do. Follow orders. Professionally, that counted.

Not getting a shootdown was a personal disappointment. But in a larger sense, all the American fighter pilots out there were riding high. Their planes, skills, and tactics had been validated. The F-14, in its first real combat test, had proved to be master of some of the best Soviet jet fighters. U.S. emphasis on relentless ACM training and tactics—the legacy of Vietnam—shared by the navy and the air force, had given them a decided edge against the competition.

The system had worked. The Libyans hadn't even made a fight of it. And Snodgrass was still young in his fighter career, which was definitely a young man's game. He was convinced he'd get another chance. And he was right.

Back at the end of the Korean War, fighter tactics had taken a dramatic shift. With the coming of air-to-air missiles, strategists had predicted that close-in dogfighting was dead. Future air combat, they said, would be fought far away from the visual arena. Jet interceptors would stand off and kill targets with missiles shot from far distances. This caused some dramatic changes.

No longer would fighters be designed for close-in dogfighting. They would be "interceptors," built for speed, range, and carrying the latest electronic wizardry. Basically, these planes would be "guided missile platforms." The McDonnell Douglas F-4 Phantom, for instance—the main Vietnam War fighter—was not a good turner. The antithesis of finesse, it was built for brute speed and climbing ability and had its own radar operator in the backseat. The navy version didn't even have a gun.

As a consequence, training began to deemphasize dogfighting

and emphasize radar intercept. The typical Phantom crew of the early 1960s, air force and navy, was well-schooled in rushing toward the distant enemy bogey, locating him on the screen, and firing a Sparrow radar missile at him before he was ever seen with human eyes. But its crew was ignorant of how to turn with a nimble Soviet-built MiG-17 or MiG-21, the primary enemy threats. The planners simply didn't think the threats would ever get that close.

But the war, tragically, showed them wrong.

First, the idea that the combatants wouldn't get close was a fallacy. Before you shoot a missile at an airplane, you've got to make sure it's not friendly. You don't want to kill one of your own. Even if you have identification gear in your airplanes, it can malfunction or be manipulated by an enemy who has broken its codes.

In Vietnam, there was no foolproof way to identify aircraft from out-of-sight distances. We had airborne and ground-based listeners for that purpose, but the navy and air force, independently of each other, frequently had planes in the sky at the same times. Even when schedules were coordinated, it was always possible that a blip thought to be an enemy was really a stray— or a friendly with its radio or other signal equipment out.

What it boiled down to was that U.S. pilots had to get close enough to the bogey to make visual identification. And when they did that, they were already in a dogfight.

Surprised American pilots found they couldn't turn as well as the MiGs. Their airplanes weren't built for it. They didn't know how. Worst, perhaps, was that they had been taught little about how to care for or employ their air-to-air missiles, which were very complicated little flying machines with narrow, restricted performance envelopes. Shot from an improper proper angle, position, or distance from the target, they wouldn't work—if they worked at all.

As the war lengthened and the North Vietnamese got more planes into the air, missed or malfunctioning missile shots and aggressive enemy fighters took an increasing toll on U.S. planes, until, in 1969, the air-to-air kill ratios were approximately even, about one for one.

Such a ratio was unheard of in American fighter annals. In

World War II and Korea, for instance, the U.S. had enjoyed ratios upward of ten to twenty to one.

U.S. pilots were dying. If the war continued, the situation could have gotten critical.

What if the Russians, who had thousands of MiG aircraft, entered?

In order to win any major conflict, you have to have air superiority, and air superiority starts with fighters winning the skies.

This was the reason for the start of Topgun, the navy's Fighter Weapons School. During the lull in fighting between late 1969 and the beginning of 1972, a small group of talented navy fighter pilots who, against official policy at that time, had kept their dogfighting skills sharp had been asked to teach the others. The Phantom was a good dogfighter if flown at high speeds. In addition, they taught missile employment and how to exploit the weaknesses of the MiGs. When the war resumed, pilots they had trained went back to Vietnam and elevated the post-1972 navy kill ratio to fourteen to one, which was a stunning, although little-known, victory.

With that victory, both the navy and the air force had learned a powerful lesson. Never again, said the new air strategists and planners emerging in the early 1970s, would they forsake what, in hindsight, was so obvious. Technology was important, but so was the pilot. You couldn't rely solely on your technology. In addition to being given a good dogfighter, the pilot had to be trained in dogfighting.

And kept current in it, meaning practiced, just like any athlete hoping to win.

The Vietnam air victory was a resounding mandate for fighter tactics training. After the war, building on what Topgun had started, all the services with fighters—the navy, the air force, and the Marine Corps—began emphasizing close-in dogfight training. If you flew fighters, BFM (basic fighter maneuvers), the actual moves, and ACM (air combat maneuvering), the employment of those moves in a tactical and strategic dogfight, became the most important things you did, what you respected and studied.

Dogfighting became king again. And if you were good at it, the rewards were ample.

Nobody knew at this time that by the end of the 1980s the teaching of dogfighting would again be receding.

Several days following the shootdown, Snodgrass found himself in Naples drinking champagne with some beautiful jet set models aboard international Saudi financier Adnan Khashoggi's 260-foot luxury yacht *Nabila*. (Khashoggi's 1986 biography is titled *The Richest Man in the World*.)

Spoils of the "conquering heroes," he wrote his dad.

As the air wing's admin officer, an additional duty, he had honchoed the press conference about the shootdowns aboard the *Nimitz* when the carrier had docked for liberty. Afterward, he had swung an invitation aboard *Nabila*, along with Kleeman and some of the other squadron members, with the help of *People* magazine reporter Logan Bently, who had attended the press conference and knew Khashoggi.

"I'd never seen anything like it," wrote Snodgrass about the yacht. "James Bond plus, complete with disco, movie theater, and more bars and decks than all of Virgina Beach [the town nearest Oceana]. . . . [We] had a big party, dinner, cranked up the discos, and sailed around the *Nimitz* drinking Dom Perignon '57. Right out of the movies."

Later, during the same liberty, Bently, who apparently had many connections in Rome, invited Snodgrass and another of his squadron buddies, Skip Zobel, to a dinner party at the heart-of-Rome palace belonging to Count Giovanni Volpi, one of Europe's noted playboys. American and Italian diplomats were there, as were film stars.

The evening ended for Snodgrass like a scene out of *La Dolce Vita*—him racing the count's 1962 LeMans champion red Testa Rossa Ferrari through Rome's early morning streets.

He hadn't gotten his MiG, yet, but the consolation prize wasn't bad.

2

If ever there was a seat-of-the-pants air warrior, it was Joe "Hoser" Satrapa. He never got a MiG, but he's a legend in today's navy, one of the best air-to-air gunners of modern times, and the only pilot ever to fly an F-14 with a big toe for a thumb.

That's right, a big toe. He blew off his right thumb cocking a grounded "Big Bertha" single-shot rifle he'd made out of an F-14's M61 20-millimeter cannon. The fatigued breech exploded, propelling the bolt through his hand as the lone bullet exited the barrel. He wanted to keep flying so he had surgeons do the transfer.

"Doesn't look like a big toe," I told him, remarking on how well the switch had adapted. "Sure smells like one," he retorted.

He was driving a vehicle with ease, and beyond its abnormal size, the toe looked just like a thumb.

I went to see him at his mountain home in Nevada City, California, right after Desert Storm. He resembled a large Gene Hackman or Keenan Wynn, I thought, but with a mustache. He had been a pass-catching end at the Naval Academy before graduating in 1964, and was easily six-two, with steely eyes, wit, and a gravely voice that hoarsed jokes and laughter.

As I got to know him, I could see a parallel with General

33

George Patton, the World War II hero. They were both born war-riors. As a lieutenant commander, he had been passed over for promotion because of some of his more colorful antics and thus was forced to retire. But then, after Secretary of the Navy John Lehman had flown with him in a practice fight, he'd made Hoser the chief benefactor of a special presidential program that al-lowed the navy to pluck talented people from retirement so he could again teach air fighting.

Satrapa's career had begun during the Vietnam War and ended with Desert Storm, and he became a bridge between the eras.

I'd already heard a lot of Hoser stories.

Like the time, when he was flying F-8 Crusaders, that he had sneaked up on an A-4 Skyhawk, suddenly popping up and plant-ing himself in front of it. He'd scared the hell out of the Sky-hawk's pilot, and came so close that he accidentally scraped paint off his tail and the A-4's nose probe.

Or another time, when at night he'd seen two wing buddies in A-7s close together and screaming out of North Vietnam after a raid on Vinh, a North Vietnamese stronghold. He'd extinguished his lights and roared head-on between them with his afterburner torching the darkness so they'd think he was an enemy SAM with their names on it—which they did.

He'd also streaked under domestic bridges; buzzed his home-town of Tujunga, California; and exploded his flight leader's F-8 with a guns shot to its fuel cell after the leader had ejected.

"It was going down anyway," he told me.

He was "colorful," as many of his friends had said, no doubt about it. But he was also very good. A guns kill is the hardest to get in the air because you have to get close, which requires the best maneuvering skills, and then hold a steady bead, which is not required with missiles.

He used at least one maneuver most fighter pilots had not even realized was possible. He called it the "pitch-moment-coupling" maneuver, a name that really made sense only to those whose job it was to throw fighters around in the sky like toothpicks. It was a quick-turn maneuver, used at the height of a slow fight—when both fighters are entwined, scissoring up, losing speed.

As he explained it, as you are about to exit, instead of flipping over on your back and pulling through and down, the way most pilots would come back around, you "tuck and roll" in about one quarter of the space and time, which, of course, turns you back on your opponent's tail much faster. The problem is that you have to endure some things most fighter pilots hate and fear.

First, the normal way to come back down is to flip the plane onto its back and pull through. This called "pulling positive G." Although you are upside down, which has little meaning high in the air, the G forces are pushing the pilot against the seat, cementing him there, which feels good and natural.

But in the pitch-moment-coupling maneuver, you go right on over the top and down without flipping on your back. The G forces lift the pilot out of his seat and force his blood and innards up, which feels bad and unnatural. Very bad. This is called "negative G." Pilots hate it. And in the pitch-moment-coupling maneuver, it's very pronounced.

In effect, from what I could gather, you didn't go over in the deep oval of a normal pull but quickly "tucked" right under, as one might do in bringing the fingertips under an outstretched hand in order to make a fist. "Your ass goes up like this," he said. "You've never felt that before. You say, Oh shit. We're out of control. We're gonna die." Then you roll rightside up [because you're inverted there for a second, just as your fingers are making the fist]. The positive G's pull you back in your seat, and you're nearly on your opponent's tail. You haven't had to go all the way down and come back up.

He said he's only fought a few other pilots who have known, or been able to execute, the move, and a former Topgun CO had gone out and tried it and broken his helmet in the unsuccessful attempt.

You have to be careful of what fighter pilots tell you. It's not that they lie, although some might. But things are happening awfully fast up there and any good fighter pilot thinks he's pretty much invincible, so they usually see the fight from a narrow viewpoint. But I'd heard the Topgun story before from other pilots. Also, the days of tall tales about victories and such are diminishing because of the use of computerized fight ranges. Most fights are now recorded as they are happening on big boards back at the base.

Satrapa had hated the Naval Academy. "Goddamn it was tough," he said. "Regulations. Cooped up." But he'd endured, barely graduating, in order to fly. "The [football] coach told me if

I performed, he'd get me jets." That's all he cared about, dreamed about. He was so afraid he'd miss out on combat that he told a summoning academy disciplinary board, "I'm just waiting to get the hell out of here so I can go to flight training and get over to the goddamn war and kill gomers."

Just to rile the board, he'd purposely worn red socks with his blue service uniform. A Marine captain noted the infraction and told him to put himself on report. "I said, 'Aye aye, sir,' and shut the door. I went about thirty feet down the hall and heard this loud, boisterous laughter. So what it equated to was that's the kind of guy we want. I wasn't bullshitting them. I said this is like sitting on the frigging bench waiting to get in a ball game and I just hope I can get over there [to the war] before the sonovabitch is over."

He did. Flight training for him was like manna from heaven. He'd lie awake nights planning his moves, envisioning performance just as he'd pictured himself making spectacular catches. He beat instructors. He had wild dreams where he would be up in the sky, godlike, seeing the vast arena, understanding what he had to do to make his plane intercept and beat another.

This carried over into his conscious flying. In the intensity and psychic explosion of important moments—especially in combat—time would sometimes slow down or speed up for him, depending on the situation, and, in rare instances, he said, he'd experience near out-of-body projection, almost as if he were extended out of the cockpit, in order to do better.

"You're watching yourself as if you're removed," he said. "If I wanted to go from here to here [I'll perceive that] I want to be inside of his turn over here so I can get the gun shot up here."

The out-of-body detachment happened to him once coming out of Vinh Sonh in 1967. He was flying a fast photo reconnaissance mission and the F-8 he was piloting got hit by triple A (antiaircraft artillery fire). The concussion knocked him out for a few seconds. He broke left and got hit again. Vinh Sonh had a gunnery school, and he realized he was in the middle of a flak maelstrom.

"I said goddamn. No warning. No RHAW gear [on-board radar warning of enemy defenses]. All of a sudden [as if detached] I saw my hands move in the cockpit. It was in slow motion. Dump the cabin pressurization. Get the ram air door open. PC-1 [a hydraulic control system] is gone. Utility pressure gone. Radio wasn't working so I knew I had a generator failure."

He was able to make it back to the ship and an emergency landing. They found several 85-millimeter holes in the plane, including one the size of a fist beneath his ejection seat.

His scariest moments, he said, were experienced while trying to land an RA-5 Vigilante aboard the *America* with the Vigi's autothrottles out. Without the autothrottles, he'd have a hard time controlling the airplane's sink rate. If he didn't make a perfect manual approach to the carrier, he'd hit it.

A bad student, he said he'd spent twenty minutes circling, trying to figure mathematically the exact fuel flow and RPM for a perfect descent and landing. No margin for error. It was a black night, no moon, and a pitching deck. On board, they were as scared as he was.

"So I'm coming in and I got a good lineup, and I said, Fuck, I'm looking good. I got sweat in my eyes. My heart's going thump, thump. This is a great chance to look bad. A fighter pilot does not want to look bad. You get shot, hit, it's not your fault. But this. I told the guy in the backseat, I'm maxed out. Don't say a fucking word. He controls nothing. Just don't say a fucking word."

Obviously, they made it.

"I've been shot five or six times," he said. "I don't scare easy. But that . . ." He didn't finish. He realized he wasn't immortal, he said, when a good friend, a pilot he thought was terrific, was killed by a freak wind shear. They were flying F-8s low to El Centro, California, at 500-plus knots when a sudden gust, traveling at a hundred feet per second, came up off a mountainside and tore his friend's wings off.

All they found of the body was a piece of the toe in the steel toe in one of his boots and the mangled Rolex watch face he'd been wearing.

"It had been crushed up like a piece of tinfoil," he said of the watch face. "His torso harness was frayed and tattered like it had been sandblasted. No blood. Nothing. He'd just vaporized. I'd been through two combat cruises and thought I was indestructible. But this guy was as good as me and something got him that he didn't even see. Absolutely no warning. Makes you think, doesn't it?"

Satrapa has a bad ear from flying, as well as a neck injury. The high noise and physical stress are to blame. ACM is a contact sport.

He told me a trick he used against F-14 pilots: Make them turn left and they'll inadvertently cross-control—give the plane contradictory commands—with a resultant loss of performance.

The reason this works is that the pilot has got to keep sight of his opponent or he'll lose. So he's turned back, not looking at what he's doing with the stick. But the force needed to move the stick at high G is so strong—about sixty to eighty pounds, depending on G—that he has to pull very hard, harder than he realizes. This causes him to not only pull right but back, which affects the rudder.

"He's telling the airplane to go right with the stick and left with the rudder. You can't do this to a two-thousand-hour [really experienced] guy. But most of them don't know it. He's wondering why the airplane is faltering. He's screwed. I'm laughing. I'm going to gun his brains out in thirty seconds."

He showed me his bow and arrow, which he prefers to hunt with because it takes more skill than a rifle. It's a formidable weapon, and he can hit a squirrel with it at fifty yards, which is no easy shot. But the most interesting thing he showed me, in my opinion, was a set of diaries he kept on his two Vietnam combat cruises. They are a fascinating account of a man obsessed with getting a MiG, as most good fighter pilots are. They provide a picture of carrier warfare and reveal an air warrior mind-set seldom glimpsed by the uninitiated.

Most fighter pilots hate to write.

But most important, in my judgment, the diaries provide a glimpse at the foundation of the current fighter era—the one I'm writing about. For it was Vietnam-era fighter pilots like Joe Satrapa who caused the change in attitude that produced Topgun at the end of the Vietnam War. (He, in fact, was involved with that.) And it was Topgun's success in the heightened Vietnam air wars of early 1972 that produced the new fighting spirit in the air force that directly led to the high levels of training and readiness achieved by all our fighter forces in the decades after.

The diaries sometimes get personal, and that is another matter. But when they talk of fighters and fighting and everything associated, they show a spirit and attitude that shaped fighter aviation at least up to the Gulf War.

The Vietnam War, therefore, is pertinent to this research:

"Just because you fly over the beach and get a few 85 mms shot at you, they say give him a medal," he wrote at the beginning of the first cruise. "Bullshit. That's what we're getting paid to do. . . . It is the weak who are cruel; gentleness is to be expected only from the strong. Those who do not know fear are not really brave, for courage is the capacity to confront what can be imagined. You can understand people better if you look at them as if they are children, no matter how old or impressive they may be. For most of us never mature; we simply grow taller. The purpose of life is to matter, to count, to stand for something, to have it make some difference that we lived at all."

I figured he'd copied that from a book, but I've got a pretty good reference library and I couldn't find the quote. He did say he was "smashed" most of the time while writing the diaries.

They start on June 2, 1967. He's a lieutenant j.g. (junior grade) in VF-111, flying sleek, single-engine F-8s (sometimes called the "MiG Master") from "Yankee Station" off *Intrepid*. "In the event that I should be shot down, captured or killed," says the first page, "I should appreciate that whoever finds this in my belongings please forward it to my parents."

Several days into the cruise, he's "very worried about Carol [his wife] and how her money situation is and why she is going out of the way to prove she is being faithful. . . . I'm down to 190 lbs, good shape, cough almost gone and jungle rot on feet has cleared up. . . . Hotter than hell, horny, depressed and pissed off. . . . Thought about folks a lot . . . wondered if they thought about me much and if they had experience in their life to match the excitement I've had in 26 years."

MiGs have shot down a navy A-4 and an air force F-4 and he's hoping to get a chance at them. On June 30, he pays a buddy five dollars to take his flight to Vinh, where he thinks the MiGs might be. Just before he arrives, an A-4 is shot down. "Gray and I were going 1.1 mach and I called him to break left as flak was creeping up his tail. About 35–45 rounds went off. I took a small hit in my starboard nose gear door. Just knocked off a little piece of the [plane's] skin."

He left, got refueled, and went back in again. "Took a few tracers. . . . No sweat. . . . Probably won't fly tomorrow. Fuck."

July 7: "Frustration waiting for MiGs. Dream of shooting MiGs.

No recognition for what we're doing." Then, "MiG trap coming up. . . . Secret. Can't wait." But he missed them again. A new pilot was joining the squadron. He'll "fly only photo escort and that will be a big deal since he's been flying A4s . . . has to prove himself."

July 9: "We lost another A4 today. SAM [surface-to-air missile] blew his tail off. He ejected and was captured immediately."

July 10: "The solitude of my cockpit is the only comforting thing I had today. No mail from Carol. Right now I almost feel I hate her for marrying me because I wouldn't be so damned worried about what's happening back home and her not writing. I feel if she would not have married me I would only have the pressure here to contend with which I [can] do standing on my head. If only I'd get a letter from her."

The next day he got a letter from her, but it only made him madder. She'd gone to a cookout and was musing about becoming a hippie so she could "do what she wanted. . . . Fuck it. . . . Thought for the day: A fighter pilot is always on the offense. If there is a MiG on his six [tail], the MiG is in a very good defensive position, while the fighter pilot is in a very poor offensive position."

They went off the line and took R&R in Tokyo, where they slept for two days, he bought a pair of crotchless panties for Carol, and they bought matching foils. "High point was when Rick and I came back drunk and ended up having a duel in the lobby of the Hilton."

Back on line, he almost got in a fistfight with a squadron supervisor, a hurricane hit them, they had to assist the *Forrestal* when the accidental firing of a missile on board ignited the worst carrier fire since World War II, and he was informed that a good friend had been shot down and was missing.

"Charlie just had gotten married. . . . Rick and I . . . in our room having a six pack of cold Millers apiece for Chuck. He and I agreed at El Centro . . . that if one of us should buy the farm we would rather the other either throw a party or get shit-faced, whichever is most convenient. . . . Since we only have a half case of beer left this is the best I can do."

A few days later he was told officially that "Charlie had bought the farm. . . . I had to beat feet out of the Ready Room cause I didn't want to show any type of emotion at all. . . . I still feel that

I am destined to do something really big. I don't know what. Maybe shoot down three MiGs in one hop. . . . That I think, is why I'm not scared of being snuffed because I haven't done anything great yet—after that I'll watch out."

August 9 was the day he got hit by flak at Vinh Sonh and saw his hand in slow motion. It was worse than he'd told me. His head had smashed the top of the canopy from the blast under his seat. The cockpit had filled with smoke "so dense I couldn't see the instrument panel." When he finally got the smoke out, the canopy windscreen was pink with hydraulic fluid. He landed with hydraulic fluid pouring out of the plane and counted thirteen fist-size holes in it. The explosion underneath him had just missed taking his feet off, and he'd been a hair away from having his controls severed, which means he wouldn't have gotten home.

Following a harrowing near-SAM hit in which he "pulled max 'G' and saw it miss me barely and explode 100–150 feet behind me," he returned to the carrier to find out that just after he'd left a target area the day before, two MiG-21s had been shot down there by F-4s off the *Constellation*.

"This war is really pissing me off. The rules are ridiculous and our role is suicide. We could end it in 2 weeks"—he meant, by mining and blockading Haiphong Harbor; bombing all their dams, MiG bases, and rail lines; and flooding the lowland. Flying over Haiphong Harbor the next night, the entire city seemingly "shooting up at us," he cursed the Russian ships below, laden with war supplies, that he was forbidden to attack. "I wanted so much to empty my guns on them," he wrote.

By late August, he was sleepless the night before with the possibility of getting MiGs on the next day's mission. "Same feeling as . . . before the big [football] game, envisioning catches . . . wondering if I'll be able to come through. Figure best thing is to see [the MiGs] before they see me, tell the photo beaney to beat feet, call a tanker for me and get some more fighters vectored in while I hold them off. One thing will be true. If there are 3 or 4 against me—I'll have the poor bastards surrounded."

By October 3, he was so frustrated he faked a broken radio and went hunting alone off Haiphong Harbor, a move prohibited by both tactical doctrine and regulations.

"Guns and Sidewinders were all set up," he wrote. He kept to a relatively low altitude—10,000 feet—and slowed to 210 knots, hoping the enemy would mistake him for a lone, defenseless prop plane. By the time he went "feet dry" (over land) his equipment told him he was being painted by North Viet radar.

But no MiGs came up.

He flew a lazy figure-eight pattern for twenty-five minutes— until he had only enough fuel to get back to the ship. But still no MiGs showed.

When he got back, he was ordered to the bridge and figured he was in trouble. But all a high-ranking officer wanted to know was how many ships were in the harbor and if he'd seen one called the *Camerusa*. "So I know now that they will turn their backs on a guy who has the balls to go trolling for MiGs alone," he wrote.

His second cruise started in June 1968. He was still MiG obsessed, but perhaps more philosophical about it.

"Sometimes I wonder . . . if all the years of waiting, dreaming and planning, the many months of training, the lying awake at night with sweaty palms, the anxiety I felt on every mission over the beach last cruise, are worth the chance of those few precious moments that may or may not come: the day I engage a MiG in aerial combat. If it doesn't happen this cruise, it will never happen."

On July 21, his roommate was shot down; and on July 29, he missed still another chance.

"Today was the day—4 MiG 17s came south . . . and I was on the port cat [catapult] for an emergency launch [a rotating security procedure and a lucky break for him]. Tension was high and I wanted to hurry up and launch so I could plug in burner and get there quickly. Then just prior to launch it was announced that VF-51's XO [executive officer] had just bagged a MiG—I knew the fight would be over before I could get there. I was so pissed and emotionally keyed up I had to pull my visor down to keep the men around my plane from seeing the tears in my eyes."

Later he wrote, "The intensity of life is in direct proportion to the realization of the nearness of death. . . . Life is meaningless and absent of thorough enjoyment unless there is a scale by which to measure its worth. . . . To some people, death is the lowest mark on the scale, and everything above is priceless. These are the weak, subdued, simple, easily influenced do-nothings with which the world is burdened. . . . Now I say, what could make life so beautiful, food taste so good, the sound of music so sincerely filling . . . than to come so close and know beyond a shadow of a doubt that you came so close to losing it, but have once again . . . tested your own limitations?

"I have always enjoyed danger. But not until a few years ago did I know why. . . . I thought at first it was for recognition from the people around me, until I found myself doing things which were dangerous with no chance of anyone finding out and still enjoying them just as much. . . . I do not mean foolish things. Things that are dangerous to some people are within the limitations of other people and are not a risk to them. The risk lies in whether you have accurately judged your limitations with no error. . . . So the final risk lies with one's own judgment and how well we know ourselves."

A UHF radio failure on his wingman's plane kept him from going after a MiG and made him suspect the man was a coward. "I will not stand for or fly with someone whom I think is afraid and my maintenance boys can't waste man hours chasing down gripes which are made up by a pilot in order to make him look not quite so bad. He was scared to death when he finally got aboard last night and it looks as though he was afraid to fly [the next night] so he said his [equipment] was down. I hope sincerely this is not the case. . . ."

He had the equipment checked out. The UHF had indeed been inoperative. Years later, the pilot, who became his good friend and clearly demonstrated that he was anything but a coward, read the entries and was shocked.

Satrapa had forgotten they were in there.

"It hurt him bad," he told me. "I wish it hadn't happened."

After learning another buddy got a MiG, and seeing an A-4 "boresight [crash into] the LSO platform," killing two, he heard rumors, on October 19, of an impending bombing halt. "What is this shit? . . . How am I going to get a MiG if the war is over? . . . Maybe Korea will flare up, or China will start World War III— Something has to happen or my very existence will be in jeopardy."

He was a war lover, no doubt about it. But there was an honesty and intelligence to him, not to mention courage. War was his destiny, he believed, and you can get very philosophical about all he wrote. If you believe in an afterlife, what does death mean anyway? Just a rebirth, although I'm very happy, thank you, to keep my distance until I'm taken kicking and screaming.

With the cessation of bombing on October 31, 1968, he took the opportunity to write down "what I have learned while being associated with the separate world of fighter pilots," including some of its "unwritten" rules.

In a kind of random, scattershot style, they were:

"The past is remembered not by the years, but by events. . . .

"Learn to focus your eyes on a particular area and scan it thoroughly with varying focal distances. . . .

"The fighter is simply a flying rocket and gun platform, and its basic qualities of speed and surprise should always be used to the greatest advantage. . . .

"Even from my early training, I never preferred the low-level bombing or strafing to the clean, exhilarating teamwork of the dog-fight. . . .

"[In a dogfight], the real danger lies when we relax and fail to keep our necks twisting."

Fighter pilots, he wrote, fall into two categories: "Those who are going out to shoot and those who secretly and desperately know they will be shot at; the hunters and the hunted."

(Evidence suggests that many of "the hunted" don't really know what they're getting into when they start climbing the fighter ladder—nor do those putting them on it know. As Satrapa later said, such pilots have the ability, intelligence, and know-how to fly the airplane well, but, ultimately, lack the aggressiveness needed down the line—the "fighting spirit," it's sometimes called.

(In training, climbing the ladder may be a challenge or a duty, perhaps a pilot's way of showing that he has what it takes or what is expected of him. For some, it might just be a simple matter of not going backward—accepting a lesser airplane or assignment when they've earned the higher rung. But there is more to being a fighter pilot than training can sometimes bring out. Only in war, when things are for keeps and you can't go back to the officers' club and review your mistakes, does the lack of aggressiveness become obvious.

(I remember a pilot I wrote about in the Vietnam War who made all the cuts, got checks in all the right boxes, and was soon on his way to a fighter squadron. But when he finally got in his first real air battle with hostile MiGs, he left rather than engage. His squadron mates, including the pilot whose wingman he was and whom he deserted, didn't get mad. They all liked him as a person and had not sensed the problem before. He was sent home. But it had taken a war, and a crucial moment in that war, for both he and them to find out that he really wasn't part of the fraternity.)

"There existed between us," wrote Satrapa, "that bond of comradeship that only those who have served and fought together are privileged to know. . . . [For instance] sitting in the cockpit prior to launch, [smelling] that strange mixture of plastic dope, fine mineral oil and J.P. 5 [jet fuel] [assailing] the nostrils and [being] somehow vaguely comforting. . . . After [getting] airborne, [feeling] the slight trembling of the stick [in your hand] as though it is alive, and not merely the focal point of a superb mechanical machine. . . . After a hop [walking] in front of my intake after shut down and [hearing] the tinkling of the compressor blades as they complete their last revolutions. . .

"We all knew the meaning of fear and felt it according to our temperaments and training. I never knew a pilot who fell outside this category; our simple duty was to control fear and live and fly with it. Once you gave way to panic, you were finished."

Hoser left Vietnam in 1969 and taught ACM to new fighter pilots at NAS Miramar, the Pacific Fleet's fighter center just north of San Diego. While at Miramar, he was also involved in the founding of Topgun by flying adversary (simulated enemy) as the new school was getting started.

But he wanted back in the war.

In 1971, he got his wish, wrangling one more combat tour when two tours was the stated limit. He finished the conflict with 156 missions—but no MiGs.

It galled him. But then he figured, "I'm young. I'll get another chance. I just wasn't in the right place at the right time."

He came back and went on a Mediterranean cruise, but it was more relaxing than taxing. Then he started flying the new F-14 Tomcat, in which he was eventually to log more than 1,600 flying hours.

In 1974, he was assigned to VX-4, the navy's special test and evaluation squadron, at Point Magu, California. And in 1976, by then a project officer at VX-4, he got a chance to at least simulate shooting down MiGs in one of the most important fighter events of the last few decades—the multipart Air Combat Evaluation and Air Intercept Missile Evaluation—or ACEVAL-AIMVAL, for short.

In the mid-1970s, the navy and air force were fragmented over the kinds of dogfight missiles that would be needed in the future. If all the different missiles the services wanted were funded, the costs would be astronomical.

To settle the issue, the Department of Defense, under a request by the Congress, ordered a secret, multiyear, air wargame exercise to be conducted in the hidden desert north of Nellis Air Force Base, Nevada. Run by the air force, AIM-ACE, as the exercise was cryptically called, was a series of tests and simulated air battles to determine exactly what dogfight missiles and tactics the United States was going to need in the coming years. That is, given the new fighters and missiles that America had and the Soviet Union was projected to have, what tactics, offensive and defensive, would we use if the two superpowers went to war?

Not everyone agreed that a simulation could approximate real airwar, but the project was funded—at an eventual cost of $43 million, according to congressional testimony—and the two services were told to pick a small group of their best fighter pilots and send them to Nellis, where they would begin preparations in early 1976.

The opposing sides in the tests were called the "Red Force" and the "Blue Force." The Red Force represented the threat, or the Soviet Union, and was comprised of a small number of top navy and air force pilots flying small F-5E Tiger IIs, often used as MiG-21 simulators.

The Blue Force—the "good," or U.S. force—consisted of a similar number of air force and navy pilots and their RIOs, flying respectively the one-seat F-15 Eagle, the air force's newest air superiority fighter, and the two-seat F-14 Tomcat.

Joe Satrapa was one of the six or so navy pilots picked to fly the F-14.

The two sides first tested various candidate missiles for their fighting characteristics in the AIMVAL portion, firing them, seeing how they performed without the pressure of combat against other airplanes. Then, in 1977, they took "all-aspect" AIM-7F Sparrow radar missiles and "all-aspect" AIM-9L Sidewinder heat-seeking missiles into simulated dogfights in the ACEVAL portion.

"All-aspect" meant that not only would the missile home in on the rear exhaust of a target aircraft, it also could lock on any other "aspects," such as front or side.

U.S. fighter planes had had good all-aspect missiles for most of the 1970s, while our enemies had not. That had given the United States a decided advantage. But now it was believed that the Soviets, through espionage, had acquired plans to the AIM-9L Sidewinder, and it was only a matter of time before their fighters also had a good all-aspect missile.

America had to get ready.

So AIM-ACE was introducing a new element in the continually evolving fighter tactics story. For the first time in jet fighter history, not only were American fighters going to enter the dogfight arena with all-aspect missiles—their enemies were, too.

"Go back to the early days of the Sidewinder," said Dan Pentecost, another of the Blue Force pilots. "You had to win the dogfight, get on his stern to shoot a missile at the bad guy. But when we got the all-aspect Sidewinder, we no longer had to win the dogfight. All we had to do was see him, and as long as we were in range, put the seeker head on him, lock him up and shoot. We had the advantage.

"Now we move into a situation where they've stolen the Sidewinder. Now neither of us has to win the dogfight. What you have to do is see the other first."

The ACEVAL air arena was a ceilinged, almost floorless thirty-mile-diameter tube of airspace hidden on Nellis's restricted range. Blue Force and Red Force fighters would enter the airspace from opposite directions and have to get a visual tally before the fight would be on. Although, for instance, in a real air battle the Tomcats would have long since used their radar-guided beyond-visual-range (BVR) Phoenix missiles, long-range missiles were not allowed.

The test was strictly for visual fight missiles.

47

"It was gutsball," said Satrapa about the fights. Everyone wanted to look good. Personal reputations and service honor were at stake. Nobody wanted to lose.

Of course, there were ways to defeat missiles shot at you, but for the most part, close-in, turning fights were avoided in the one-versus-one, two-versus-two, and four-versus-four fights of ACEVAL. Most of the time, said Dave Bjerke, another of the Blue Force pilots, the Tomcats would just "blow through" the Red Force fighters "as fast as we could, shoot and get the hell out."

Because the Red Force F-5s also had AIM-9Ls and were driven by pilots he knew were good, Bjerke said he didn't want to allow them to get him in their heat-seeker envelope. There wasn't much slow fighting in the test unless it was prearranged, and usually it was done somewhere else besides in the AIM-ACE arena, which was electronically monitored by the Nellis Air Combat Maneuver Range.

"Conversion to beam and stern attack was avoided [by the Blue Force Tomcats] due to the bogey's ability to fire any time he could pull his nose onto the F-14," states the Blue Baron Project report, the navy's independent study of AIM-ACE, which I recently got declassified. "The all-aspect threat made it necessary to stay away from the bogey if at all possible. Survival required staying at long range, sneaking up on the beam or tail, or staying close to the range boundary for a quick bugout [exit]."

"We were changing tactics exponentially," said Satrapa about the benefit of having the range's real-time mapping and analysis of the fights every day. One contingent would go out to a fight and be surprised by something the other contingent did, come back, and spend hours devising something to counter, then use it the next day.

Sometimes it worked and sometimes it didn't.

Bjerke said the tactics that eventually emerged, which are still mostly classified, basically boiled down to "exploiting their weaknesses and using our strengths, which is always the way it has been."

The Blue Force fighters had better radars than the Red Force and could usually find them first. But the Red Force planes were smaller and harder to see, which was a benefit in regard to the visual acquisition requirement for shooting. There was even competition within each team. Because the navy Blue Force F-14s had zoom-in television to better see the little Red Force fighters, the air force Blue Force F-15s mounted telescopes in their cockpits, which worked very well.

The innovation stuck in the F-15—until a better method came along.

Most of the kills by the F-14s came from Sparrow "face shots," said the Blue Baron report. In order to counter those, said Bjerke, the F-5s exploited a problem with the F-14's radar: It couldn't track a target if the target went perpendicular to the line of its radar beam.

Thus, coming head-on at a Blue Force section of F-14s—but still out of range of a "face shot"—a Red Force section of F-5s would suddenly split to the left and right, going out perpendicular to the Tomcat's radar beam and causing the F-14s to lose them.

The F-5s, however, couldn't use that tactic with F-15s, said Bjerke, because the Eagle radars were better and could hold the Tigers in the perpendicular.

Other tactics were "devious," said Blue Baron, or "cautious," said Satrapa, such as "dragging" or "rope-a-dope," where one fighter hung back or otherwise goaded opponents to attack in their "home" airspace while a wingman or other section mate waited unseen to shoot them if they took the bait.

Fear of getting shot and thus losing a reputation got so bad, said Pentecost, that some of the participants would simply roar through the arena without any intention of entering into a fight. Friends stopped talking to friends over the competition, said an air force F-5 driver. And interservice rivalry brought charges and countercharges of cheating and spying.

In addition, said Satrapa, there was at least one midair. An F-15 and F-5 collided nearly head-on. Both were so intent on the mission that they apparently failed to see each other.

"Nobody got killed, which was amazing," he said. "But when you got two guys closing beak to beak at over 1000 knots, it's damn tough to get out of a midair."

Satrapa himself had actually shut down his engine for a few seconds—a very dangerous tactic—in order to deny an attack F-5's Sidewinder his engine's heat signature.

"You'd do anything to stay alive," he said. "It was such hot competition for the number one jock."

But out of AIM-ACE emerged the data base for all-aspect tactics that would come to rule U.S. fighter aviation as it moved toward Desert Storm.

All-aspect, along with "off boresight"—the ability of a missile to track and hit a target even if the aircraft is not pointed at it—were to be the major missile advances of the 1980s that would dictate how a modern fighter pilot fought.

Satrapa, by the way, won the navy competition, finishing ACEVAL with the best kill ratio and just nipping Bjerke, who came in second.

Following AIM-ACE, Hoser left VX-4 to teach electronic warfare countermeasures (ECM) for a year, and then went to NAS Oceana, Virginia, the Atlantic Fleet's fighter headquarters, to instruct in the improved F-14A/A+ Tomcat until his first retirement, in 1984.

For a year and a half, he flew firefighting planes for the California Department of Forestry. But when Navy Secretary Lehman arranged for his recall to the navy in early 1986, he jumped at the chance, resuming his old job as an instructor at Oceana—and with a promotion to full commander.

Almost twenty years had passed since he'd first started chasing MiGs, and he was beginning to feel his age. Once he found himself gasping for air while pulling seven G's in a demanding dogfight. It happened again in a three-minute fight with Topgun instructors.

It wasn't a heart attack, he knew, and it didn't happen again, so he sloughed it off, keeping the episodes to himself, and worked out all the harder.

"I didn't smoke. I was doing push-ups and pull-ups. It scared me a little," he said. "When you're a young harddick, you go down to Key West and fly three hops a day, drink all night, and chase pussy. When you're forty-two or forty-three, you fly two hops a day, have a couple of beers, and go to bed by 2230 (10:30 P.M.). When you get to be forty-seven or forty-eight, you have one hop, eat dinner, and crash."

He was fifty.

Nevertheless, the Gulf War gave him new life.

"This was it. Destiny. It was going to happen," he remembers thinking. "I was going to get my MiG."

He was working at "Strike U," the navy's increasingly important air warfare center, in Fallon, Nevada, when the war broke out. He wasn't in an operational squadron, but Roy Gordon (a fighter commander discussed in the next chapter) said he'd give him a seat in the squadron if he could get qualified, as did another fighter commander.

"The adrenaline was really pumping. This was my last chance and I knew it. Nothing was going to stop me. If I'd have known I was going to die getting my MiG, I still would have gone."

But the navy knew he was no spring chicken. The toe-thumb was a good way to hold him back. He had to pass a battery of medical tests.

"Vision. Heart. All kinds of things I'd never done before. I think they were trying to find something else wrong so they wouldn't have to base it on my hand."

He passed them all, even took glee in casually using the thumb to tie his shoelaces, remove and replace his glasses, and do other tasks with it in front of a medical board, appearing unaware that they were scrutinizing the thumb but actually "working as hard as a dog to keep it looking good."

He got a unanimous thumbs-up, but by the time he got back to Strike U and was ready to leave, the war was over.

The realization was devastating.

"I said, Jeeez. I can't believe it. Didn't make it again. Everything ready. At least two seats waiting for me."

Depression set in. "But then I said, well, maybe somebody's trying to tell me something."

The next few dogfights he got in left him mentally and physically tired. "I said, well, I guess I'm going to cash in my chips and do something else."

He'd already bought a place in Nevada City, California, up on a beautiful, tree-covered mountain. He retired for the last time and now lives with a new wife and pretty young daughter—on whom he dotes like a Jewish mother—again flying firefighting planes.

I asked him if he ever wished he'd been a fighter pilot in World

War I or II, where the chances of getting kills were so much better (because of the large numbers of fighters and air battles then)
than they were after that.

"Since I was seventeen or eighteen," he said. "Target-rich environment. Sound of the piston engines, smell of the aviation gas
and the roar. I always liked the P-51s in Europe."

But, in truth, I don't think he ever really dwelled on it.

Satrapa was a modern warrior, and modern warriors fly jets.

3

THE F-4 PHANTOM JET was a great fighter for its day. It replaced the F-8 Crusader that Joe Satrapa had flown as the dominant navy fighter in the Vietnam War, and had always been the air force's choice. It was fast, powerful, and heavily armed, and once pilots learned to fly it as a maneuverable fighter, instead of as a point-and-shoot interceptor, it began to rack up impressive kill ratios, especially in the navy.

The Phantom will probably go down in history as one of the all-time jet classics. "Rhino," "Thunder Hog," and "Big Ugly" are just some of the names this great plane with the hunkered-down, two-engine fuselage; bent wings; and downward-pointing tail fins acquired while performing so admirably over the decades.

But by the early 1980s, the Phantom was getting old, as an experience by Roy "Flash" Gordon, a young ACM instructor in 1981, illustrates.

An F-14 fighter squadron commander by the Gulf War, Gordon, a lieutenant then, was having the time of his life in Key West back in the early 1980s in one of the best-kept secrets in the navy: VF-171 Det. The "Det" was a permanent detachment from the larger Oceana, Virginia–based VF-171, the East Coast F-4 RAG (replacement air group). New Phantom pilots were sent to the det by its larger parent to learn to dogfight their newly assigned fighters. It really wasn't a secret, but you had to be there to appreciate it. A little coral island with one of the wonders of the fishing and diving world in your backyard—the beautiful, clear, warm Caribbean—and nonstop, no-hassle, freewheeling, perfect weather dogfighting two to three times a day, almost any day you wanted.

"It was the type of place that if they'd just forgotten about you and left you there for ten or twenty years, you'd have stayed there happily," he recalls.

He'd just been married. He and his det mates had frequent parties at their houses on the canals, and they frequented the great local watering holes and restaurants, like the Boca Chica Bar on Stock Island, or Sloppy Joe's, where Hemingway used to hang out, on picturesque Duval Street. The Pig was good for black beans, yellow rice, and roast pork.

They'd show up for work at six A.M. in shorts and sandals, and after their hops, head on out to the reefs with beer and fishing rods or spearguns. A det was different from a full-blown squadron on a big base with admirals. With eight Phantoms and four A-4s, three of them souped-up Echoes, they were pretty much the navy there. The RAG, huge VF-171 up in Virginia, would send down a group of students for five weeks and it would be Gordon's and the others' job to teach them basic ACM.

He was a Topgun graduate, as were the other instructors, so they knew what they were talking about. And despite the casual lifestyle, they took their business seriously, making sure that when the students left, they had a strong indoctrination in how to fight the ornery and hard-to-handle Phantom, which they'd all come, through the tough work of mastering it, to love.

Unlike the new "fourth-generation" fighters (as they were sometimes called) that had entered service since Vietnam—like the navy's Tomcat and the air force's F-15 Eagle—the Phantom was controlled solely by hydraulics, pressurized fluid that moved its control surfaces. No electronic wizardry. No state-of-the-art gadgetry. It took strength and art to make the Phantom respond. It was much more of a "seat-of-the-pants" fighter than the newer models, and definitely less forgiving.

"No margin for error" is the way Gordon describes it.

If something went wrong in the air, the pilot better know how to correct it, he intimated, because the Phantom wasn't going to help.

It was a brute, and responded with brute force.

But back to the problem:

On this particular day—it was late afternoon, the last hop of the schedule—Gordon was up showing Lieutenant Joe Strange, a new RIO instructor in his backseat, a guns defense maneuver they used against the MiG-17.

They were at 15,000 feet, in a left turn.

Basically, when the 17 got close—as the A-4 Skyhawk MiG simulator behind them had—and started "pulling lead" (moving its nose to one side of the target) so it could fire at a position ahead of the Phantom (the only way the bogey's bullets could hit him because of the relative speeds and angles), Gordon would "unload" (accelerate straight ahead and down in afterburner), extending far enough away to ruin the bogey's tracking solution.

When the bogey tried to compensate by rolling over to "reacquire" the Phantom, Gordon would pull back into him, thus causing the bogey to try to roll back again. Each time the bogey tried to reacquire, Gordon would roll or pull lead. And because the Phantom had a superior roll rate, the bogey would always be playing catch-up and could never draw a proper bead. Eventually, the Phantom's more powerful engine would extend it out of the bogey's gun range and new options were available.

It had worked in Vietnam.

But as Gordon began demonstrating the defense, something went wrong. He suddenly couldn't stop the roll. Rather than easily swinging back to wings level, the Phantom started a downward plunge, rolling incessantly, boring a hole through the air like an airborne drill going crazy.

They were in excess of 550 knots and accelerating.

This was twenty tons of metal basically spinning like a top, the view outside the cockpit rotating from blue-green sea to mango-colored sky in dizzying sequence. Manipulation of the stick had absolutely no initial effect in countering the emergency. He considered ejection briefly, but realized the air blast outside—because they were going so fast—would kill them.

They were in a critical situation.

The solution Gordon finally came up with after descending nearly seven thousand feet in this corkscrew and trying everything else he could think of, was reducing power to a minimum and standing hard on his left rudder pedal, literally smashing it to the floor and holding it there with great exertion. Somehow those two actions stopped the roll, albeit very precariously. In addition, after some very delicate experimentation, he found a combination of left rudder pressure and stick that would allow approximately five degrees of left turn out of the airplane without going back into the roll—but he couldn't deviate a hair from that combination or the spinning would start again.

With darkness approaching, they limped home, Gordon rigidly holding the controls and throttle in exact position, cramping, exhausted—but never faltering. Even so, several times they started to roll again, electing at the last second not to eject because the unstable aircraft would behave once more.

The point of all this is that when they finally did get back, landing with zero margin for error and receiving medals for doing so, they found out that a little bolt connecting the stick controls to the flapping aileron had backed out of the aileron's control rod, causing the malfunction. Way back in the Vietnam War, someone had serviced the Phantom with an inferior part, and similarly caused emergencies were increasing among Phantoms throughout the world by 1981.

When Gordon's tour was up, he decided he wanted out of the aging F-4, as did a lot of other young fighter pilots in the navy and the air force, both of which were phasing out the planes—at least as fighters.

In Gordon's case, it was a matter of wanting a more combat-capable yet forgiving airplane—and knowing that if he didn't get F-14s, his road to advancement would be blocked.

For others, especially brand-new fighter pilots, it was more a matter of wanting the newer, more exciting jets; the "electric," better equipped and better performing "fourth-generation" fighters.

The superfighters of the 1980s—such as the one then–Air Force Lieutenant Rob Graeter flew.

The phone call from Colonel Taylor was terse: Pack a bag and be at the air terminal by midnight. They might be away for an extended period.

Rob Graeter didn't need more. This was his commanding officer talking. It was a little after midnight, September 1 (Far Eastern Time), 1983. The young air force F-15 Eagle pilot knew a huge Korean Air Lines 747 passenger jet had disappeared over Soviet waters in their vicinity and he had heard the rumors. The Russians had cold-bloodedly shot it down, claiming it was on a spy mission and they'd given it repeated warnings.

He didn't believe the Soviets for a second. His base, Kadena, Okinawa, four hundred miles south of the main Japanese islands and home to his 12th Tactical Fighter Squadron, had access to highly classified information. It told a darker story: The passenger jet had strayed and been blasted without warning; missiled, as it was, out of a frigid Pacific night, its 269 passengers—at least those of them still alive—screaming in seemingly endless terror as their plane hurtled nearly seven miles down into a black and pitiless ocean.

The airliner, Flight 007, carried women and children. It carried Americans. It was believed that no one survived. Graeter had seen distraught families waiting at Seoul airport, the flight's final destination, on television. It could have been his own family on that plane. His wife, Debbie, and eleven-month-old son, Adam, lived with him at Kadena. They were to fly back to the States within the week. The grandparents hadn't yet seen Adam. But now that he was being ordered to go with the select group of pilots to Misawa, a small forward base nearer to the disappearance site, how would Debbie get to the airport?

The problem worried him after he hung up the phone.

Debbie, herself, wasn't happy when she heard the order. It would be the first time they were separated for any extended period since their marriage two years before. While they'd planned for the trip back home, this was sudden and different. He was going into harm's way. The mission would be to guard lumbering P-3 search planes from Soviet fighters as they looked for the KAL wreckage and possible survivors. If the Russians had shot down an unarmed airliner, what would they do to the P-3s? Was this the beginning of World War III? Would she ever see him again?

"Things were pretty tense," he says. She remembers "worrying about him being shot down, yelling at [him] for something." He remembers, "I forgot my bag. She had to run back to the house . . . meet on that big boulevard on the base. That was the first time I'd seen her so upset. She wasn't one to be that way."

But he was glad to be going. It was an honor to be picked. He was the only non-IP (instructor pilot) of the six who had been chosen. IPs were up at the top of the F-15 squadron pecking order. They were the pilots who checked out the others, made sure they were mission-ready, certified them. The only reason he wasn't an IP already was that he didn't yet have five hundred hours in the F-15, a requirement over which he had little control.

But he was well on his way, getting all the flight time he could. Only a first lieutenant, and barely three years out of ROTC at East Texas State University, he had just been made a four-ship flight lead, which was the job most of the IPs had. The four-ship lead was the quarterback in the basic Eagle deployment of two pairs, or "elements," of F-15s. When given a mission, he conducted the brief, commanded the other three Eagles in the air. It took exceptional ability and knowledge, which was why most IPs and four-ship leads were higher ranking captains or majors.

"Rob wore the F-15 like a suit," recalls his friend and former flight leader from those days, Sal Speziale, now an American Airlines pilot. Big like a football halfback, quietly confident, the black-haired, dark-eyed son of a career air force officer, Graeter had always thought he'd fly large C-141 transports like his father until he'd witnessed an F-15 stand on its tail and shoot straight up at an air show during his basic pilot training.

"The pilot did a short takeoff," Graeter, who was born in California, remembers. "Then he stood it on its tail and pulled it right into the vertical ... seven thousand feet straight up.... I was [training] in the T-38, which is reasonably powerful, but nothing like that.... It was eye watering."

From then on, he'd set his sights on fighters. Graduating at the top of his class, he'd won an Eagle. It was a big fighter, he remembered, "pretty."

Built in response to Soviet advances, plus the dogfight problems air force pilots encountered during the Vietnam War, the F-15 was now the air force's main fighter. It was a pure air superiority machine with no other purpose than shooting down enemy planes. Twin-tailed, twin-engined, and bubble-canopied—all like the navy's fourth-generation F-14 fighter, which it resembled—the Eagle had stronger engines than the Tomcat. In fact, at the time it was delivered to the first U.S. combat squadrons, it was the only American fighter with thrust that exceeded its weight. This was almost a revolutionary upgrade from previous fighters, and the reason it could go straight up, actually gaining speed while climbing. Previous air force fighters had to climb at a distinct angle. Stand them on their tails and they'd fall backward, possibly go out of control.

They simply didn't have the power.

But the Eagle's thrust—25,000 pounds of it in each Pratt and Whitney F-100 turbofan—meant it could turn without excessive energy loss, a tremendous advantage in aerial combat. In addition, the new C-model Graeter's squadron was flying had a souped-up radar with four basic search modes, enabling it to find elusive targets over a hundred miles away, as well as to automatically lock on and shoot—with gun, radar, or heat-seeking missile—bandits already engaged at shorter distances.

At Kadena, they called the new C-model Eagle the "Big Dick Dog." While it resembled an F-14, its wings were larger in area and fixed rather than swing. To aid the pilot in a dogfight, it had two innovations: "HUD," the heads-up display of all necessary flight data, projected on the glareshield in front of the pilot; and "HOTAS," the hands-on throttle and stick, meaning all the switches needed during a fight were at the pilot's fingertips on either the stick or throttle. He didn't have to lean or stretch to reach any of them. All told, there were some eighteen of these switches to choose from—it was like playing a clarinet, some said—including radar search modes, missiles and guns, and radio frequencies.

Thus, unlike the pilot of an F-4 Phantom in Vietnam, the Eagle pilot didn't have to move his eyes or hands much in order to take a shot. He could keep his eyes on the bandit, which was so important in a dogfight. In a business where milliseconds were often the difference between life or death, such advantages arguably made the Eagle the deadliest killing machine in the air—in the hands of the right pilot.

"Rob was the type you only had to show once," says Speziale. Quick. A fast thinker. "Very intelligent, both academically and common sense–wise. It's hard to find people with both." He was like the character Iceman in the movie *Top Gun*, says Jim Meyer, another American Airlines pilot and longtime friend from pilot training. "He didn't brag about golden hands or being the toughest around. He didn't have to. He didn't have to prove anything to anybody—except maybe himself."

The assignment to Misawa was his chance, the first time he might be tested in actual combat, a fitting culmination to his air force training so far.

He looked forward to it. But was he good enough?

A reluctant and apprehensive Debbie dropped him off at the darkened air terminal, they kissed and said good-bye, and after the bag-forgetting incident, he boarded, at around five A.M., a small T-39 business jet, with Colonel Taylor, whose call sign was "Hawk," and two of the other selected pilots. The balance of the contingent would help fly the Eagles up to Misawa and sit the first twenty-four-hour alert.

Misawa was a small, picturesque U.S.–Japanese-run airfield at the northern tip of Honshu, the main Japanese island. It was one of the closest Allied bases to the Soviet Union, being only two hundred or so miles from Sakhalin, the long, thin Russian island hugging the mainland over which the KAL airliner was said to have been missiled before it crashed into the Sea of Japan just north of Hokkaido, the northernmost Japanese island.

Because of its location, it was a key intelligence-gathering base.

They arrived at around eight A.M. There wasn't much there—a few old hangars, a tower and communications building, several Japan Defense Force planes, and green fields, some with antennas, surrounded by hills and lakes. A navy F-4 squadron would arrive later and be caught up in the alerts, too. It was the end of summer and the weather was cool with foggy mornings.

As dawn broke, they set up headquarters in a small tractor trailer on the far side of the field. Both the trailer and the field had last been heavily used during the Korean and Vietnam wars. They furnished the trailer with an old couch, a coffeepot, and radio equipment. Outside, on an old parking ramp, they parked their six gray Eagles, the distinctive "ZZ" on their tails. A runway was nearby. They later set up lawn chairs and a croquet game, two of many items supplied by the base commander, an air force colonel there to ready the base for a future air force tenant.

"It was like those movies you see of the pilots in the Battle of Britain," recalls Graeter. "The enlisted guys had a big pavilion tarp and we'd play games or lounge around reading or soaking up rays. We even had one of those hand-cranked sirens for scrambles. This colonel was like our black market guy. He kept asking us if there was anything he could get us. He had lots of cash because of the [unit] coming in, and got us food, videos, TVs."

But the first few days were tense.

Early on they were given clearance for top-priority classified information arriving on the shootdown. They had brought an intelligence officer with them.

"He was a real go-getter, high-strung, emotional," remembers Graeter. He carried a folder and made trips between the base intelligence office and the trailer. "We had maps in the trailer with pens in them, and he would open his folder with the latest information and show us what was happening. We plotted it on the maps."

The hot spot was the suspected KAL crash site in the Sea of Japan off the southwestern tip of Sakhalin. The Russians had fighter bases on Sakhalin—at Smirnykh, in its center, and Dolinsk-Sokol, at its southern end—and at Vladivostok, on the mainland near the North Korean border. Swing-wing MiG-23 Floggers, with medium-range Apex missiles, were the most numerous threat. There were also Vietnam-era MiG-21s at the bases. But the first day of the crisis, the Soviets ominously flew a new MiG-31 Foxhound from Sakhalin's Sokol down to Vladivostok.

"We weren't concerned about the Floggers or Fishbeds [MiG-21s]," says Graeter. "They posted a minor threat. The Eagle is better on all counts." But the MiG-31, recently introduced to Russian units, was a mystery. All they knew was that it was an "enhanced version" of the MiG-25 (interceptor) and that it had made the Vladivostok run at record speed—2.3 Mach, or around 1,500 miles per hour—at 65,000 feet. Graeter: "We didn't have anything that could fly that fast at that altitude except the SR-71 [spy plane], and the MiG was carrying missiles."

The Russian pilots were also somewhat of a mystery. They were perhaps the best pilots of all the U.S.'s Cold War enemies, teachers of the North Koreans, Libyans, and Syrians, among others, which hadn't as yet won them any honors. But although Soviet pilots tended to be rote and less skilled than American pilots—perhaps reflecting their country's authoritarianism, as well as a lack of regular and innovative training—the pilots in the Far Eastern Sector, as the Russians called their air force in that area, tended to be the country's best.

"I don't know why," says Graeter. "Maybe it's because they're farther away from the bureaucracy in Moscow and left alone. They are really out in nowhere. But they have some know-how. It's not like messing with some of those Third World pilots."

Nevertheless he believed he was better trained and better prepared. Hell, he was raring to "smack 'em," he says. He and Speziale, a handsome Sicilian-born immigrant who had once worked as a model and actor in New York before attending the Air Force Academy, had been practicing for years for such a fight.

Aware that the safest shot was before the "merge"—before they could even see the bandit with their own eyes—they both nonetheless preferred the close-in, slow fight for testing their dogfight skills. And they both knew that they had that luxury, since the Russians didn't have a good BVR (beyond visual range) missile—at least, nobody had seen one.

Speziale: "Compared to Rob, I was kind of small—five-foot-seven. So it was like David and Goliath. But we were great friends and both dedicated fighter pilots. We both wanted to learn. So we'd go out and have these great fights, me as the flight lead and him as the wingman. We'd come back all sweaty and exhausted."

Graeter: "The movies or TV can't show you what it's really like. The rapid closure rates. How fast things are happening. . . . If your head weighs ten pounds, the G forces are making it feel like ninety . . . your chest is crushed, making it hard to breathe. The world goes upside down, rightside up. You go up, down, around . . ."

At least once, their competitiveness almost ended in disaster.

Air force safety rules dictate that dogfight practice cease below five thousand feet, and that planes stay at least one thousand feet apart and two thousand feet above a cloud deck. But neither Graeter or Speziale were about to call "knock it off" as they teetered nose-high in a slow-speed battle that they didn't realize was rapidly approaching the minimums, their planes nearly entwined, each waiting for the other to make a mistake.

"We were standing on our tails," recalls Speziale, "basically no airspeed, no control."

Something had to give.

It did. Both Eagles fell off to opposite sides, diving into dense clouds, their pilots becoming disoriented because of the low visibility. They fought to regain controlled flight, knowing that the sea below was rushing up. The only way they could get the air sufficiently back on to their wings and start flying again was to continue powering straight down—at about one thousand feet per second.

"It was a scary situation," says Speziale. "I'm fighting to get the nose up. We're talking to each other. 'Rob, where are you?' " He said he didn't get the plane flying again until he was approximately one thousand feet from the ocean.

Another second or two and he could have reached out and touched it.

"When we came out of the clouds," he said, "we both saw each other. We flew straight and level to get our heartbeats back. It's one of those times when you realize you've unknowingly done something you never want to do again. But we would really push those jets."

The good ones always did. Neither wanted the indignity of going home the loser.

Graeter and Colonel Taylor took over the alert the afternoon following their arrival at Misawa. Their watch was uneventful and they were not launched. Both sides were looking for the airliner's black box. Details about the shootdown trickled in from Intelligence: The Russian pilot had made a visual identification of the airliner. He had radioed back to his headquarters that it was too big to be a spy plane. He had not warned the airliner before complying with an order to shoot it down.

The Russians were clearly aware that it was a passenger plane with civilians aboard, said Graeter. America vehemently denied that it had put the airliner up to any spy mission, a position that gained credence in years after the incident as Russia admitted more culpability and the United States stuck to its denials.

"We were getting real-time info and the more we heard the madder we got," Graeter added.

The situation with the P-3s also deteriorated.

The search planes were nervous as they flew unprotected in the northern Sea of Japan. MiG bases were all around them. But they had to go it alone. Authorities running the operation—ultimately reaching all the way to the Reagan White House, which was very mad about the shootdown—did not want the Eagles to accompany them for fear of escalating the crisis. Only if it was determined that the P-3s were in real immediate danger would the Eagles be sent to their CAP station.

So Graeter and the others had to wait.

But as they studied the CAP that had been given them, they realized they had a problem. The orbit was placed at a cushioning distance from Soviet airspace, again in order not to be provoking. The trouble was that warplanes from at least one of the MiG bases—Sokol, on the tip of Sakhalin—could get to the P-3s in half the time the Eagles could. There were rumors that the MiGs were going after the P-3s. After high-level deliberations, the pilots were given a second, closer CAP. But it was only to be used if the situation warranted.

In the meantime, accounts that human remains were washing up on the northern shores of Hokkaido came in, as did a photo of a MiG harassing a P-3 on the first day of the search.

The photos pushed everybody to the brink, said Graeter. "What arrogance. First they shoot down a civilian airliner and now they're trying to keep us from finding the black box to see what happened. They didn't know that we'd made recordings of all their comms [radio communications], so we already knew what had happened."

He said he believed the MiG had actually bumped the P-3's wing in an effort to intimidate it. "We wanted to go up there and smack them. Those were Americans they'd shot down, and Americans in the P-3s."

On the third day he was there—his second alert shift—he finally got his chance to act.

"The [Intelligence] lieutenant called and said the P-3s are up and MiGs are being launched," he recalls.

It was a cool, overcast afternoon. Graeter and Taylor were on standby, and they manned their Eagles to sit and await instructions. In about ten minutes, the lieutenant "came running out of the hut with a map." He climbed up to Taylor's open cockpit, where Taylor and he conferred. Graeter was too far away to hear what they said, but as the lieutenant left, Taylor gave the signal to start engines.

They were going.

Graeter, heart pounding, didn't need any more information.

They'd briefed on what to do earlier. He was the wingman. He'd follow the colonel.

It was the first launch of the mission. "All the maintenance guys came running out to watch, so we blasted off. I remember we were loaded with three [fuel] tanks and eight missiles so we were pretty heavy [approximately thirty tons, or nearly double the normal weight]. The airplane really shuddered as we turned left toward the CAP."

He was disappointed that the haze prevented him from seeing the skiing mountains around Sapporo, where the Winter Olympics had been held in 1972. "But all the Japanese and Americans were watching, so the adrenaline was flowing pretty well, and I've got a big smile on my face. At this point it's a lot of fun."

But as they climbed farther north, "the adrenaline started to fade and you begin to think, Uh, oh, I'm really going. Why exactly have they scrambled us? I don't really know. Maybe there's something big going on that we're going to jump into? . . . You worry about the unknowns. Am I good enough? Am I trained enough?"

Were they about to start World War III?

He'd been training all his military life for this, but "it's totally different when the fight's for real. Nerves become a major factor. Your hands will shake on you if you let them. Your palms sweat. In training, you go home and brief after a guy shoots you. In a war, you're not coming home. This had the potential to escalate. . . . I remember thinking, God, how will we ever defeat these guys? It's such a huge country. They have Fencers [Sukoi attack planes] and Black Jack bombers that could attack my home at Kadena where my family was."

He was confident of his and Taylor's abilities. But what if the situation demanded more?

Born in Vacaville, California, in 1957, Graeter had known he wanted to be a pilot since his eleventh birthday. As a present that day, his father took him flying in a Piper Cub. He was so set on the profession that when he enrolled at East Texas State, he volunteered "flying" as his major. Told there was no such course of study, he ended up in computer science.

"Back then it was just being able to look down at the ground and being free and floating around," he said, "seeing all those houses as little specks. You weren't tied to the road or sidewalks. It was such a neat sensation. You could go directly to where you wanted to go."

He was a fairly good student in high school, but because of injuries he quit football for track, where he was a shot-putter and discus thrower. At East Texas State, he stayed away from sports altogether for fear of hurting his knees and thus his flying career. He was elected president of his social fraternity, Delta Tau Delta, and became commander of the Air Force ROTC detachment, getting a military scholarship in the process.

He got through basic pilot training fairly easily and married Debbie, an enlisted clerk at one of his training squadrons, right after graduation. Their courtship almost cost him his dream. Women, formerly only in the WAF (Women in the Air Force), had recently been integrated into the regular air force. The service was sensitive about fraternization. When he'd been reported at Debbie's on-base quarters after hours, he was threatened with loss of his hard-won F-15 assignment. But when his superiors realized the relationship was serious, they backed off.

He and Debbie were married in an all–air force ceremony.

He ate bugs and got dunked in parachute harness at survival schools, and in late 1980, after fighter lead-in, a two-month course where they weaned him from the smaller training command T-37 and T-38, he and Debbie drove to Luke Air Force Base, outside Phoenix, Arizona, for his initial training in the F-15 (the RTU, or replacement training unit).

"It was pretty awesome," he remembers. "When you're fresh out of ATC [Air Training Command] and all you've seen is the little white airplanes, those gray monsters [the F-15s] are awe-inspiring. I remember just being overwhelmed by their size and power."

Learning the sophisticated systems—weapons, the complex radar, central computer, inertial navigation—was the hardest task, he said: "All confusing." The T-37 and T-38 had been elementary by comparison. But he studied nights and weekends and slowly caught on, until, at the end of the four and a half months, he was showing signs of innate talent as he winged through fifteen introductory sorties of BFM, the basic fighter maneuvers used when fighting another airplane close-in.

"The bottom line in BFM," he says, "is your ability to maneuver the airplane, make it do what you want it to do."

Like a gifted athlete, he was instinctive. He didn't think a lot in the air. He just performed.

And he had the gift of SA (situational awareness).

"Most guys can master the mechanics of the systems," he says, "but it's instinctive to be able to assimilate all the data, get a big picture, and react offensively. Not a lot of guys can do that."

In August 1981, as the Reagan administration began to pump more money into the armed forces after the Carter depletions, including giving him a smile-prompting pay raise, Graeter reported to far-off Kadena, one of the Pacific Air Force's busiest bases.

"It was a little numbing," he remembers. "Okinawa is eleven hours ahead of the States. So you're out of whack timewise, and stranded on this huge base with tankers and AWACS [airborne warning and control system planes] and F-15s scattered all over. The air base is one of the biggest in the world. It was pretty neat."

Although he'd finally graduated, he still had to be tested. The 12th Tactical Fighter Squadron was operational. It was great that he'd passed all his training command requirements, but they needed to know if he actually could function in the real fighter world. If they were called into battle, he was going to have to perform at a professional level.

Their lives depended on it.

An IP would put him through MQT (mission qualification training). Basically, this tested a pilot's ability to fly the Eagle as a wingman, the low man in the two-ship element. Adding to the difficulty of qualifying was the fact that the squadron had recently received the new C-model Eagles, which had more powerful radar than previous models.

At Luke, he'd learned on the simpler A-model.

Typical of the squadron's IPs was Mike Straight, a Nellis Air Force Base, Nevada, F-15 Weapons School graduate on his way to becoming an award-winning tactician. The fair-haired Straight was an expert on F-15 performance and a demanding airfighting scholar who would become F-15 Weapons School Instructor of the Year. But Graeter passed his MQT in minimum time and was posted to a routine alert in Korea the very next day.

"I couldn't believe how lucky I was," he says. "I remember waking up at night and thinking it was a dream, then realizing I really am flying F-15s in an Eagle squadron."

But he still had a lot to learn. And it wasn't until a year or so later, and countless hours of fighting practice and briefing instruction, that he finally began to feel that he'd "arrived" as a fighter pilot. In particular, he remembers a fight he and Sal won working as a team in the wing's semiannual "Turkey Shoot," an ACM competition among the wing's four squadrons.

It was a canned setup, he remembers. He and Speziale were fighting a senior IP positioned a mile and a half behind them.

With the call "Fight's on," the two defenders broke into hard seven-G turns.

"I can't even begin to explain what that feels like," says Graeter. "If you weigh two hundred pounds, seven G's makes you weigh fourteen hundred. It's the ultimate roller coaster. Your cheeks droop, your mask slips off. You have a hard time seeing because your eyelids are flapping."

G-suits ballooning, grunting to tighten stomach muscles and further prevent upper body blood from pooling and draining sight and consciousness, the two-ship curled in side-by-side half circles at 450 knots. Still just beginning the turn, fighting off "graying," a preliminary to blacking out, Graeter forced his G-heavy head back to catch sight of the bandit.

"He's going to come down between us and try to force one of us out," he explains.

Simultaneously, his fingers were selecting a radar mode on his stick—"playing the piccolo," they called it. In this case his middle finger bumped the vertical scan mode. With the attacker descending, it would provide a lengthy up-and-down swath. His weapons were already on. He had only to catch the bandit in the swath and then select heat or radar missile for a mile-plus shot, or guns if closer.

Two thirds into the turn, with the fleet bandit merely a rocketing speck out in front of him, Graeter saw that the IP was faking. Looking like he was going after Speziale, he was dropping his nose slightly, a preliminary to suddenly reversing direction and switching back to Graeter—which he promptly did.

But Graeter's SA had already projected the move.

Rather than continuing in his horizontal circle, as the IP had figured he would, Graeter had done the unexpected. He'd exited his turning circle straight up and gone over on his back, teetering precariously, as the surprised IP, nose still downward, had roared beneath him.

Upside down, slowed to about 250 knots, furiously working the foot pedals and stick to keep his inverted hover, Graeter knew he had several seconds to watch his prey. It would take that long for the IP to pull his nose up because of gravity.

The IP was obviously going to try to come back up and over him, Graeter deduced, which at least would have prolonged the fight, possibly kept it neutral.

But then the IP made a mistake.

Rattled, fighting gravity while Graeter now had it as an ally, the IP abandoned his plan of attacking the younger pilot and turned hard and horizontally back toward Speziale. The move presented Graeter with an opportunity to pull down hard and on to the IP's tail.

Graeter took it.

"It's really a fast turn because I'm slow and I've got gravity with me," he said.

More crushing G's, swirling horizon. He straightened out, rightside up, and was closing on the IP, who was curling in front and knew he was in trouble.

"As soon as I'm coming down, I'm trying to lock him up for a shot," says Graeter. Because he had the IP so close, he switched to supersearch mode, a compact, more powerful beam. All he had to do then was get the target in his "reticle," a small aiming circle on his HUD, and pull the trigger.

Because he was so close, he'd gone to guns.

The IP jinked and slowed, trying to evade. But Graeter kept his distance—and his lock.

"You have to roll with his jink, slap power back. The reticle's jumping. You make corrections."

Modulating power to keep within minimum range, he fired.

The guns automatically calculated proper solutions.

Score!

From "Fight's on" to "Knock it off," the entire engagement had taken only fifteen to twenty seconds, great time for the exercise, and a big win for his squadron.

Two other times that day they fought the IP in different canned setups, Speziale getting a kill, and the two of them sharing a third.

Three to zero! And over a pilot with many times their experience.

They were stars—at least for that day.

But they didn't gloat. Maybe a few private "shit hots" as they climbed down from their planes and walked back on the tarmac, but "that hand-slapping is Hollywood crap," says Graeter.

It wasn't professional.

"The guy who loses is technically dead," says Speziale.

And they still had to see the gun camera film to make sure the shots were valid.

They were. And the IP, just as cool at the debrief, backhanded some compliments. "He said something along the lines of, 'I didn't expect you to do that,' " remembers Graeter, and " 'I was really surprised you were in my shit so fast.' "

Graeter, quietly, had thrived on the comments.

In time, winning had become routine. He and Speziale had been selected outstanding pilots of the Turkey Shoot—and of two more in the following year. They'd received plaques, buzzed Russian trawlers together, played jokes on new young pilots who were as green as he had been when he'd first come to the squadron.

He'd come to believe that he was worthy.

But that was during training. This KAL mission was for real.

The two Eagles streaked in the battle formation that was called the "Wall": close together, line abreast. The formation was almost synonymous with Eagles, especially a four-ship. It allowed them to mass their considerable firepower. "Everything in front dies," is the way they liked to explain it.

Don't mess with the Wall.

But the mission was for naught.

They arrived at the CAP station only to be told by AWACS that the MiGs had turned around. They could see them eighty miles away on radar but they were fleeing. Taylor asked permission to chase. But permission was denied.

"I would have kept badgering," said Graeter, "but Hawk, after arguing, said that was it. I was young and I wanted to go after them real bad. But I guess in hindsight that was the best call. No telling what would have happened if we'd killed a few."

They didn't like it, but they stayed on their CAP.

"It was frustrating," said Graeter. "We wanted to show them who they were messing with, that we could kick their butts."

Two hours later they went back to Misawa. In the days that followed, Graeter and others would scramble again and play the same game. Although they toyed with each other on radar, it became apparent that whenever the Eagles rose, the MiGs would retreat.

"That gave us some satisfaction," said Graeter.

But not a lot.

At one point, says Speziale, there was even talk of sending up a decoy to sucker an attack. But the mission was called off.

Within a week, the Russians became conciliatory, and tensions dropped.

In six weeks, Graeter was back home.

He'd missed this chance to test himself. He didn't know it but he'd get ample compensation in Desert Storm.

4

"MONGO" WAS HIS call sign, a moniker he'd gotten, he said, for putting his head through a "beer machine." He didn't elaborate. As we talked he put some chewing tobacco under his lip and began spitting into a cup.

Captain Steve Robbins was his real name, and he was an instructor at the air force's F-15 Fight Weapons School (FWS) in Nellis, Nevada. I had come to Nellis knowing it was the center of fighter piloting in the United States.

The low-slung, modern building we were in housed not only the F-15 FWS but similar schools for the F-15E, the bombing version of the Eagle; the F-16 Falcon, the air force's newest fighter; the A-10, the F-111, air warfare controllers, and intelligence officers. Young air force standouts came here to become experts in their "weapons platforms," as they call their planes—flying them, fighting them, shooting their missiles and guns—and then go back after the four-month courses and become their unit's "weapons" officers, responsible for keeping the unit current.

Since the Vietnam War, Nellis, once a dusty World War II Army Air Corps gunnery school, had steadily grown in influence, giving birth to such important fighter training programs as

MiG-simulating "Aggressor" squadrons and "Red Flag," the massive air-strike exercise designed to give bomber and fighter crews as realistic a dose of air warfare as is possible in peacetime before they have to learn the hard way in real combat.

Nellis was a mecca. Everybody who is anybody in fighter aviation, regardless of service, eventually comes here. Not that there aren't other important fighter bases in the United States. There certainly are. Miramar, Oceana, and Eglin come to mind. But Nellis, because of its huge northern ranges, enveloping a sizable chunk of the heart of Nevada, and the nearly five thousand square miles of restricted range's isolation from populated areas, is the one with the most going on.

The Stealth fighter, for instance, was tested and housed on one of its secret ranges for years without the general public's knowing about it.

As a consequence, nearby Las Vegas owed its rise almost as much to fighter pilots as it did to gangsters.

But that's another story.

Mongo had an unsettling look, the kind I'd seen before games when good opposing players had measured me. Not that it was personal, or that he even considered me in the same league. But he was calculating—cold blue eyes, confident manner, blunt speech. And because of his position—instructor to F-15 pilots deemed the best in their squadrons—there was no doubt he was a top Eagle pilot.

He'd just returned from Desert Storm, where he'd had a strange experience—time compression. A SAM had been shot up at him and he'd had to make a high-G, 180-degree turn to avoid it.

"It seemed like it took forever," he said, "but it actually had taken about five to eight seconds. . . . Adrenaline. Your mind is on a different plane. . . . It's so receptive to input that the normal time frame is slowed down."

It was his first time in combat, which always serves to heighten sensation. He had gone as the Eagle weapons school's representative to find out about the Iraqi pilots, who he said weren't much once their command and control had been destroyed and they had no one to tell them how to fight.

He didn't get much time in the air and never saw an enemy airplane, except on the ground, where he strafed a four-engine Soviet transport called a "Candid." The other thing that impressed him was lasting snapshots of "very specific things"—for instance, humans on the ground.

"I rolled down, it seemed like for half an hour, and then I remember flying by and looking over the side and clearly seeing some Iraqi ground troops standing there looking up at me. I can still remember their faces, and it seemed like that lasted for five minutes. But then everything went back to normal."

But the war was now receding and he was back at his job training superior F-15 pilots to be better. Strangely, he said the hardest thing he'd ever experienced in his military life was not combat or near accidents, but getting through the FWS as a student in 1985.

"It's not show up and you're going to graduate," he said. "You've got to perform. . . . I remember during the BFM phase sitting up in the middle of the night wondering how the fuck did he do that? How am I going to beat that? . . . It was intense, real intense."

Not only do students have to fly well, duplicating what their instructors do, but they have to be able to convincingly brief and debrief—get up in front of the instructors and talk insightfully about what they are learning. "I kept saying, God, how am I going to do it?"

The highlight came, he said, when he and three other Eagle drivers—two instructors and two students—went against twelve Vipers (F-16s), in a class exercise, and killed ten of them without the Vipers getting off a shot.

"Best Eagle sortie I ever had . . . I remember going into the merge with a guy named Jess Hamilton, the epitome of the killing machine. He's got the world's greatest eyeballs. . . . He'd call a tallyho over here and then I'd follow and pick off the strays. . . . Where are you ever going to get into a fight with Vipers and not have them get off a shot?"

Back at his squadron after graduating, he said he had "the best year I've ever had in the air force.

"I had a great commander. His call sign was 'Cowboy.' He basically gave me free rein to run the weapons program as I saw fit. . . . People would come to you for help. . . . We'd have bull sessions on Friday afternoons. Get out a bottle and go to the chalkboard, and throw up a problem."

After that he was asked to come back to the Fighter Weapons School as an instructor. That was in 1988.

"Tremendous challenge. I taught AIM-7 [Sparrow missile] and BFM, which meant I spent a lot of time researching. It's real technical. So I can teach it at an appropriate level. We consider this to be the Ph.D. of fighter degrees. It's not an electronic engineering course . . . but a fighter pilot's course in how the missile works, what goes on, much more in depth than anybody will ever get anywhere else on what the thing does."

The flying in the job is the best he's ever had, he said, but the most "rewarding" aspect is "seeing a guy that comes in maybe not confident in his abilities. He knows he's good in the air but he's not real good on standing up and being able to talk, to be able to instruct, brief, and to debrief and think quickly on his feet. And then over that four months see him really progress to someone very confident in himself as an instructor and a pilot."

He had a "very aggressive" fighting style, he said, but "you win with basics. . . . If I had to lay two foundations for Eagle employment they would be mass firepower and do the basics very well. . . . We don't do anything cosmic. What we do is the basics very well. That kicks anybody's ass."

What are the basics?

"Mass your firepower [as in the Wall] . . . operating the radar, taking the offensive advantage, placing your jet in a position where you have a weapons advantage . . . utilizing his weaknesses, like [a less powerful] radar . . . where you can come in and deny him radar contacts. Any of these advantages to get you in the first position to employ weapons before he can.

"Then from there, to execute defensive basics if needed. For instance, if you get in a position where you missed your radar contact . . . You are now defensive to him. [If you are beyond visual range] you react accordingly. You haven't lost the ball game yet. You're just momentarily defensive before you retake the offensive."

He hates to lose, he said, but losing in training is a must.

"Losing in combat in unacceptable . . . so you have to learn from your mistakes. . . . You will see some fighter pilots who cannot lose—at least in their minds. What you end up with there is a brick wall. No matter how good the guy is he's never going to be the absolute best he can be because he refuses to accept a critique. . . . I've had my ass shot in training plenty. And I'll be the first to admit it. But I'll learn from it. I'll try to avoid making the same mistake again. . . . So yes, I hate to lose and being competitive is good. But the guy who makes excuses is the guy who is going to die."

If a student persists in not acknowledging his mistakes, there are two ways to handle the situation.

"The way I start is by leading the first two missions and letting them lead the next two missions . . . and when it's our turn to debrief—after they've led the mission—I go through and critique all my mistakes and let him see that . . . if anything, I will be harder on myself than I will be on them. So they'll see, hey, these guys are willing to hit their own mistakes and to do it very severely.

"If they don't see it from that, then I'll sit them down and go, Look, asshole, if you don't start learning to accept critique and admitting when you're wrong, this four months is going to be miserable if you are lucky enough to make it through. So you try the sublime approach first. And if that doesn't work, you directly confront him with it's time to change your attitude.

"The latter happens occasionally. . . . You still get some hardheads and you wonder if they're just kind of nodding until they can get out of here and graduate. . . . You wonder how they are going to be when they get out in the field. But I'd say the vast majority turn out real well. They learn that you don't have to be shit hot all the time. In fact, the guy all the young guys are going to respect is the guy who will admit he made a mistake and tell you how he is going to fix it. Not the guy who goes, No, I never made a mistake. That guy is quickly seen as a bullshitter. Very quickly. People aren't stupid."

We talked for an hour, but you're not going to get a lot in a first meeting.

Doug Cantwell's call sign is "Stretch." No explanation needed there. He is tall and lanky, with blond hair and all-American looks, a hint of a smile when he talked. Thirty-seven years old, he'd been an instructor at the FWS since 1990, and in F-15s all his service life, which is roughly fifteen years.

Like Mongo, his dad had been in the military: Mongo's a navy chief petty officer during World War II; Cantwell's a career army officer. He had been born in Frankfurt, Germany; had been captain of the swimming team at North Plainfield (New Jersey) High School; and had not been interested in flying—unlike Mongo, who said he'd "always wanted to be a flyer"—until he'd received an ROTC scholarship at the University of Texas, from which he graduated in 1975.

Among his distinctions were several little cloth silver stars sewn into his flight suit sleeve above the wrist, each signifying five hundred hours in the F-15. He was one of the most seasoned Eagle instructors. He had also taught Saudi Arabian pilots in the mid-1980s how to bomb in the Eagle, a skill he'd acquired before the fighter, in the new form of the F-15E, had been adapted for bombing.

Similar to Mongo, he said the high point of his career had been when he was selected to attend the F-15 FWS as a student—"I had wanted that more than anything else in my business life"— but once there, that honor turned into a low point.

"It was a very frustrating time for me because of the high level of capabilities you had to demonstrate and what they expected of you. There were times when you'd get in a slump and find it very difficult to get out. . . . For the professional aviator, this is the most difficult course there is. . . . It's at least a year's worth of work crammed into four months. It's all-consuming."

The most "demanding" part of the course, he said, was the last "dissimilar air combat tactics mission" each student had to perform successfully before earning the looked-up-to "bull's-eye" patch. "I can't remember the exact force levels [he had gone through in 1983], but in the current syllabus . . . it's six of us against twelve adversaries, at all altitudes, from three hundred feet to fifty thousand feet, and it takes place in a very small piece of airspace.

"There are a lot of airplanes out there and, as the leader, you've got to have total control over the entire engagement." This was the elusive SA. "That to me was the most demanding thing because it can't be free-flow. . . . It has to be structured. It has to meet the objectives of the mission that you lay out during the briefing. To do that, you've got to keep it under control."

What were the objectives?

"Your objective is to defend your piece of airspace. . . . You may not be able to kill every one, [but] if you make them turn around and go away, that accomplishes your objective. But certainly you've got to be able to detect all of the threats to your flight and effectively apportion those threats to the other members so that the most important are targeted and weapons employment is maximized. . . . Our objective is to shoot 100 percent valid shots at all targets."

He said he failed the first attempt but passed the second. "It was a learning experience."

His first squadron had been at Bitburg, Germany, which, until the Cold War ended, had been the air force base from which experts figured the first American fighters would fly should a war with the Soviets start in Europe. It was 1977, the F-15 had recently been introduced, and he had been one of the first young lieutenants out of the training command to get an Eagle assignment.

"I almost felt invincible. . . . All the other guys were old F-4 guys who had converted to the F-15. They were looking at the lieutenants as the new breed. . . . So I was right on the ground floor and felt like I couldn't do anything wrong and could get away with anything. . . . We were close to the Luxembourg border. Very beautiful terrain. And the flying was very challenging because of the weather there and all the different political borders and nationalities you flew against and with."

Three friends died in accidents there because of the weather, he said. One, his wingman at the time, got disoriented, they surmised, while taking off in a storm, and they lost him.

"It was the worst feeling I've ever had while flying—number four [the friend] not answering the radio when he was challenged for a response. And then having to hold while the flight lead then tried to find his aircraft accident site to verify that he had, in fact, gone down and there was no survivor and so forth. You always hope that he's able to eject before the airplane hit the ground. A lot of thoughts go through your mind, but you still have to fly the airplane."

He'd been lucky and not had any accidents himself. One of the scariest he ever saw, he said, was another friend having a fuel tank explode on him in the air, enveloping the entire aircraft in flames and pinning him against the cockpit as it pitched over into a "negative G kind of flight," out of control. Luckily, the friend was able to eject and is now a general at Davis-Monthan Air Force Base, Arizona.

Just prior to coming to Nellis, Cantwell had served in Iceland at a remote base intercepting Russians.

"They fly routine flights up over the ice cap to monitor its progression," he said of the Soviets. "Obviously, that's for their submarines, which like to use the cap for cover. . . . The flights would take them close to [Allied military zones], and our job was to intercept them if they entered and escort them out."

Once he'd intercepted a Russian Bear bomber "actively engaged in antisubmarine warfare at a very low altitude . . . had its bottom door open, dropping sonar buoys and that sort of thing. . . . I dropped down low to take some pictures for Intelligence purposes . . . that was pretty interesting."

But he'd kept his distance. "You know there have been instances documented where Soviet aircraft may be engaged in laser operations against our pilots. Spotlights at night focused on our airplanes to maybe create some blinding type situations and that sort of thing. Over the years we've tried to avoid instances like that and since then we've developed an agreement and understanding with the Soviets to limit or prohibit those types of operations. . . . Quite frankly, a lot of air activity has decreased and there haven't been many instances of that kind of hostility for a long time."

One of the most interesting things he told me was about training in Oman in an exercise much like the Gulf War.

Shortly after the Iran hostage crisis, he said, experts began to feel that America's next war might take place in the Middle East. The Omanis were friendly to us, although not openly, so the air force and the navy began holding secret exercises in the sultanate, which borders Saudi Arabia.

"It was a kind of a Red Flag," Cantwell said, alluding to the huge, multiweek exercises mounted from Nellis and often involving over one hundred fighters and bombers, "only you didn't have any constraints placed upon you whatsoever. The airspace was wide open. You didn't have to worry about Salt Lake City or Los Angeles and their air traffic. . . . We lived in tents for a month and did pretty much the same thing that our forces are doing over there [in the Gulf War], only it was in peacetime. . . . It was pretty exciting."

That night, after spending the day interviewing at the FWS, I went to the "O'club," part of a spacious building on the base that looked, inside, with its tile floors and dining and sitting rooms, like any American country club. This was the place on a base where the pilots were supposed to let their hair down and tell you, once served and relaxed, what they really think.

It was Wednesday night—"Lingerie Night," a small sign at the lounge's door announced. Models from Las Vegas were in the featured attire, and they walked smilingly amid the sea of green flight suits that packed the place, many different patches on their sleeves. Most were at Nellis for a Red Flag, which was in progress.

"Love Shack" by the B-52s—being played by a disc jockey on a bandstand—blasted over the club's speakers as I walked in. After being given a "Jeremiah Weed" bourbon, which is a drink wildly popular at Nellis, I was introduced to a crazy, tough game called "Crud," which is a favorite at air force fighter base O'clubs, especially the one at Nellis.

I still don't understand it well, but it's played on a pool table with certain cue balls but without the cue stick. You pick up teams, about four guys on each, usually made up of your squadron or crew mates, and then each guy takes a turn fast-rolling the cue ball down the felt on the table, knocking in other balls, and running like a halfback to a position at the other end. The next guy up on the other team can block you from making it to that other end for your next shot, and, believe me, he'll do so with reckless abandon, throwing himself at you, hitting you, hurting you.

I may not have the rules exactly right, but guys have broken legs and arms playing Crud, say devotees. The object, I believe, is to eliminate as many players as possible until one guy remains standing. He's the winner and usually gets his drinks free, or some such. Fighter pilots like the game because of its competitiveness, said Major Greg Kries, the Nellis public affairs officer at the time.

I'm not that competitive, but I did enjoy the game until I got "morted" on a procedural error I was not aware I was committing. The rules are pretty complex. There were groups of flyers waiting to take their turn in the Crud room, a kind of lighted, sunken adjunct to the darker main lounge, so it was back to the bar and more Jeremiah Weed, which has a much higher alcohol content than other bourbons, I'm told.

I didn't have that much, not being a big drinker, but it was flowing freely. Around the bar, on the walls, was a makeshift aviator's history of the goings-on at Nellis through the decades—entire wooden walls and bar furniture, preserved in chunks, from the old, smaller O'club, which had been remodeled into its present larger one: a piece of the polished bar that must have stood in its middle, nautically wooden table tops, all mounted and displaying, under lacquered varnish, the etched signatures and sayings of waves of pilots and crews passing through.

"Whacko," "Suck," "Psycho," "gunslingers," drawings of planes, "Don't give me any of that Yuppie do da," and "Snake," were just some of the many names and epitaphs etched into the remnants and the new walls. I'd seen more of the same on displays in the Fighter Weapons School Center lounge—things like "Anything else is rubbish" and "Go for your gun Commie and die." It was a kind of neat shorthand for men who prefer—but are certainly not limited to—talking with their actions or their hands.

There were a lot of girls in the bar. Obviously, they'd come to meet the aviators. This lingerie night Crud tournament was a good time. It was camaraderie, as fighter pilots like to call it. Most of the pilots had flown all day in a demanding, skill-testing scenario. They were with others who had done the same, understood, and appreciated what it took. You couldn't bullshit about who you were and not eventually get caught, which is often not the case in less dangerous, more cerebral civilian jobs. In a squadron, you generally knew who and what your friends were.

The commandant of the Fighter Weapons School, Colonel Lawrence Johnston, a young-looking, gracious, thirty-year veteran from Oklahoma City, Oklahoma, was leaving for a new command at Shaw Air Force Base, South Carolina. In his honor, there was a little farewell party of Jeremiah chugs going on over by the bar.

Earlier, Johnston had told me:

"These kids here are dedicated and committed. Of course, it takes a toll on the families. . . . Most guys, if the schedule permits, won't go home after eight hours, because there is always something else you can do to strop your razor a little bit. . . .

"You don't find many sons of stockbrokers or wealthy landowners or businessmen here. . . . That's certainly no hit on the wealthy . . . but people of means usually have other opportunities open to them. . . . Our guys come from middle-income, middle America . . . small-town-type areas.

"The picture I'm trying to paint here is that most of them come from places they would like to leave, or at least don't want to spend the rest of their lives in. I am sure there are exceptions. But what that means is they are going to have the opportunity to travel . . . get to see strange and unusual things that they didn't get a chance to see in Choctaw, Oklahoma. . . .

"I'm building this [discussion] from the least important [aspect]. . . . You [a fighter pilot] will not become a rich man . . . but there is the opportunity to make sufficient salary to feed your family, take care of your sick grandparents, buy the most expensive whiskey you'd ever want to buy for your friends. And send your children to college. . . .

"Now all this starts to become a pretty good proposition when you're doing something that is so hysterically fun—the flying of an airplane. . . . And you're doing it with your bros . . . men just like you, tickled to death to be pulling nine G's and seeing things that so few men ever get to see . . . and the proposition includes preserving the freedom and way of life of our country.

"Now that sounds like such horseshit . . . waving the flag and all that. But, in fact, it's true. . . . I think it's very good that our country now will go to battle for righteous causes. Blood for oil? Holy shit. Yeah, it's blood for oil, but it's blood to keep us from being held hostage to Hussein. . . . That is why this group is so cohesed now.

"Two years ago, three years ago, when you had these spotty situations, the reasons for doing battle were very sparse. . . . But we're doing some righteous stuff here . . . worthwhile stuff . . . stuff worth dying for. . . . And when I can do it with my bros . . . I mean, it doesn't get any better than that."

Everybody was toasting him, and you could see the genuine emotion from him as he bought the drinks— which was the custom—and from them as they drank them.

I left early and was not able to confirm this, but I was told the next day that the colonel was bodily carried out into the O'club parking lot by some of his charges, stripped of his flight suit in one of those memorable good-bye ceremonies that only good friends can think up, and left naked to fend for himself in the rain.

That Jeremiah Weed is powerful stuff.

The strangest story I heard concerning Nellis—and, for that matter, about fighter pilots in general—was the following. It came from Tom Skanchy, a former F-15 FWS commander, Vietnam veteran of two hundred combat missions, and miraculous survivor of an F-4 ejection almost point-blank into a runway that broke so many bones he spent a year in the hospital mending. I'm citing all this to show what a hard-boiled fighter pilot he was, and, consequently, that he was not one to be easily swayed.

In early 1980, Skanchy was vice commander of Red Flag, responsible for operations. He got a call that there had been a midair collision over a remote area on the ranges involving three fighters whose pilots had been killed. All were friends of his, one especially so. He immediately called a helicopter unit and began organizing a search and rescue.

Very shortly after getting the call, he got another call, this one from a psychic who lived in a small Nevada town and had heard of the accident. He asked Skanchy if he'd received his letter predicting it. Skanchy had not, and said he didn't want to be bothered. But the next day the letter arrived, postmarked several days earlier. It did predict the crash and had other correct pertinent information.

Skanchy still wasn't interested, because, as he says, "Fighter pilots are rational people and they really don't like to think about such things."

But they couldn't locate one of the bodies, belonging to a black officer. The psychic called Skanchy, correctly identified the missing man as black, and insisted he knew where the body was. He could see it in a vision he was having during a séance at his house. He said the body was intact, sitting in an ejection seat—which he called a "rocking chair" kind of thing—near some springs and old mines.

Skanchy said it didn't add up. Most midairs result in the fatalities' being found in little pieces, and there weren't any springs or mines in the area of the midair.

But the psychic persisted. He kept phoning that in his trance he was sitting with the dead officer in a kind of small canyon or depression. Without any other way to go, and impressed that the psychic had nothing to gain and did not want money, Skanchy finally agreed to let him try and direct, while in a trance state, one of the helicopters to the site.

At first they had no luck. The psychic said he could hear the helicopter in his trance, meaning it was nearby, but the heli-

copter pilot could not find the canyon or anything else the psychic described. Then, after about twenty minutes, in an area
where the searchers had looked down and seen nothing, the psychic said he saw the helicopter overhead.

Unknown to the psychic, the helicopter was a red, white, and
blue Department of Energy aircraft, but he described it as such—
"which absolutely buckled my knees," said Skanchy.

The helicopter came lower and found the body, intact and still
strapped into the ejection seat.

It was later determined from aircraft videotape that the nose of
the plane he had been in had been pointed in the direction of the
canyon at the last millisecond, but witnesses had not seen that in
the huge explosion. That was why he had ejected so far from the
debris.

"Of course it spooked the whole base," said Skanchy, "but it
made a believer out of me."

5

SECOND LIEUTENANT KEITH BEAM, call sign "Beamer," made the mistake of going to his radar too soon.

A twenty-three-year-old F-16 "Fighting Falcon" pilot at Utah's Hill Air Force Base, he had just lifted off on a training flight into a dark, moonless night of horrendous weather. His instructor, "Moose" Mullard, was already in a climbing westerly turn two nautical miles ahead of him.

His first task was to follow.

He didn't want to mess up right at the start.

So, making his own climbing turn, only seconds into the flight, he looked back inside the cockpit to check for Moose on his radar screen, a glowing green rectangle between his knees. Thus, he eliminated his main source of spatial orientation—sight of the outside.

"What I should be doing is looking at my instruments, flying the airplane by cross-checking all the gauges, and looking back out," the future air force F-16 Fighter Weapons School instructor recalled. "Radar trail," they called it.

But he was preoccupied with the radar.

Not that sight outside the cockpit that night would have made much difference.

85

It was winter at Hill, February 1983, and the storm they were banking into over the Great Salt Lake was a black, cloud-filled mountain of rain nearing snow. It billowed from an 800-foot floor to a 15,000-foot ceiling, and was probably fifty miles thick—an immense, rain-slashed rectangle with visibility of barely a few feet and no hint of the orienting horizon.

Beam's mistake in these first few seconds was about to chillingly introduce him to the most common cause of accidental flight death in the air force (and probably the navy, too)—spatial disorientation, often called "vertigo"—and begin for him a night of contained terror and surrealism he'd never forget.

In fact, Hill had recently had two F-16 crashes from spatial disorientation, one resulting in the pilot's death. Both jets had gone into the Great Salt Lake, according to Scott Logan, a fellow student with Beam who also roomed with him. There had been so many such crashes, according to Logan, that a local newspaper cartoon showed F-16s clogging an effort to drain water from the lake with a pump.

But a new plane—as some of those in the lake were—was going to have its troubles, and so Beam, a confident pilot and former soccer star at the Air Force Academy, from which he had graduated in 1981, was not dwelling on other pilots' misfortunes.

His attention was focused solely on the green radar screen.

It wasn't more than twenty seconds into the flight that he found Moose. The instructor was also flying a Falcon—or Viper, as its pilots preferred to call the nimble little single-seater. Powered by a lone, potent Pratt and Whitney engine with afterburner, the Viper was the air force's newest fighter, although its relatively modest twenty-five-mile-range radar was not one of its touted features.

In order to be nimble, the fighter had to give up some long-range capability.

Revolutionary, however, was its new "fly-by-wire" flight control system. Previous jets had used slower, harder-to-move hydraulics to transmit the pilot's will to the control surfaces. But the "Electric Jet," as the F-16 was sometimes called, used lightning-fast electrical impulses, plus a computer, to quickly and precisely steer the plane.

If the pilot wasn't exactly correct in his movement of stick and rudder, the computer would compensate.

The light F-16, which also doubled as a bomber, was a maneuvering marvel. Just a slight amount of pressure or movement on the jet's small, side-mounted stick (another innovation) was all it took for the pilot to instantly send the plane into a nine-G turn, which was about the limit of any pilot's endurance. But precisely because of its smoothness, the jet gave no seat-of-the-pants indications of trouble.

Even the wind roaring by outside was barely audible.

Beam couldn't feel he was in danger.

"I was at about two thousand feet and supposed to be in a slight, thirty-degree turn to the right," he remembers. But having found Moose and glancing at his instruments, he was surprised to see that he was in a much harder turn, approximately sixty degrees. "I'm getting slow. My nose is pointed much higher than I wanted."

In fact, the bubble-canopied jet was rolling upward, and as a result slowing from 300 to 150 knots and in danger of departing from controlled flight, which, at two thousand feet, left Beam little time or space in which to recover.

"We have a warning horn in the cockpit, so I think I would have heard it," he said, reacting to the possibility that he would have gone right on over and crashed into the ground or the lake (whichever was below him). "But you never know. Things were happening pretty fast. I'd gone into the weather and gotten a little disoriented. . . . My body [with no references from outside] was telling me we were still in the turn, but my eyes [on the instruments] were showing something else."

It took him a few seconds to react. "You're confused. You say, Hey. What's going on here?"

He checked a backup attitude direction indicator (ADI). It verified the main ADI, showing he was in a much steeper turn than he thought.

His slowing flight speed cinched it.

The jet was teetering on the brink of stall or worse. The delicate motion sensors in his ears were deceiving him. He knew he had to act fast.

He quickly added power, while at the same time dipping a wing lower, putting the plane in a suddenly steeper turn. This dropped the nose quickly, slicing it downward, enabling the wings to catch air and start the jet flying again, albeit in the wrong direction—toward the ground.

But the quick dive increased airspeed and he was able to pull the nose back up. In a matter of seconds he was back on course, following Moose.

It had been a close call.

"Once it's over it makes your heart pound a little," he says. "But it could have been worse. I'd rather have my nose pointed up and getting slow than all of a sudden popping out of the weather at eight hundred feet and seeing the ground rushing up."

He settled down.

He didn't know it, but that was only the beginning.

He was now three and half miles in trail and climbing, which was something the F-16 did very well. Its thrust-to-weight ratio, or ability to accelerate while going up against gravity, was as good as or better than the ratio of any other jet in the world at that time. He felt better with Moose on the radar and he was watching his instruments carefully.

Since starting flight training a year and a half before, Beam, a bachelor, sharing a condominium with Logan and Mike Loida, another Viper student, had been briefed adequately on the possibility of vertigo and disorientation. The solution, his instructors had always emphasized, was trust your instruments.

Still, many students, having just been through what he had, would have alerted their instructor. But Beam was very competitive, about to graduate from the RTU (Replacement Training Unit) and be assigned to his first operational squadron. He didn't want to jeopardize that—not that alerting would have hurt his standing. It was just the principle. He'd distinguished himself by even getting picked to train for the Falcon, which was few in number at that time and given to only the best basic flight students. He was now getting known as a "natural," which was ironic for a guy who'd "puked [his] guts out" on his first basic training flight and then taken half the course to begin to feel comfortable.

But he felt he was now in control of his disorientation. This was his first night flight alone in the F-16 cockpit. He'd gut it out.

At about 15,000 feet they broke out of the weather into a black, moonless void; first Moose, then Beam. "Darker than crap," he remembers. Only a few stars and the lights of Moose's jet were visible; blue on the right wing tip and fuselage, red on the left.

It was like flying in outer space—no way to tell where the

ground or horizon was, just pinholes of light twinkling in the void.

Moose started a gentle turn, the lights of his plane moving eerily in Beam's vision.

They were going to get gas.

Perhaps fifty miles away, a four-engine KC-135 jet tanker streaked toward them unseen. It was above them at approximately 20,000 feet, on the downward leg of a huge, racetrack-like orbit, which the two Vipers would enter for their rendezvous after the tanker had turned in front of them and started its return.

They'd approach the tanker from behind.

Tanking was one of two major tasks in the training flight; bombing, which they would do next, was the other. Moose was in contact with the tanker as he started his slow, climbing turn toward it, dipping his wings slightly, about thirty degrees.

As they'd briefed earlier, Beam now closed the distance between his and Moose's jet by cutting across Moose's soft arc to join him close abreast and a little below. The two jets then continued the turn in unison, Beam tucked under Moose, keeping good visual on his leader, concentrating on his colored lights in order to maintain their very slim separation; Moose giving all his attention to the coming rendezvous, which would be especially dangerous in the moonless night.

In the fleeting seconds as their duet continued, Beam felt the turn getting steeper. Soon he believed it was a full ninety degrees, which was exceptionally tight, perhaps putting their wings perpendicular to the horizon, had they been able to see the horizon. But he didn't dare take his eyes off Moose. The two jets were dangerously close and he didn't want a recurrence of what had happened when he'd looked inside his cockpit before.

"I wasn't sure what he was doing," he says about his leader. "All I could see was his wing. I was just hanging on for dear life." And since Beam hadn't mentioned his earlier vertigo, Moose wasn't radioing that they were, in fact—contrary to what Beam was now feeling—still in the gentle, thirty-degree turn. "I'm getting the 'leans' real bad, but I think that's just because we're in this severe turn."

As had happened earlier, the tiny chambers in Beam's inner ear, deprived of other input, such as vision, were deceived again—but this time in an opposite way. Where before he hadn't realized he was in a curling climb, now the fluids, which jostled hairlike nerve endings to give him a sense of balance and direction, were tricked by the smoothness of Moose's gentle turn and were sending Beam's brain signals falsely indicating he was in a hard right turn.

He reacted accordingly.

"If I'm in a ninety-degree turn," he says, "then I'm going to have to be rolled up under [Moose] pretty tight." In effect, he moved a little closer to Moose, who was still not watching him, increasing the danger of their proximity.

"I think I'm looking up at him over my left canopy rail," he remembers. "The closer I get to him, the harder it is to see him as the turn gets steeper."

At least that's the way it appeared to Beam.

In reality, he wasn't below Moose—he was above him. When he thought he was moving up to Moose, he was actually moving down.

In the near-mystical black void, he'd totally lost his sense of up and down, just as two objects revolving around each other might do in outer space. There was nothing with which to judge his relative position. His only visual reference was Moose's blue-lighted wing tip, to which he had welded himself without cognizance of the horizon or anything else.

In addition, reaching the point in the turn that put them in a straight course to the tanker, Moose, aware of the disorientation dangers of such a night, had gently leveled his wings back to the horizon, thus ceasing the turn, which was why Beam was finding it harder to see him. By leveling, Moose had changed the positional relationship between the two jets. Beam was having to look harder over his cockpit to keep his instructor in view and in proper alignment. But he did it, unknowingly leveling his own jet in the process and maintaining the precarious slight hover, leans and all.

Luckily, they finally sighted the lights of the tanker, which alerted Beam that something was wrong. Because of the radio communication, Beam knew they were climbing to get gas. But the tiny lights coming toward him in the distance seemed below him—at least that was the way he was perceiving them.

"The tanker's saying he's at twenty thousand and we're to come in at eighteen," he remembers. "That's when I thought,

Whoa, something's messed up. How can he be two thousand feet above us when I'm looking down towards the ground at him?"

The realization was startling. He looked at his instruments. In addition to showing that the ground was actually in the opposite direction, they indicated that he and Moose had straightened out into level flight, although he was slightly above Moose. "I thought, Oh man, I'm screwed up again."

It was a scary feeling. In effect, he'd been flying blind, unaware of where he really was, not in control of where he was going. Thinking he was below Moose and turning, he now realized he was above and flying straight and level. Worse, he had to maintain that level flight path despite the contrary turning feelings his inner ears were still giving him.

"It was so hard," he remembers. "You keep glancing at the gauges, saying, 'We're not in this turn [that he kept feeling he was in]. We're straight and level. We're straight and level.' It's the hardest thing to make yourself do. . . . You want to do one thing because of the seat-of-the-pants feeling . . . [but] you force yourself to do the correct thing because of the facts."

He still wanted to turn, curl up "under" Moose, which, in reality, would have forced the two planes dangerously closer. But "you say to yourself, 'Get your ass down. Get your ass down. . . .' You've got to fight it or it'll end up killing you."

Again, he didn't tell Moose. "I probably should have, because he'd mentioned in the brief that something like this could happen. You can fly on autopilot, get away, and watch your gauges until you're all right. But I thought I'd just gut it out and [the disorientation] would go away."

He was partially right.

The tanker turned in front of them and he fought the urges, watching his gauges, staying straight and level. They made their way up behind the large, four-engine tanker, and Moose positioned his Viper beneath its giant tail.

An operator looking out a window extended a long boom to a small, lighted receptacle on the F-16's fuselage. Meanwhile, Beam, still struggling, moved up to a position a little above and perhaps ten yards off the tanker's dark right wing tip to await his turn.

"Once I got on his wing, the leans started going away. I'm feeling better. Up feels like up. . . . But it was still really dark and the tanker had this light ... A nacelle light, I believe, somewhere over the wings on its fuselage ... It was really bright. It was blinding me."

He tried a few different positions, but the light was always in his face. "It was bugging me. I couldn't see anything."

He decided to maneuver the tanker's wing between him and the light, hoping that would give him some perspective. He flew forward and down a little bit and finally thought he was okay until the tanker's eight-foot-wide wing tip suddenly stabbed at him out of the dark.

"It was a big chunk of metal, not more than a foot from my canopy. I wasn't supposed to be that close. It kind of scared me and I obviously moved away."

His disorientation had eased, but now he was blind with or without the light. "I had no depth perception. I had to do something."

Moose had briefed him on a procedure: Ask the tanker to turn down the nacelle light and turn on its dimmer landing lights, located where the wing met the fuselage. When they complied, everything cleared up. He could finally see the wing and where he properly should have been positioned.

That's nice, he remembers feeling.

He waited his turn and then got his own gas.

It took five minutes to fill his tanks. They'd been in the air approximately half an hour.

But now, in order to take their practice bombing runs, they had to go back through the bad weather.

He was not looking forward to it.

They went into close "fingertip" formation—their wing tips barely three feet apart—Moose leading, and descended into the weather. The range, called "Eagle," was about thirty miles away. They were to drop to the storm's bottom, come out underneath it, and commence some low-level bombing passes.

Back in the soup, Beam started getting the leans again.

The weather was moving in a direction opposite to their course. They broke out of it at about two thousand feet, fifteen miles from the range.

"Once we got past the squall line," he remembers, "there were like a bizillion stars, but no moon and no horizon." The range had lights on it but they just blended in. "You couldn't tell where the ground was. It was like a black hole. I just had this sensation I was flying upside down."

They'd moved farther apart by this time, but he could plainly see Moose's jet, about one hundred feet away.

"I felt like I was looking up through my canopy at the ground, but I kept looking over at Moose, and he was flying the same attitude that I was. If I was messed up, so was he."

He, of course, also checked his instruments. They showed he was straight and level.

"It was just the weirdest, strangest feeling," he remembers, "the worst I'd been all night."

He didn't like it, he said. He was scared. But that was to be expected. At least he understood what was happening this time.

"I know that the more I feel like this, the more I just have to concentrate on my instruments. They're what are going to keep me alive."

Unlike a few moments before, he was now back at 2,000 feet, a very short distance between him and a crash.

"You keep cross-checking your gauges," he says. "Nope, nope, nope. There are the stars and there is the ground. Am I climbing or diving? Is my altitude changing? No, altitude's staying the same. ADI says we're straight and level. His airplane is doing the same thing as mine so we've got to be straight and level."

He says he decided that if he didn't come out of it soon, he'd radio Moose and "go home."

But the focus on his instruments—perhaps the cross-checking with Moose's airplane—finally paid off. Half a minute before they arrived at the point where they were to split and begin separate runs, he began to feel more like he was rightside up.

"My body is starting to say it's getting better. It's getting better. We're not quite so upside down anymore. I'm just flying the instruments. I'm not looking outside."

By the time they were on their actual run he was back to normal.

But he knew how insidious the disorientation was.

As he had been briefed previously, he then took the lead on the second run—a low-level route back through the bad weather with him showing Moose the way. Moose was characteristically silent.

The rest of the flight was uneventful.

When they got back, Beam finally told Moose about his disorientation. Moose wasn't happy. Beam should have told his instructor, he said. Vertigo is a dangerous affliction. Suppose it had occurred during combat? Then he told Beam something Beam wasn't expecting—he (Moose) had experienced disorientation when Beam had been the leader.

The son of an air force sergeant and a British mother, Beam had an international, if somewhat rootless, childhood, growing up in Japan, Nebraska, England, and Colorado. Sports and athletic competition were major factors in his life. He was a baseball pitcher as a kid in England but got tendinitis in his elbow and switched to soccer. When his father was transferred to Colorado Springs and a job at NORAD, the center of the U.S.'s missile defense command, he started thinking about going to the Air Force Academy, which was located there.

Soccer took off for him, and he was offered several scholarships, including one to the academy and one to Brown University in Providence, Rhode Island. But after a visit east, he decided he preferred to stay closer to home. "I like the West. The other thing was the economy at the time. [It was the late 1970s, inflation was high, and it was cheaper to stay at home on scholarship.] The air force guaranteed a job and a really good education."

But he almost quit. "If it hadn't been for sports, I would have. The academics were very hard there and high school hadn't prepared me." He focused on "the athletic competition and keeping my head above water in the academic and military side. . . . I suppose it was good for me," he said about the academy's rigors and discipline, "but to tell you the truth, I wasn't ready for it at the time."

He had a free spirit side to him, a quality his friends in pilot training will attest to. He hated the restrictions, the forced confinement of the academy. "I wanted to skip class and not get in trouble for it." But he learned to cope and succeed. "It wasn't that I improved my grades so much. It was just that my study habits got better and I learned to do more with less effort."

He had not planned to be an aviator. In fact, he'd gotten sick in his junior year in the academy's little Piper Cub–like T-41 trainer. "It was very embarrassing," he recalls. But he didn't want to go through the doctors and scorn required to get out of the fifteen-ride indoctrination series that was used to ferret out unqualified flyers, so he continued. "It took me about eleven rides before I wasn't sick anymore and it sort of got fun."

But he still didn't want to fly. His plan upon graduation was to do his required five years in the air force in a management job and then get a job with a major air force contractor like McDonnell Douglas for "big bucks." But being pilot-qualified, he didn't want to have to "go through the hassle" of explaining to everyone "all the way up to the superintendent" why he wasn't going to take advantage of what they'd trained and processed him for.

So he didn't.

In June 1981 he reported for basic flight at Williams Air Force Base, Phoenix, Arizona—the first of many courses he would take before he would get his wings and be assigned to a specific airplane—"and had the best time of my life. . . . The training was tough but Phoenix is such a great city to have fun in. I guess I tried to live out four years of academy life in one year of pilot training."

He got airsick again but fought it, and in about a month he was "able to look out the window and go, boy, this is a blast." Between nights at Bobby McGee's, a popular Mesa, Arizona, nightspot, and rides in the T-37 jet trainer ("after I'd gotten to a point where I was ahead of the airplane"), he was having a ball.

"I went out with this guy, an IP [instructor pilot], on kind of a fun, freebie ride. It was like monkey see, monkey do. He'd do a maneuver and I'd do it. It was like he had some confidence in me. I said, Hey, this is fun. And then once you started thinking it was fun, then, combined with maybe a little bit of natural ability, you start getting good."

One day at Williams they had an open house to show the students what they might fly once they'd graduated. "They had an F-15 and an F-16," he remembers. "I'd been leaning toward the F-16 simply because it was the newer jet, but I didn't really know what the differences were. But there they were together. The Eagle was so big, but the Viper just looked like a sleek little sports car. Like it was made for me. I sat in the cockpit and it felt like it was just built around me."

He knew what he wanted.

He had all the attributes of a good fighter pilot—good eyes, good eye-hand coordination, awareness of what was going on with his plane and in the sky around him. And he was aggressive, recalls Stu Johnson, who would meet him in fighter lead-in, the next phase of their training. "I'm not talking about stupid aggressiveness. All fighter pilots are aggressive to some degree. But Keith was able to take the plane to the edge, to know when and where to do things with it, and many times they were things other pilots would hesitate to do."

The aggressiveness stemmed from the competitiveness: the drive to excel and win; a hatred of losing and being beaten. "I think it was just something in him," says Johnson. "It was there in everything we did, whether playing baseball or cards. I can remember as a class getting out there and doing some things together and having some of the biggest arguments and fights I've ever seen."

But in most everything else, says Johnson, Beam was a "pretty laid-back guy," a "night owl," who was always staying up into the wee hours, "even if it was just to watch TV." He was good on the dance floor, adds Mike Loida, another of his RTU roommates, "the disco kind of thing." Adds Logan: "You never saw him with an ugly woman. He always had a pretty one, and they'd go out of their way to get close to him."

With short, curly, brown hair, and the build of a middleweight boxer, including a somewhat flattened nose that looked like it had been broken but wasn't, he had a straightforwardness that complemented his confidence. "I thought he was a smart-ass when we first met," says Logan, "but then you put that aside when you got to know him. He was a lot of fun to be around and he could back up what he said."

They came to call him "GQ" for his propensity to go on sudden shopping sprees for fashionable clothes. "He'd bring home three hundred dollars' worth of sweaters and shirts," says Logan. "The rest of us weren't so stylish. We were strictly jeans and tennis shoes." Beam liked high-energy rock, fast cars, but had the good humor to "just laugh" when Logan spun his new Mazda. He became notorious for sleeping, and at the RTU condominium, he didn't have a bed, just some blankets. "He could nod off at a moment's notice," recalls Logan. "He'd push it all night and then go in his room and you wouldn't see him for twenty-four hours," adds Loida. "The only guy I ever met with a sleep pattern like that."

In addition to learning about the deceptions of flight, Beam and his fellow RTU classmates were introduced to the rudiments of Viper air-to-air fighting.

"Our main job is putting bombs on the target," he says, "but to do that, we have to get there. . . . There are only so many ways to drop a bomb. But getting there [through the enemy's varied defenses, including radar-guided artillery, surface-to-air missiles, and well-armed fighters] is an art."

This was more so because, unlike the other superfighters of the era, the F-14, F-15, and F-18—the F-16 did not have a long-range, or beyond visual range (BVR), missile. This meant it had to use special maneuvers and deceptions, such as sudden right exits and releasing chaff and flares, to evade long-range missiles shot at it and in order to advance to the close-in visual fight, where it could use its advantages. But once within visual range of its adversary, the Viper was as deadly as any fighter in the air.

The RTU students, however, weren't yet experienced enough to use those advantages. So what their instructors hoped to do in this initial training was introduce them to a few basic but important concepts: how to maintain the offensive advantage in a fight and how to defend from being killed.

Beam, Logan, Loida, and the others in their class were given approximately five "hops," or flights, of instruction concerning offense, five concerning defense, and several more to demonstrate how to fight as a team.

They started with the most important—offense, a simple one plane versus another, called a "one v one," where they would be positioned in what was called the "perch": about a mile and half behind an adversary, near his six o'clock (tail), the perfect position from which to begin trying to get a kill.

"The point was to start out easy—in a point-and-shoot position—give us a feel for what was a valid shot," recalls Logan, who had been a pilot-training instructor prior to being selected for the RTU class.

But simply being behind and in good position wasn't enough. First, no adversary is going to sit there and let you shoot him. Second, even though the F-16 had a good heat-seeking AIM-9 sidewinder missile, and a more sophisticated AIM-9 coming in the future, its primary weapon at this point was the AIM-9P, or Papa, version of the Sidewinder and its 20-millimeter cannon, both of which worked successfully only within certain parameters, or "envelopes," outside of which they were useless.

The AIM-9P, for instance, was not "all-aspect," meaning it couldn't be fired with any hope of success at every part, or "aspect," of the target. This meant that a head-on shot would be fruitless. In order to home on the bandit's exhaust, the Papa had to be shot from somewhere behind what was called the target's "3-9 line," which was roughly behind a line extended through its wings (the tips of which corresponded to the three and nine o'clock settings on the fighter pilot's mythical position clock).

The missile also, as all missiles do, had a distance requirement, meaning it had to be shot within certain ranges. Too far or too close wouldn't do. The ranges were something on the order of a maximum five miles, and a minimum just inside one mile. And the closer the shooter got, the more precise his shot had to be. The missile worked only when fired within a certain imaginary cone extending out from behind the target's exhaust. The cone got narrower as the attacker got closer.

These were a lot of variables they had to learn and operate within as they maneuvered furiously to get a kill. An air-to-air fight is a quick action, lasting no more than thirty seconds on the average, according to records. Within that space of time, the pilot has to make literally hundreds of decisions based on his speed, altitude, and position relative to his target.

The gun, too, had its envelope. Although less complicated than the missile, it was effective only at the closest ranges, which were the most fleeting.

With the call "Fight's on," the "defender"—the fighter being attacked—would break hard and downward, trying to maneuver out of the attacker's firing solution. "You accelerate hard after him," says Logan. "The F-16 can pull nine G's, which is a very tight turn. He's trying to negate your attack, increase angles on you [so he can turn and attack you], turn his 3-9 line away from you. . . . You're trying to get in a position where you can employ your ordnance, having to cope with all the different changes in angle, aspect, closure rates—all the weapons employment restrictions that you have."

In the chase, both fighters are employing basic fighter maneuvers (BFM), which are the tools of the air-to-air fight. For instance, the attacker, seeing the defender break hard and down in front of him—which, itself, is a basic fighter maneuver—might turn quicker and in less space by going up and down in a sudden "yo-yo," which should enable him to drop back on the defender's tail, in position to again press the attack.

"You're learning to maintain the offensive position, which is the primary objective in any [dogfight]," says Logan. "You want to get in a position to employ your weapons. . . . But you don't want to be so aggressive that you can't turn quick enough or slow down fast enough to not give up the offensive advantage."

In the defensive lessons, the roles were reversed. The defender was trying to stave off the attack, capitalize on the attacker's mistakes.

"You're trying to move out of his firing solution," says Logan, "deny your vulnerable cone by increasing angles to complicate his weapon's employment, which is extremely hard looking over your shoulder. . . . 'Lose sight, lose fight,' they say, but it's tough to know your altitude, fuel, and airspeed looking behind you. . . . You have to develop a timing in your brain to know when to check [front]."

The defender has two basic choices: increase range from the attacker so he can turn and maybe bring his own weapons to bear, or decrease range to force the attacker into a guns envelope, which is easier to defend against, or an overshoot, which immediately makes the defender the attacker.

"Defensively," says Logan, "the thing to do is survive as long as you can while maintaining your energy [ability to maneuver]. What you want to do is move from defensive to neutral to offensive. But even if you're neutral, you're surviving."

Beam was only now beginning. As he got better, instructors would increase the degree of difficulty of the lessons. It would take him years to develop a style that would make him one of the best F-16 drivers in the air force.

But the seed was being planted.

Years later, during Desert Storm, he would echo other fighter pilots by saying, "You won't find many warmongers amongst us. Every now and then yes. But fighting is what we've been trained to do. . . . When the time comes, what most of us want to know is how, as a man, as a person, how am I going to face death or possible death? So far, all it's been is fake—fake bullets, fake bombs, fake bad guys. But how am I going to react when real people are shooting at me and I'm trying to kill real people?"

The question and the camaraderie would motivate him throughout the decade.

BOOK 2

A GATHERING
OF EAGLES

6

COMMANDER JIM ROBB is a big man, tall, long-legged. His call sign could just as well be "Bear," instead of "Rookie." The Topgun CO has a certain ranging restlessness about him as he talks in his small office, or walks the Topgun halls. But he is candid about himself and the command he heads, known formally as the Navy Fighter Weapons School.

It's at Miramar Naval Air Station, California.

Born in Corpus Christi, Texas, Robb is a veteran F-14 pilot and squadron commander, former Topgun graduate himself, 1977 Atlantic Fleet Fighter Pilot of the Year, MiG-simulating "adversary," and air show pilot, the last of which he called a "cocktail circuit" job that entailed "some of the scariest flying I've ever done.

"It's a very dynamic environment. . . . Not formation flying. . . . You're max performing the airplane at low altitude, close to the ground. The plane really flies down there, I mean it has all kinds of thrust . . . seven-, eight-G turns at five hundred feet . . . or going over on your back at four thousand feet and doing a split-S [which takes you toward the ground]. . . . It's not something you'll normally do."

He said he'd been on "a pretty fast track for a long period" back then, "running pretty hard." The navy was different in the 1970s. But luckily he met his wife. "She probably saved my life," he said.

He had a picture of her behind him.

She wasn't there, so I couldn't ask her about his shipping out, which, of course, was probably none of my business. But it's always been a problem in the navy. One wife had told me navy wives break down into three categories: those who adapt nicely to the navy family concept, where squadron members' wives become like a second family; those who cheat; and those who just can't handle it and go nuts or worse.

I'd heard of at least one suicide in that regard.

But that had nothing to do with Jim Robb, who seemed to be very happily married and had four children.

He said his dad had been a navy flier, and he'd grown up a quiet kid who had played trumpet in the school band and liked to play pool. He'd gotten an engineering degree from Rensselaer Polytechnic University in 1972 and a master of science degree from the University of West Florida in 1973.

ROTC had been his route into the navy.

Training programs such as Topgun notwithstanding, he said the best training is always actual combat. For him, he said, that had been off the coast of Libya in the late 1970s, "because you never knew what was going to happen."

Like Dale Snodgrass, whom he knew and had flown with and against, he and his squadron had gone out against Gadhafi's MiG-21s, 23s, and Sukhois, for tension-filled jousts, always maneuvering so the Libyans couldn't get a stern shot, which was their only threat.

"The guys prepared for it and then they went and did it. They worked at it. They talked about tactics . . . looked real hard at themselves, about whether or not they were prepared for combat. . . . You gotta test people to the edge of their ability. In other words, you don't want to lose airplanes . . . or send anybody to a mental hospital, but you do want to weed out the weak flyers . . . put them under enough stress that you know very well before you go into combat what they are going to do."

He said that, as a squadron commander, he'd work his officers "hard on the ground . . . send them out [flying] at night . . . watch them in severe evolutions."

And in bad weather.

"Down in the ship, in the Air Traffic Control Center, all the COs sit down there—it's COs only—and you watch your guys get worked up out of the ship and then come back. And there are guys that land and there are guys that don't land. From the ship's point, this is very important. Safety-wise, you need to be able to land and not hit somebody else or you need to be sent home.

"If he's having troubles then you have to know the guy well enough to know if he has capability and is he mentally preventing himself from doing it. And then you have to talk to the LSOs [the landing signal officers, who direct and grade carrier landings] or him in the air and say, Hey, you are gonna land tonight. Here we go. I've sent guys back to the beach to land to get more fuel and come back after a real bloody session and eventually they landed. That happened all the time when I was a deputy wing commander. If they didn't hack it, then we got rid of them."

He said that was happening a lot in the Gulf War, which was still going on when I visited. "There's a very short chain for guys who can't hack it." One CAG, he said, had already "sent six guys home. Immediate action. When you're talking about launching forty airplanes at night and you're gonna tank and rendezvous with no lights, go bomb over vast distances, and then come back and be able to land, there's got to be no question that it's going to be there. . . .

"So, in training, that's what we're trying to do. We're trying to push these people to their limits to allow them to get the capacity, the inner peace, that they are capable . . . get them beyond the 'can I' stage of their career, [where they are asking,] 'Can I do this? Am I good at aerial combat?' [to where they are confident that] 'I am a good pilot. I can lead in combat.' "

Robb heads a staff of some thirty officers, most of them instructors or instructors-in-training, and approximately 145 enlisted, most of them maintenance for the A-4s and F-16s the instructors fly as adversaries against the students, who bring their own planes.

In addition to teaching promising young fleet pilots how to be better, the school instructors fly air combat training missions against fleet squadrons and collect intelligence, most of it secret, on potential enemy pilots, aircraft, and tactics, which basically means on the Russians, who are the main suppliers of most of the potential threat aircraft and tactics.

Robb took the time to give me an extensive blackboard talk on the school and threats in general, the gist of which follows:

The heart of what they do is classified, but, basically, they try to find out as much as possible about the threats in order to minimize guesswork about potential enemy capabilities and tactics. They always assume the worst, on the theory that if you can beat their best, you don't have to worry about the rest. The threats are changing rapidly, so training changes a lot.

The navy fighter picture is complicated by the requirement that its fighters always give priority to defending the carrier. This means that their tactics and training are more geared that way than, for instance, the Air Force Fighter Weapons School (FWS), which can generally devote itself purely to air-to-air, or air-to-ground (bombing), as the case may be.

The Phoenix missile, unique, at least up until now, to the F-14, is a direct result of this emphasis on guarding the carriers. It's the longest-range air-to-air missile in the U.S. arsenal (up until the Gulf War), capable of hitting, under the right conditions, an enemy plane at maybe a hundred miles away. The requirement for that kind of missile grew out of the fear of waves of Russian bombers with long-range missiles of their own attacking the carriers.

Tactics, specifically, have changed dramatically in the last few years. It used to be that only the United States had airplanes capable of hitting other airplanes in their forward quarters. U.S. planes could just maneuver out of a potential enemy's ability to hurt them. Now the enemy has the forward quarter capability, so U.S. pilots have to be careful.

Real careful.

The Russian MiG-29 and Sukhoi-27, for example, can locate targets at long distances, certainly beyond visual range (BVR), which is a big catchphrase today in fighter aviation, and send a missile out to kill it. These highly maneuverable, fast, and sophisticated threats can shoot from just about anywhere.

So tactics have gotten more cautious, although there is still a minority contingent of fighter pilots who say to hell with all the sophistication. It's hurting the fighter pilot's aggressive spirit. Within reason, just gutsball it and blow their asses off.

But generally, aside from that debate, everyone agrees that you want to kill if you can before you get to the merge. You want to know more about your adversary than he knows about you. If he's targeting you, or has already shot at you, you want to do something to defeat his missile as well as shoot your own. If he forces you to just defend yourself, you've lost the offense, which in fighter piloting is a prescription to die.

The whole thing is extremely complicated, with literally endless scenarios depending on types of aircraft, missiles, altitude, distance, speed, weapons envelope, fuel situation, and numbers of attackers and attackees, to name only a few of the factors.

For instance, some missiles, like heat-seekers, can be shot and left to track on their own. However, most radar missiles demand that the shooting aircraft keep the target locked until impact. That means that if you are the shooter, you have to hold a relative stable position even if you know you've been shot at by the target and a missile is on the way to hit you. You're going to be hampered in your ability to evade.

Conversely, if you know your missile has a longer range than your adversary, or if he has not seen or targeted you, you can shoot without fear of being hit yourself. But be smart. Fight only when you have the advantage, unless you're forced to do otherwise. Be aggressive but not reckless.

I'm in the back of Classroom 2, a large, low room filled with Topgun students about to get a mass briefing for their one-versus-one exercise, one of the most important in the five-week course, Jim Robb has told me.

It's a kind of final exam. One airplane against another. Nothing fancy. Just what they learned the first week. Core ACM. All the other exercises in the course—one versus two, two versus two, two versus four, etc.—build on one versus one. The next week the class goes to Nellis for Red Flag and secret program training. This is effectively it at Miramar.

The school has purposely scheduled the one versus one final three weeks after the students had the instruction so they can see how rusty they've gotten in the intervening time. One of the running lessons at Topgun is that to be good—or "proficient," as they call it—a fighter pilot has to practice regularly and often. Lay off just a couple of weeks and you'll see the difference. You won't be as good as when you stopped, which is a lesson for the congressional budget cutters who think that Desert Storm–type performances just occur whenever our military takes the field.

But in addition to being the wakeup call the instructors want, the one-versus-one exercise is also probably the best test of the student's newly acquired abilities. One on one is down and dirty. Nobody can help you or make you look good. Just you and an instructor fighting to the death, because one of them is going to die—at least that's the way it would be if it were real combat.

Although the students, in flight suits, are milling around, eating, and joking as they find their seats in preparation for the brief to begin, inside they're deadly serious. Their reputations are at stake. They want to be good. They are pumped.

You can tell by the quick laughs, perhaps louder than normal; by the edginess as they mingle, or sit and fidget with small notepads and pens they will use to take down important information about the flights. Each will simply get a time and a place to show up, in the air, not knowing who or what will be there. It could be several A-4s, in which case the threat would be "second generation"—as opposed to "first," "third," or "fourth generation" in Topgun parlance—meaning no forward quarter missiles, capable of certain speeds and maneuverabilities that they will quickly have to adjust to in their fighting plan.

(The "generation" designation was never fully explained to me, and, I suspect, involves some classification. But my sense was that "first-generation" planes would have been the older, less advanced, Vietnam-era fighters, like the MiG-17 or the F-4 Phantom. They, for instance, presented less of a threat than "fourth-generation" fighters, like the MiG-29 or F-18 Hornet, which had much more sophisticated weapons and performance.)

Of course, the students first must find the bogeys on their radars.

If they don't, they'll be killed right off the bat.

But in this exercise, they'll eventually be pitted one-on-one with an attacking instructor, and it will be in that fight that they will most have to show their stuff.

Rock music is blaring as the instructors enter and start setting up things. At this particular moment, it's Oingo Boingo's "Just Another Day," a very driving, fast-paced song like something from the movie *Top Gun,* which is certainly appropriate.

The classroom is similar to any spacious boardroom, with meeting tables and plush chairs, except that on its walls are pictures of former Topgun classes, maps of the Middle East (including Iraq), maps of the Nellis ranges in Nevada, and a handsomely painted portrait of a World War I aviator in a green uniform and brown leather breast strap.

But what really catches my eye are the television sets hung from the ceiling. Four of them. They're playing gun camera film of real MiG kills in past engagements. This is the film from the nose of a fighter that captures whatever is in front of it in an engagement. The film is gritty, obviously rerun many times. In its center, eventually, come fleeing, darting MiGs, trying to escape.

They can't.

The round or square "pipper" sights, visible on the various films and accompanied by similarly visible rapidly flashing computations of speed and distance, are locked on and won't let go. You can't see the enemy pilot because his cockpit hides him from view. But in many of the films you are probably close enough, and despite Oingo Boingo's rather thrilling accompaniment, you can sense his frantic fear.

The MiGs twist and turn, but nothing they do works. The pipper bears down, relentless. You can imagine the MiG pilot shooting a look behind, terror in his eyes. Suddenly, from the pursuing plane, a pencil-thin line streaks in from the side. It's a missile. It homes to the MiG. Massive fireball. It's hard to imagine anyone surviving, but some do. The gun camera flies through the explosion and fire and on comes another fleeing MiG.

Rock music and "dealing death," as Jim Robb terms the art of loosing missiles. It's a chilling combination when viewed for real, but one, I must admit, that holds fascination—like watching an execution.

(One Topgun instructor from the past was, in fact, called "the Assassin," a name he got not from his actions in any war but for his ability to tame hotshot students who thought they knew everything.)

The briefing begins with preliminaries as Lieutenant Chris "Lumpy" Chamberlain, the instructor who will conduct the brief, writes some rules on the board: "Know your limits." "Know your aircraft." "A training violation is a kill." Then a surprise: the unexpected entrance, in full Arab headdress and robes,

of several other instructors. Saddam Hussein's or Muammar Gadhafi's finest, is the implication. They are followed by Jim "Pops"
Papageorge, the instructor who is also this class's manager (in
charge of the class), in dark blue North Korean uniform and
funny, slant-eye glasses.

A little laugh before the sweat . . .

Stan O'Connor got mad at his parents and joined the subma-
rine service. Now he was XO of Topgun, Robb's second.

What happened, said the tall, soft-spoken lieutenant commander, was: "I had a falling out with my parents and went downtown to Santa Cruz to enlist in the Marine Corps. But the Marine
recruiter was out." So he signed up with the navy recruiter, who
had been a submariner and put him in for the same.

But he did so well in boot camp that his brother, a highly
touted high school baseball catcher who was being recruited by
numerous colleges, including the Naval Academy, was able to
get an academy athletic scout to send Stan to an Annapolis
preparatory school, which was all O'Connor, a good athlete as
well as a good student, needed.

He loved the academy and went on to win the light-heavyweight
national collegiate boxing championship for it in 1976; earn a degree in oceanography, a subject he loves; and be selected for jets,
which he'd admired since being a skinny kid riding his bicycle
for miles to watch planes at the airport.

"My parents had certainly instilled a lot of self-discipline in
me," he says. "And even though we had our differences, there is
a lot of love there."

O'Connor didn't seem like a boxer—or, for that matter, like
most of the other fighter pilots I'd met. I might have guessed he
was a late-night FM announcer, so mellow were his voice and his
personality, at least to me. But his lanky, muscular physique, and
obviously broken nose, bespoke action.

In fact, in 1989, he'd ridden a flamed-out (engines extinguished and thus powerless) Topgun A-4F for three desperate
minutes, including trying to guide it over populated San Diego
areas, finally ejecting over vacant land at a mere five hundred
feet, just missing the fireball when the jet crashed.

"It was one of the few times where I felt like I was not in control," he recalled. "Fighter pilots want to think they are in con-

trol of their destiny. But that was to a point where it was time to say a prayer. And I did. . . . I knew that if the [ejection] handle didn't work, if it didn't fire, I was dead. . . . And then the chute had to work. . . . The [proximity to the] fireball was unexpected. That was like, 'Oh man, I'm closer to it than I thought.' "

Fortunately, the wind blew him clear.

He had been a nugget (new) F-14 pilot on board the *Kittyhawk* in the Indian Ocean when Americans had been taken hostage by Iranians in late 1979.

"We were briefed that day that we were going to war. I remember them saying, 'Some of you guys may not be coming back,' and the guy next to me saying, 'Probably talking about you, not me.' " He said he'd never seen more bombs, missiles, and mines in his life than were on the carrier. "We were maneuvering up north to Gonzo Station and getting ready to launch the first strike. In fact, the guys were walking to the airplanes. . . . My mind-set was, Yeah, I'm ready. . . . But it was called off at the last minute."

He said it was the challenge of "mentally figuring out how to get a positional advantage" in a three-dimensional sky and the "freedom of the mission"—being able to "roam, search out, and destroy the enemy"—that made him want to fly fighters.

"I'm very competitive, although I think people are surprised at that, as outwardly I don't tend to come across that way. . . . I'm not an animal who starts frothing when the bell rings, but I do like the sport of it, and I like the feeling of satisfaction knowing I can hold my own and prevail in most cases."

As XO at Topgun, he was being groomed for command, if not at Topgun, then with a squadron.

Fighter piloting started to "gel" for him, he said, on his second cruise back in the late 1970s under the tutelage of John "Black" Nathman, a name I would hear more than once when asking naval aviators who they thought were the best among them.

He remembered one fight in particular. The two of them were flying a slow scissors, ribboning around each other, both trying to maneuver behind to get an advantage. "I thought I was flying it about as perfect as you could possibly do."

When Nathman suddenly dove, O'Connor thought he had him. But then, just as suddenly, the teacher came back up and over in a "beautifully pirouetted" barrel roll, which landed him right on

O'Connor's stern. "I remember it as clear today as when it happened. . . . It was a finesse move, smooth. . . . His timing was impeccable. . . . I was doing well but it showed me there is always room for improvement.

"The other thing I liked about John was that he was very creative. . . . We would go out and fly a CAP mission on different stations and save fuel. I worked my tail off to save every ounce of fuel I could, so at the end of the mission we had this 'period of vulnerability,' he would call it . . . five minutes where we would try to work the radars to gain an undetected entry on each other, and then merge where we would fight. . . . We did this on every hop."

He said such sessions with Nathman taught him how to "exploit opponents' mistakes, gain positional advantages, and control airspeed. . . . You want to target a particular airspeed because if you are too fast [you can't turn as well as you should.] What ends up happening is what we call an arc. You're turning with this huge radius and your opponent is flying at a slower airspeed and can turn inside that radius and gain a positional advantage.

"I really developed stick-and-throttle, seat-of-the-pants-type flying with him, where I never came into the cockpit to look at anything, like airspeed. . . . If I needed information, I'd ask the RIO. . . . He taught me a lot about reconstruction, how to write down the fight so when we came back we could identify those areas we needed to improve on, break out the models . . .

"You need to think a fight through. . . . It's hard to say where a fight begins and ends, in terms of what you're going to teach and how you're going to progress. You may make one mistake that's really evident, but because of the nature of the fight, you didn't have the opportunity to make other mistakes, so they'll show up in other fights. That's how you build your bag of tricks so you can put it all together and go out there and fight."

I was told that back during the Vietnam War, when the Navy Fighter Weapons School started as a detachment, Dave Bjerke, one of the original Topgun pilots, got the idea of painting MiG silhouettes of Topgun graduate shootdowns outside on their hangar wall. I guess it was similar to putting a star on your aircraft.

Smaller silhouettes now line the walls flanking the steps leading up to Topgun's paneled offices—MiG-17s and 21s from the Vietnam days, and more advanced MiGs for the few navy kills that have come later. The silhouettes have the names of the crews beneath them and the dates of the kills.

It's a logical introduction.

I've never met a fighter pilot who actually wanted to physically kill the enemy pilot, although I'm sure there are some. For instance, Pete Pettigrew, a navy Vietnam MiG killer and another of the early FWS founders, told me that after his 1972 kill he was hoping the MiG pilot had survived so he could shoot him down again.

For most of the good ones, I think, the really important thing is the thrill of the contest, doing the best one can at something that, at its height, is so viscerally pleasurable to some of them that it has been likened, on occasion, to orgasm, however fleetingly.

Of course, flat-out besting the other guy and "lording over him" is certainly part of the attraction. It's an ego thing. And fighter pilots have egos. Huge ones. Not all, but most current and former FWS instructors, navy or air force, will quickly volunteer, when the subject approaches, that taking the "me" out of the practice fighting with students—meaning the "I—*me*—beat you"—is a must if they're going to be successful teachers.

In keeping with that predominant philosophy, the school's teachers make a conscious effort not to outwardly flaunt their superiority or be flamboyant, as the conventional image portrays them. For instance, unlike their students, most of whom wear numerous eye-catching patches and other regalia on their flight suits announcing who they are, the instructors wear only a single shoulder patch—the distinctive "MiG-in-the-pipper" (the pipper being the center dot of a fighter's optical gun sight, thus signifying the wearer's dead aim)—and have only a small, gold "TOP-GUN" embroidered on their rawhide name tags. (All flying graduates of the school win the patch upon completing the course.) Most don't even wear rank insignia on their flight suit because, they say, that, too, distracts from the lesson.

Operations Officer Joe Christofferson says that if any Topgunner goes to the officers' club—or anywhere else, for that matter—and starts boasting about how good he is, he'll be in trouble with his peers. There's a story about an ace who came to the base with "MiG killer" on his license plates. The Topgunners are said to have asked him to remove the plates. "Our reputation is earned, not bragged," said Christofferson, which is certainly true. But it's also true that everyone in the fighter business knows what the Topgun patch means, so who needs to brag?

The true situation, I think, is captured somewhat in a plaque on one of the Topgun walls. Entitled "Ode to Top Gun," and somewhat tongue-in-cheek, it says, "Given to a bit of swagger, which no one questions—rather envies and imitates . . . none is your better; few your equal. . . . In a single day you may joust with Richthoffen, Tomb, Hartmann; fight the battle of Britain . . . then with a turn of a head and quick change of armour, quietly, suavely slip into the role of teacher, lecturer. . . . Timid souls beware . . . but you (TOPGUNs), charged with firm resolve and mellow boldness; fly, fight, win."

And there's even a little elitism inside the school, and rightfully so.

When a new instructor arrives at Topgun, even though he's a course graduate and has the distinction of being so good he was invited back to teach, he's not allowed that privilege until he's passed rigorous air and classroom examinations that, on average, take a year.

These include becoming Topgun-proficient in the A-4 and F-16, and delivering a lecture on a weapons topic that has been likened to preparing a master's thesis.

"I can honestly tell you," said Christofferson, "that the first year around here you're not really an instructor at all. You're a student like you've never been before. . . . You go out and you're flying against a nearly perfectly flying opponent. Even subtle BFM [basic fighter maneuvers] errors [simple maneuvers] will give them position. . . .

"And then you come back and you're expected to debrief the fight as an expert. . . . The syllabus for the A-4 and F-16 is killer. It takes the wind out of anybody's sails. . . . The lecture is even bigger. . . . I mean we've had guys walk in here who were so confident it was oozing out of their ears, and halfway through they were on their knees."

Although the work here is deadly, humor and wit are used to get it across. A plaque on one of the walls is entitled "Lessons Learned." "Beware the Hun in the sun," it says. "Don't blow your beets.... When bee-bees are flying, it's time for your last best move.... Use the sun, but remember everyone else is there."

One of my favorite plaques is the French School of Aerial Combat's 1917 definition of fighter pilot characteristics. In addition to skill, cunning, and purpose, the plaque says, the good fighter pilot must also be "endowed with great Sangfroid," a funny word that actually does mean great self-possession, "often cold-blooded," in the face of danger, according to Webster.

I still think it's funny, and I think Topgun does, too.

Lieutenant Rob "Ice" Ffield was a younger instructor than O'Connor, polite but measuring. He might have been a ski bum, he said, if he hadn't decided to continue college. That was in upstate New York, at a small school named Clarkson.

Ffield, about five-nine, was blond and slightly built and looked like a skier.

"The big thing I had done when I was young was ski racing," he said, "so I was heavily into it." He went to the division-one national championships as part of Clarkson's ski team in his sophomore year, and wondered, "Shoot, should I be a ski bum for the rest of my life or continue college?"

It was a "crossroads," he said, but he opted for the schooling, earned a degree in mechanical engineering in 1981, and worked for a year for Boeing in Seattle as a flight test engineer before deciding to go to Pensacola. "I'd always been interested in flying," he said, but he saw that "it would take considerable time and money to get a commercial license." Pilot friends advised him "to go military because that's how to really learn and they pay you."

He was one of the first junior officers selected to fly the F-18 Hornet, the newest fighter in the navy arsenal, which, in keeping with growing budget restraints, doubles as a bomber. "Black" Nathman, he volunteered, was one of the senior pilots transitioning with him to the new fighter.

I wanted to find this guy Nathman.

"He was a very impressive individual," said Ffield, "and typically we would get a lecture from one of the RAG instructors, and they'd say, 'Okay, you got a clear to go.' And he would go, 'Okay, everybody stay here.' Then he'd sort of tell us how things really worked, so to speak. Not to put down the instruction . . . but he was such an excellent pilot and someone like me . . . well, with 278 hours and he has thousands and has been a Topgun instructor and so forth. You listen to those guys."

Ffield's first cruise flying the Hornet was on the *Coral Sea* in the Mediterranean. Following a terrorist bombing of a West Berlin discotheque in which one American was killed and fifty people were injured, he had flown CAP to protect the carrier after the April 1986 retaliatory raid against Libya.

The raid had been precipitated by another of those "Line of Death" exercises that had led to the 1981 shootdowns. Ffield said a lot of navy jets had dogged the tails of Libyan pilots in the days before the raid, careful not to give them opportunities for good shots. The rules of engagement (ROE) had again prevented the Americans from shooting first.

On one occasion, he said, he'd had a chance to scare a MiG-23 pilot—but only with his intelligence camera.

"I don't want to get into tactics too much," he said, "but we have a way of sweeping in low and undetected by the Libyans. Their radars have a difficult time picking us up. The resolution [on the screen] is such that they don't know exactly where you are or where you're coming from. But their controllers have told them you are out there. So they are looking for you and all of a sudden you pop right up next to them. The guy looks over and goes, 'Whoa.' Then you take his picture."

On this particular intercept, said Ffield, the MiG pilot just "hunkered down in his seat and kept on flying." But he knew of other situations where the Libyan pilot had produced a camera and taken intelligence pictures of his own. "They're looking at what kind of missiles you have, that sort of thing. Same as us."

He was selected for Topgun after the Med cruise and, in 1988, was asked to return as an instructor.

A good fighter pilot has got to be aggressive, he said, "not in the physical sense, but have the heart of a lion. . . . You have to be someone who is going to go after something and then get it. . . . Don't get me wrong. You can be mild-mannered, but you have to have the will to win."

He said situational awareness in the really good pilots was the result of what they sometimes referred to at the school as " 'Karma,' where you just sort of feel where things are." It's the same sense, he said, that a running back in football has—although he's not looking at the tackler, he moves at precisely the right moment, leaving the tackler to eat dust.

"The best guys are always at the right place at the right time, and they can just feel when it's right to do something. A lot of that comes with timing, and, again, it's natural for some people. They pick it up quicker than others, or are just born with it. Other guys do it enough to where they start to develop it, like a sixth sense, so to speak."

He was skeptical of the press and worried that America's success in the Gulf War would make the public think that good fighter piloting was something that just came naturally for Americans, and that therefore funding for the training, which is so vital to keeping skills honed, would be cut off (which, in fact, has happened since the war).

Even the best fighter pilots will get rusty if they are not flying and fighting regularly.

"We'll find ourselves right back where we were in the late 1960s," he said. "It happens after every war. After World War I our military turned into a flying club concerned more about formations and looking pretty than how they would fight."

He said you get "very patriotic" working at Topgun.

"Guys have been here since six o'clock in the morning, and they won't leave until eight at night. They do this day in and day out. . . . What really ticked me off about some reporters during [the Gulf War] was that they looked at the military and went, Man, you . . . you guys are terrible. What do you mean, you know, what's this collateral damage here? [Pilots] are laying their lives on the line and they're not getting paid anything. . . . Compared to the airlines, if I got paid overtime, I'd be a millionaire now."

Lieutenants Jeff "DD" Dodson and Jeff "TJ" Naven were not happy. Topgun students, they had just been "killed" in the big one-versus-one exercise: the final, put-it-all-together, end-of-course knife fight.

An F-14 crew from VF-154, Naven was the RIO and Dodson the pilot. "We were out there to do some damage and kill the guy," Dodson said later, "and we just kind of . . . in our blood thirst, made a few mistakes."

They weren't sulking or kicking chairs or anything like that, but you could tell this was not a triumphant return. Dodson, in a soiled flight suit, as was his RIO, was slow in setting up the gun camera videotape. He regretted being too eager, too quick to go for the throat. He knew he should have been a little smarter, a little more patient.

They had done badly on one of the first section hops, a two versus two. But they'd done very well in a recent division hop, a four versus four, so they had momentum going into the final.

Stan O'Connor, the instructor they had fought and lost to, was low-key as he sat down and asked Dodson if maybe fuel or mechanical problems had hampered them.

No, sir, said Dodson, a drag car enthusiast who had found the ultimate speed machine in fighters. "We just could not get a lock on."

He did not want to make excuses.

No problem, said O'Connor, sitting down.

What was about to start was a vital part of the learning process—the student coming back and conducting the debrief, showing he could dissect the fight and learn from it.

O'Connor looked up attentively.

Dodson, the son of an engineer, had grown up in Washington, D.C., and paid his own way through school at New Mexico State to earn a chemistry degree. He turned on his tape and began by recounting the beginning of the fight, trying as much as he could to avoid using the personal "me" or "we" and referring to himself and Naven as "the F-14" and O'Connor as "the A-4."

The A-4 got sight of the F-14 first, he said, which was not unusual. The Tomcat is twice as big. Once they did see the A-4, it was about two miles away, barreling toward them.

Seeing an A-4 instead of an F-16 meant that they were not dealing with a fearsome adversary like the MiG-29. It was more like a 21. They could be a little more aggressive, less cautious about a face shot or incredible maneuvers.

Their initial plan had called for 500 knots at merge. But they realized they were lower than they had planned for, and so tried to reduce speed so the F-14 would turn better at the lower altitude. The lower speed would also help them keep from going below the floor of the fight, which was 5,000 feet. That would be a safety violation and cause instant elimination.

He noted that the sun shouldn't have been a factor in the fight because of a shielding layer of clouds.

The A-4 looked very fast to Dodson as it blew by them. They both made right turns, meaning they were turning away from each other to circle as quickly as they could in opposite directions. The turns, in fight pilot parlance, meant that the fight was going to be "two-circle," as opposed to "one-circle," which would have meant the fighters had turned toward each other.

From a god's-eye view—if the plane movements and directions could somehow be magically highlighted—an observer looking down would see two parallel circles emerging from the circular movements of the aircraft. The circles would be tangential, or side by side, the planes, each in its own circle, curling back toward each other.

Because of the relative strengths and weaknesses of the two planes, Dodson wanted the fight to be two-circle. He had a better turn rate than the A-4, and therefore probably would get around his circle quicker and gain an advantage.

So everything, thus far, was going their way.

But then the A-4 had suddenly zoomed up, "out of plane," meaning out of the two-dimensional circle it had been traveling parallel to the F-14. It was a "very aggressive, nose-high maneuver," Dodson briefed. "Don't know if it quite becomes a pure vertical, but it's certainly in the seventy-degree, nose-up attitude."

O'Connor, not wanting the two-circle fight because of the advantage it gave the F-14, had made the first offensive move. Dodson almost went up with him, because he had tremendous power and thought he could catch him. But he decided to wait until they'd merged again.

The fight, however, had now shifted in O'Connor's favor. By going up and changing direction as he had, the two planes were now in a one-circle fight, meaning that instead of going in opposite circles to meet as the circles met, they were, in effect, chasing each other around one circle.

Realizing this, Dodson knew he'd better do something quick. With O'Connor at the top of the turning circle, and Dodson coming around the bottom, he decided to try a quick-turn-up maneuver, which would rapidly point him toward the A-4 and, as he accelerated toward O'Connor, enable him to shoot off a missile.

It was a kind of do-or-die move, but if he could pull it off he could negate O'Connor's sudden advantage and get a quick win.

He went for it.

The problem was that by going up he was going to lose speed rapidly. Conversely, his target, the A-4, was already up and would be coming down, gaining speed—or "energy," as they called it. "Speed is life" is always the rule, and while many times there are optimum speeds for various maneuvers, and the F-14's power was considerable, you always had to be leery of the trade-off.

Dodson got the nose on the A-4, target distance and missile envelope parameters were good, but couldn't get a radar lock.

They had only a few seconds to do so.

By the time they got up to where they wanted to be, they were down to 200 knots and couldn't sustain a rapid climb. Making matters worse, O'Connor had seen what they were doing and was diving down to curl back up on the F-14's tail and maintain advantage.

"F-14 knows he's committed a pretty fundamental error right here in selling the farm for one shot that may or may not pan out," said Dodson, drawing the situation on the debrief chalkboard. "It's starting to feel a little bit defensive here."

He knew he was in trouble and hoped that maybe he could regain the offensive. He thought that maybe the A-4 wasn't as fast as it should be coming down and he therefore might be able to get some angles on it once he got more speed on his jet.

But he was wrong again. And then he committed another fatal error. He lost sight of the A-4. It was only for two seconds. But the saying is "Lose sight, lose the fight," and by the time he reacquired the smaller adversary it was coming up behind him and O'Connor called "Pipper on," meaning he had a guns shot.

Dodson wasn't sure he heard the call, and he maneuvered some more, but the fight was already over.

If it had been a real fight, he and Naven probably would have been killed.

O'Connor didn't make too many comments at the debrief. He complimented Dodson on making a good move to take away a simulated Atoll shot the A-4 wanted to make. But he said the initial move up toward him that Dodson had contemplated and then abandoned at the beginning of the fight had been slow and "arcing," and therefore had allowed the A-4 to turn quickly and gain the advantage.

Two months later, and back at his squadron, Dodson called the fight the "high point" of his time at Topgun.

"Winning's great and all that kind of stuff," he said, "especially in actual combat. You gotta win in combat. But in training, you can lose or not do so well and still come away with learning points."

He said he'd still be aggressive but "be smarter about it. . . . We maneuvered aggressively to take a shot, what we felt would be a kill shot, an end-the-fight shot. We sold the farm to get that shot and when it didn't happen, when we didn't get a lock on as quick as we wanted . . . we were out of energy and out of ideas. . . .

"In engagements like that—personal, one-on-one engagements—opportunities for getting locks and taking shots are very transitory. It's not like you have fifteen or twenty seconds. It's a split-second type of thing . . . a battle of seconds out there, looking for delayed reactions of the other pilot, getting lock ons, stuff like that. . . .

"You gotta temper that overwhelming desire to kill 'em fast, and be smart. . . . I should have taken my time and worked on the problem for thirty more seconds or something like that."

7

LIEUTENANT JOE CHRISTOFFERSON nudged the big Tomcat forward and began his descent.

Only three weeks out of F-14 training, he was a new member of the VF-2 Bounty Hunters, recently judged the best West Coast fighter squadron in the fleet. Although he would later become a respected Topgun instructor, this was early 1982, and as a young nugget he was about to attempt, in the inky skies off Hawaii, one of the most dangerous feats in naval aviation.

It had to do with one of the main differences between flying fighters in the navy and in the air force.

Night carrier landing.

Naval aviators pride themselves on carrier landings. They are a measure of their skill. Most air force fighter pilots, however, say it just detracts from ACM time. And they are right. But it is still one of the hardest things to do in all of aviation, and night carrier landing is downright scary.

Making matters worse for Christofferson, the weather was terrible.

Day carrier landings are hard enough. But night landing is like garaging your car at 140 miles per hour, blindfolded, the garage moving. It is threading a needle with a bullet; in bad weather, it is controlled crashing onto a bobbing parking slab.

Further, this was Christofferson's first attempt as a new member of the squadron.

He had made a few night carrier landings in training, but with an instructor in his backseat and good weather. Now he was a fleet pilot, expected to hold his own. The RIO behind him was a no-nonsense veteran lieutenant commander. This was the big leagues.

"Let's just say I didn't want to screw it up," the handsome, dark-haired Naval Academy graduate recalled. "I wanted to do well."

That sense of competitiveness had been with him all his life.

The son of a career navy surface ship officer, he'd been a recruited quarterback and second baseman in high school, and well-rounded enough to win an appointment to Annapolis, where he'd continued athletics at the collegiate level. Exposed during summers to submarines, surface ships, and the Marine Corps, he'd chosen aviation and then won fighters precisely because of the challenge.

"Joe's a real image-conscious, competitive guy," recalled his VF-2 skipper, Chris Wilson, a navy captain at the Pentagon in 1992. "He's a high-ego type, and I don't mean that in a derogatory sense. He's always done well at everything, been looked up to by his contemporaries."

Christofferson, married, was a leader, the kind who would rally a team to a winning score and then play a practical joke on them. With tall, dark features, all-American good looks, and an easy manner, he was a head-turner and an organizer who had been heavily sought by the other fighter squadrons that had had an opening.

Wilson said the Bounty Hunters, one of the first squadrons to get F-14s, had actually forgone earlier possible selections they'd been offered in order to be assured of getting Christofferson and another good pilot later. In effect, Christofferson had been one of the fleet's top draft choices out of the training command—a fact that only added to the pressure he now felt.

He knew key members of the squadron would be watching him.

They'd returned to the ship from a night training mission to stack in orbits a thousand feet apart. There were a number of planes behind him, including his flight lead, Bob "Rat" Willard, a fighter pilot with the kind of reputation Christofferson hoped to earn. He wished the weather was better, but that was nothing he could control. Starting his straight-line descent at 6,000 feet and 250 knots, he'd be hitting the *Ranger*'s deck in the next few moments.

It was approximately twenty-one rain-soaked, invisible miles ahead.

Everything was synchronized. The "push" had come at a pre-arranged time, as would the lowering of his wheels, even the "trap," or landing. For the bulk of the descent, he'd be flying at 250 knots, then slowing to about 150 after lowering his gear. Simultaneously, he'd be "dumping" gasoline in measured amounts. The cables stretched across the landing deck, which would stop the Tomcat, were set for a maximum weight. The big fighter was heavy as it is. More weight than maximum, in the form of extra fuel, might rip the cables from their moorings, not to mention cause a holocaust should there be a crash.

But he also had to be careful to keep enough fuel to continue flying if he unexpectedly "boltered" (failed to engage the arresting cable and had to keep flying) or was waved off before he hit the deck. "Fuel management," the pilots called the skill. And, as he neared the ten-mile-out mark, where he would "dirty up" (lower his landing gear, flaps, and tailhook), he radioed "Max trap," confirming he had the optimum amount, which, in this case, was 7.8 thousand pounds.

Everything was going as expected.

He was gaining confidence, getting closer.

At six miles out, he still couldn't see the carrier, but he and his backseater were passing through 1,200 feet and had slowed to the prescribed "on-speed," approximately 138 knots. At three and a half miles, he pushed the F-14's nose over slightly for his final descent. It was then that he caught the first glimpse of what had to be the ship.

It looked to him like a "tiny white flashlight," and he could also see the faint light of the destroyer behind it, over which he would soon be passing. He now had visual proof that everything was going right. But just as soon as they had appeared, the lights disappeared, extinguished again in the stormy darkness.

It didn't matter. He already had to trust his instruments—"fly the needles," as they called it—in particular, his azimuth and glide slope indicator. If it showed a perfect plus sign, he was on the right heading and glide path. If it didn't, he had to make corrections—bring the two thin lines into a perfect cross.

Nothing he'd ever done had ever taken such concentration. It took excellent eye-hand coordination; it was the ultimate video game, life and death in the balance.

"They're not talking to you much," he later recalled from Fighter Weapons School, when I called him about the incident, "only if you're really off. . . . My heart's going pretty fast. . . . I'm making line-up corrections . . . working the power . . . working the airspeed."

He was descending closer to the water, entering the crucial zone, where the ship's lights would come into play and every correction was critical. He especially had to watch out for vertigo, the distortion in sensations and perceptions that could make him fly into the sea—or worse, into the back end of the carrier.

He wished he could see the ship again. "We always preach 'Scan your instruments, fly your instruments.' But one peek [of the ship] is worth a thousand scans."

Just inside a mile, he got his wish. He caught sight of the "ball," a mirrored device on the ship's port side that, along with a line of vertical lights, would be his only designated outside visual aids. The ball moved up and down depending on whether he was above or below the glide path.

The ship itself was still invisible.

To his great relief, the ball was centered.

The aircraft was exactly where it should be.

For the next few seconds, for almost a quarter mile, he had to continually scan his instruments and the ball, smoothing his power, making line-up corrections. The ball was his lifeline. He had to keep it correctly centered.

At three quarters of a mile, his RIO "called the ball," sent a radio message to the LSO, watching him from a perch astern, to monitor outside control.

"Roger ball," replied the LSO, who would remain silent except to give voice corrections if he felt they were needed.

All Christofferson's senses were heightened; every movement was critical.

Only a few seconds to touchdown.

The big fighter whistle-roared through the stormy darkness, seeming to hang in suspension as it dropped toward its target, its swing-wings plied in full extension, its pilot scanning his instruments and the ball with the intensity of a high-speed computer.

"Don't settle," radioed a calm LSO.

The caution was like a subtle arrow shot imperceptibly into his focus.

He knew that high winds were a challenge, in that just a small reduction in power caused the plane to sink measurably. Not only were the winds heaving the *Ranger*'s deck with huge waves, but they were increasing the "burble," or "sink hole" across the closing stern "that wants to pull you in."

If he relaxed power, the plane would drop much faster than if there was a lighter wind.

To prevent the settle, he overreacted.

"I came on with a little too much power," he remembered. "That drove me a little high, so I reduced power ever so slightly. But it wasn't enough to get me back down."

The plane drifted slightly to the right.

"Come left for line-up," said the LSO.

"We're only talking a couple of feet here," said Christofferson. "If you land more than about seven or eight feet either way of centerline, you run the risk of clipping your wing across the nose of a parked aircraft."

He had only a nanosecond. He made the last correction, but in so doing, again added slightly too much power. The Tomcat's wheels crashed onto the flight deck but with the plane's nose slightly down, and, consequently, its rear slightly up.

There are only four cables across the deck. His tailhook hit just ahead of the three wire and skipped over the four wire. Landing at full throttle, he was already taking off when he heard the LSO say, "Bolter, bolter."

He'd blown it—not a rarity on night carrier landings. But that was little consolation.

He continued on up. They told him to climb back to 1,200 feet, turn back around, and make a second approach.

"I am just . . . I can't tell you the feeling after boltering," he remembers. "You can be the most confident guy in the world, but after that, you just feel terrible. I was beside myself. . . . all sorts of things go through your mind. . . . I'm going to be in trouble. . . . I wonder if I can do it?"

His RIO, a senior officer, critiqued him as he headed back astern, but Christofferson knew he couldn't dwell. "You've got a lot of flying left to do. . . . If you let it distract you, you're going to kill yourself." He had to concentrate. Compartmentalization, aviators call it, and it enabled him to put the problem behind him, focus on what was ahead. "Okay, I boltered once," he remembers thinking. "That's not the end of the world. Other guys have done that. . . . Let's go for it."

He found new confidence (as those who had picked him to get this far believed he would).

He traveled ten miles back astern and they hooked him back in for another straight-line descending approach, holding back the other fighters above him, forcing them to fly extra orbits.

This second approach would be quicker and shorter, but he was well aware that he had disrupted the operation. Everyone holding would have to be that much more precise, would have to work that much harder managing their gas, flying longer.

It added to his pressure.

But the approach went like clockwork. "I just knew we were going to do it this time."

He called the ball, dropping down in the darkness, scanning his instruments. Although he was apprehensive, everything looked good. In the final seconds, he could taste the landing. . . . And then he did the same thing again—powered just over the four wire.

"I was high this time and he told me to come down a little. . . . I was nervous, having already missed, and it was dark and scary and everything. . . . I didn't want to come back on the power and have a big settle and scare everybody."

Second bolter.

He'd done it again.

He lifted back into the night.

"I'm not panicking or anything . . . but I'm upset. . . . I feel like I'm embarrassing myself, my squadron, the ship."

In addition, there was a new concern. His fuel state. "Max gas" was usually enough for three bolters, no more. Then he'd have only enough to fly to a "divert" base, which, in this case, was Barber's Point, five hundred miles north of Oahu, near Pearl Harbor. Unless—and it was a big unless—they refueled him in the air with an air wing tanker.

But he'd only refueled once at night—earlier that evening. Only at that time it hadn't been so dark. While he didn't like the idea of having to go to Barber's Point, with the personal failure and special operational problems that would represent, the thought of having to tank under these conditions didn't thrill him either.

Air refueling always meant high chances for midair collision. At night—and with a novice in suspect weather—the chances were even greater.

Then he heard the ship telling the tanker, a converted A-6, to move close to him. "That really put a chill down my back."

Starting the third approach, he told his RIO this was probably it, a fact the veteran, now icily silent, was well aware of.

It was another short approach. "I'm more nervous now because I've missed twice," and there was "a lot of anxiety" because of the possible tanking.

He called the ball. "They're talking to me. 'Hey, you're looking pretty good. Keep it coming. Don't settle' . . . I can tell I'm their special project, their special child that night. . . . It feels good."

But as he came to the final seconds, trying to relax and make it easy, he got behind on the power and started to settle.

The LSO called for slightly more power.

Overreacting, he gave it too much again. Still, maybe because of the rise and fall of the deck from the heavy seas, he landed where he should have—right in the midst of the wires. But the Ranger was an older carrier. Its arresting cables weren't raised, as newer carriers' cables are. They lay flat. Now, because his Tomcat came down in an incorrect attitude, its tailhook skipped over the three and four wires. He launched back into the night.

At first the ship told him to climb to 8,000 and tank in preparation for another try. His heart sank. Then they asked his fuel state. He told them he was right at the minimum to make Barber's Point, about 5,500 to 6,000 pounds. Another trip around to try and land and he'd have to ditch if he didn't make it.

They diverted him.

As he pulled back on the throttle to conserve fuel, and headed for Oahu, he thought his naval career might be over. "They're going to throw me out. . . . I'm done as a pilot. All the thoughts in the world go through your head."

His RIO wasn't any help. "He goes, 'We still got a lot of work to do. You've never been to Barber's Point. I haven't been there in a hundred years. It's night. We're low on fuel. We don't know what the weather is. . . .' "

The tension between them got worse when the A-6 tanker received special permission to try to run them down in order to give them gas.

"When he [the RIO] found out that the tanker was, in fact, on its way . . . he comes up and says, 'Okay, no screwing around. We need some gas. No messing around here.' Like I'd been fooling around all night?" he recalled thinking. "I'm just kidding here. I don't really want to get aboard."

He was miffed. He shouted back, "I'm doing my best!"

In truth, he had mixed emotions about the tanking. He welcomed another chance at landing, hopefully proving that he could do it. But he dreaded the tanking operation, with which he was unfamiliar, especially under such adverse conditions.

"The one thing I wanted to avoid was having to [night] tank for the first time because I had to have the gas. And, if I had to divert, having to scare myself because I didn't have the gas. . . . I wanted the conditions to be, Hey, I got plenty of gas. I'm just going to go up here and practice. But it didn't work out that way."

It took the A-6 about ten minutes to catch up with them. They were approximately eighty miles from the ship. The tanker pilot knew the F-14 didn't have the fuel to join on the tanker, so he moved ahead of the Tomcat and joined on it.

"Unbelievable," said Christofferson, marveling at the tanker's action. "They don't join on you. You join on them."

From its lower rear, the tanker extended its fifteen-foot metal hose with the basketlike drogue at the end. But Christofferson couldn't see anything but the plane's running lights.

"I'm talking about a pitch-black, unbelievably dark night at sea."

There was no way they were going to get gas if they couldn't find the pump.

His RIO volunteered a solution.

The Tomcat took inflight gas through a probe protruding from its nose. The probe's tip had a small, red identification light, used chiefly to determine that it was extended.

They could see the diffused red light.

"My RIO says, Well, the only other thing I can think of is just drive up there close to where you think the drogue might be and maybe the probe will light the basket."

Both planes were speeding at around 300 knots. He was going to move up toward the A-6's belly, his only reference points the tanker's tiny green running lights. Somewhere in between, spearing in front of them, was the drogue.

It could be lifegiving—or come crashing through their cockpit.

The probability of midair collision increased greatly as they got closer.

Up they inched. "I was trying to stay calm. I'm a pretty calm guy . . . but there was no doubt in my mind that I was nervous."

But almost as soon as they started looking, the probe light illuminated the hose.

"I just sort of walked it back and it showed me the basket."

That was the easy part. Now he had to make the connection.

"It takes finesse to get it in at any speed, and finesse to keep it in, especially at night, especially when the thing doesn't have lights on it."

After "three or four stabs," he said, he finally connected. "I don't know how to this day I did it. . . . My hands were shaking. . . . I think the Lord helped me. . . . He just took over the airplane for a few seconds. . . . Somehow, I was able to stay in. . . . It was unbelievable."

The tanker gave them about 6,000 pounds. It took about two minutes, but to Christofferson "it felt like forever." Knowing he now had enough fuel to make a few more passes, the ship told him to come back.

He thought about telling them he'd go on to Barber's Point and come back tomorrow, but then it was "refocus time . . . no time to dwell . . . I'm back in the game."

They flew back to the ship. Every plane but his and the tanker had recovered (landed).

Christofferson went first, the tanker holding back in case he needed it again.

He'd hardly let himself think about it, but the one time he'd night-trapped a Tomcat in training he'd boltered, landing on his second pass. Before he'd trapped that night, however, he'd let himself think the unthinkable—that it couldn't be done. That he might die trying it.

Now, he said, he knew he could land. It was just bearing down and doing it.

He hoped.

This fourth pass was probably "as challenging a moment" as he'd had in naval aviation, he says.

He dropped down and caught the four wire.

The feeling was "unbelievable," he remembers—"total ecstasy. I can't tell you how happy I was. There just is no feeling like escaping death and landing safely on the ship."

His skipper, Wilson, was waiting for him, as were the LSOs. He got a special debrief. Everyone was very understanding. What took a while to sink in was that more experienced pilots than he had boltered that night. And since the ship was soon to go on cruise and could be ordered into combat, the squadron had been testing him, seeing how he would react under stressful conditions.

He'd passed.

It was months later, and Christofferson, working hard to prove himself as a fighter pilot, thought he finally had Rat Willard, premier aviator, where he wanted.

The two were practicing dogfighting above the northern Arabian Sea, Willard driving his Tomcat in a searing turn; his pupil, Christofferson, bearing in. The burly blond flight lead, a Topgun graduate and former RAG tactics instructor, always beat his inexperienced wingmen. That was expected. Not only would Willard come to be known as one of the best fighter pilots in the navy, but beat-and-teach air-to-air practice was the training process he'd set up when he and his wingman had saved some gas after a mission.

But this time, Christofferson, tactically aggressive for a nugget, and a highly intuitive pilot, sensed his first victory.

It would be oh so sweet if he was right.

Since making that first fleet night landing months ago, he'd been getting beat on a regular basis, then enduring long postfight debriefs by Willard, who seemed never to tire of pointing out his mistakes—in minute detail.

It was getting him down. He needed a lift. "Everybody's friendly and helping you," he said, "but you wonder if you're really worthy of being in the same room with these guys."

But that was history.

Now he was sure he was gaining. The two Tomcats swirled parallel to the horizon, the sun glinting off the ocean below. Only a few more seconds and he'd have the advantage, maybe have a shot. "That's when Rat would go vertical," he remembers, "do some loop-de-loop reversal that I couldn't follow, come back and shoot me."

Back to frustration. Back to the doubts. They'd been on Gonzo Station off Iran for three months, and he didn't seem to be making headway. "I knew I could do it [dogfight well] . . . but unless I'm seeing myself win . . . it just doesn't feel very good."

And if he wasn't practicing against Willard, he'd fly with Chris Wilson, his skipper.

Wilson, a former F-8 Crusader pilot with Vietnam combat experience, was one of the original F-14 instructors. In the late 1970s, he'd been a member of the handpicked navy contingent sent to Nellis Air Force Base to fight in ACEVAL-AIMVAL, the wargame tests that had pitted some of the best fighter pilots in all the services against each other to see what air-to-air combat in the future would be like.

"Willard and Wilson [both renowned slow-fighters] were the best F-14 drivers and teachers on the West Coast," according to Christofferson, "but you don't realize that at the time. All you realize is you're a bum because you're not doing very well."

The dogfight style Willard was teaching was called "position" fighting. Simply put, it was a game plan in which the pilot used his aircraft's best turning ability to quickly gain angle advantages, or "position," on his opponents and then hold them, or increase the angles until he was within shooting parameters.

Turning, after all, was what a dogfight was all about.

Position fighting was a more aggressive fight, as opposed to "energy" fighting, which was more patient (although each mixed elements of the other). It depended on the pilot's knowing the aircraft's optimum turn rate and turn radius (among other factors). Every aircraft turned quickest and in its smallest circle at a certain optimum combination of speed, nose attitude, G load, and altitude. This didn't occur necessarily at its fastest speed, nor at maximum G's, but at a perfect combination of all factors that, when achieved, meant the aircraft was "max performing"—turning at its absolute best.

If a pilot was fighting a similar aircraft—meaning one with a comparable turn rate and turn radius—he, at least, would never get outturned and, thus, outadvantaged, presuming he kept his aircraft max performing. And if it had different turning abilities, he'd max perform against his opponent's weaknesses.

Students like Christofferson were told what the max performance figures were for the Tomcat. Six-and-half G's, for instance, for one maneuver, and several degrees nose low for another. But the trick was in being able to sense the subtle variances in speed, nose position, and the other factors determining turn rate and radius while simultaneously fighting heavy G's in the fight and not daring to look inside the cockpit for instrument cues for fear of losing sight of the opponent.

As they liked to say, "Lose sight, lose the fight."

Good position fighters just "felt" the combinations; they knew instinctively, through endless practice and familiarity, when their jet was max performing and when it was not.

But it usually took years to become that instinctive.

In addition, there were moves, or maneuvers, and countermoves to those maneuvers, that students had to master. Until he experienced them—had them used against him in a fight—a pilot usually couldn't do them or defend against them. Then he had to become so good at them that their use became—like max performing—second nature.

Finally, just as in a chess game, a really good dogfighter, position or otherwise, had to become so familiar and instinctive with what he'd learned that he was able, prior to the fight, to formulate a game plan. And then, once the fight commenced, he had to be able to instantaneously change that plan depending on what was occurring in the actual fight and where exactly in the sky he projected himself to be as the fight progressed.

This last part was the putting-it-all-together skill, according to Willard, a former Naval Academy defensive end in his college days. He called it "offensive countering."

Instead of merely reacting to an opponent's moves—as one did in "defensive countering"—a really good fighter pilot controlled and dictated the fight by initiating one, two, even three or more moves ahead. Thus his opponent had to react to him, not vice versa.

The "offensive" (initiating) pilot was always ahead of a "defensive" (reacting) pilot.

"The quickest way to, I think, take advantage of an airplane's maneuvering capability," says Willard, a captain preparing to take over a nuclear carrier when I talked to him, "is to maximize its turning rate all the time. Get the [aircraft's] nose pointed where you want it pointed to kill the other airplane. So my philosophy . . . centers around immediate reaction time. Certainly having a game plan. But beyond the game plan, having knowledge of all the countermoves and the offensive countermoves and the counters to the counters."

It took strength, concentration, and intelligence to "position" or otherwise fight an F-14. The pilot had to constantly keep his twenty-five-ton Tomcat at the edge of its performance envelope while simultaneously processing a myriad of data—gauge-given and seat-of-the-pants—as he rocketed, rolled, and tumbled through a weight-exploding, consciousness-graying (sometimes consciousness-snuffing) set of high-G maneuvers.

Willard: "If you can keep your wits about you . . . think your way through with minimum reaction time . . . focus on your opponent . . . always assessing what he's going to do . . . max perform the airplane . . . through however many turns it takes . . . these are the principles that are going to make your airplane a killing machine."

Christofferson had been competitive with Willard when their jets had stayed in the same planes of motion, generally called the "horizontal plane," the plane roughly parallel to the horizon. But when Willard had taken his jet "out of plane"—in a direction other than the one the two of them had been swirling in—especially up into a vertical slow fight, Christofferson had run into trouble.

"I just couldn't make the kind of timely reversals [quick turn-backs] that [Willard] could," he remembered. "Going uphill was hard enough."

Spacial orientation—knowing exactly where you were in relationship to the horizon—was harder in the vertical. Losing speed, the Tomcat was harder to control, especially reverse.

"You can't just point the nose like you would if you were faster. . . . Below 150 knots . . . it takes quite a bit of rudder input to make it go where you want. . . . You almost have to use opposite stick [push it away from the direction] you want to go. . . . It's

An F-14 Tomcat from Brian Fitzpatrick's VF-103 "Sluggers" flies over a carrier during Desert Storm. The U.S. Navy's preeminent fighter after Vietnam, the Tomcat was designed to protect carriers, and had both dogfight maneuverability and exceptional firepower. Because of its long-range Phoenix missile system, a single Tomcat could simultaneously target and hopefully destroy multiple enemy planes at distances approaching 100 miles. U.S. Navy F-14s "opened" and "closed" the 1980s with air-to-air kills against Libyan fighters.

(*Above*) Two who forged reputations as among the best fighter pilots in the post-Vietnam Navy: (*left*) Dale "Snort" Snodgrass, talented, personable "golden arm," and (*right*) John "Black" Nathman, soft spoken on the ground but a "methodical executioner" in the air. (*Below*) Navy F/A-18 strike fighter Hornets en route to a Gulf War target. The new but controversial Navy fighter bomber, which entered service in the early 1980s, was the only Navy fighter to score air-to-air kills in the Gulf War.

(*Above*) The Air Force's lack of a good air superiority fighter in Vietnam gave birth to the F-15 Eagle, a pure dogfighter with exceptional maneuverability, acceleration, and weapons systems. F-15s got most of the air-to-air victories in the Gulf War, with the majority of those being won by members of the 58th Tactical Fighter Squadron, known as the "Gorillas." (*Below*) Two of the Gorillas responsible for that record were (*left*) Cesar "Rico" Rodriguez, who shot down a MiG-23 and ran a MiG-29 into the ground, and (*right*) Chuck "Sly" Magill, a Marine attached to the 58th who bagged a MiG-29. Magill was the only Marine to get an air-to-air kill in the war.

Gorilla flight lead Ralph "Cheese" Graeter shot down two Iraqi F-1 Mirage fighters early on the first night of the Gulf War. The kills are represented by stars flanking his name on the rim of the cockpit of his F-15.

Joe "Hoser" Satrapa, a Vietnam flyer who became known as the best "guns kill" shooter in the post-Vietnam Navy, shakes hands with Dale Snodgrass (sunglasses) before a final dogfight in Tomcats and dress flight suits on the occasion of Satrapa's first retirement. He was later called back to active duty by the secretary of the Navy, who wanted him as an instructor.

Young fighter pilot Keith Beam sits atop his Corvette in front of the Air Force's other air superiority fighter, the F-16 Flying Falcon, or "Viper," as its pilots like to call it. The Viper's comparative light weight and "fly-by-wire" control system make it the most agile air-to-air fighter-bomber in the U.S. arsenal. Beam became a Fighter Weapons School instructor in the nimble jet.

Larry Pitts, airborne in the cockpit of his F-15. The "Gorilla" Eagle driver shot down a MiG-25 and participated in secret missions in the Gulf War.

Larry Pitts

"Hoser" Satrapa in the early days.

Mark Fox, one of the Navy's two Gulf War MiG-killers, sits in a Hornet cockpit aboard the U.S.S. *Saratoga*. He missiled an attacking MiG-21.

U.S. Navy

(*Above*) Nick Mongillo (*extreme right, flat-top*) with friends aboard the *Saratoga*. The young VFA-81 Hornet pilot was with Fox when he shot down another attacking MiG-21. (*Below*) A promising young VF-154 Tomcat crew: Jeff Dodson, pilot (*left*), and Jeff Naven, backseater (*right*), attended the Navy's Fighter Weapons School, known as "Topgun," together. The intense four-week course is designed to make such crews fighter tactic experts for their squadrons when they return.

Jeff Dodson

Jeff Naven

Viper pilot Keith Beam in dress blue.

Francis "Paco" Geisler, storied F-15 pilot and squadron commander who built the 58th.

Brian Fitzpatrick as a tester of an early F-18.

Hornet pilot Scott Speicher (*at right*), believed to have been shot down by an Iraqi MiG-25.

Fighter pilot Valhalla: Nellis AFB's 4477th "Red Eagles" at their secret base in the Nevada desert. The best of the best were assigned here to fly enemy aircraft against other standout pilots in the Air Force, Navy, and Marines. Paco Geisler, one of their leaders, is on the extreme right. Jim Robb, a future Topgun CO, is inside the World War II jeep.

an art. . . . And both Willard and my skipper were the fleet standard at it."

Teetering at the brink of 110 knots, his feet furiously footing the rudders, cross-controlling the stick (putting in controls to go one way and then reversing to go the other) or just holding it neutral, Willard would suddenly flip the Tomcat over onto its back and pull it down in a quick direction reversal. Upside down, diving, he'd be regaining the speed he lost, aiming for the kill.

Christofferson still would be trying to react, hopelessly disadvantaged.

Position advantage for Willard.

"He was pretty good at changing his game plan," remembers Christofferson. "He could always show me a new wrinkle, something I hadn't seen before. . . . One time we started an attack, and instead of coming at each other at the same altitude [as they normally did], he drives his airplane up and over, almost like he's barrel rolling over me. . . . If you haven't seen that before it can be a very deceiving maneuver."

By the time Christofferson countered it was too late and Willard was already drawing a bead.

"I was fighting for the particular turn," says Christofferson. "In other words, the turn we were in right now. I'm looking at him and trying to remember, 'Okay, my parameters are this. This is my airspeed, this is how much G I have on the airplane at this particular moment'. . . . He [Willard] was thinking two or three turns down the road. . . . 'Okay, I'm going to do this on this turn, and if he [Christofferson] does this, I'll do this, and by the third turn' . . . I just couldn't think that far ahead."

And so it went, Christofferson learning what he was taught but always running into a new move that again "put him in the box." He was made the squadron "powerplants" officer, a typical nugget job in which he supervised the mechanics keeping the Tomcat engines working. He learned "loose-deuce" section tactics—staying relatively abeam and thus in mutual support even while turning suddenly, as would happen in combat. But the in-flight training continued—lengthy debriefs always dwelling on his need to improve, little to point to in the way of his own personal accomplishment.

"I got better and better, but I'll be honest with you . . . No matter how hard I tried, and, I mean, we got into some really good fights . . . I never got to a point flying on Rat's wing where I felt I'd arrived. Every time I flew with him I always felt, well, he beat my butt again."

He'd always excelled. He wasn't used to being second.

"The crux," observes Mike McCabe, a Bounty Hunters RIO at the time and a Vietnam MiG killer, "is the pursuit of excellence." For the really good fighter pilots "it's not just a matter of flying fighters and getting the girls . . . 'Hey, I'm Topgun. Look at me' . . . They blow right through that. . . . They want to be perfect. . . . Call it the Dick Butkis [former great Chicago Bears linebacker] school. He didn't care about the press. He didn't care about the adulation. He wanted to hit. He wanted to beat you."

One day in August, Willard had mechanical problems with his airplane and Christofferson got another flight lead, a pilot several years his senior.

As usual, after the mission, they squared off for a practice fight. Starting a mile or two abeam, the two planes merged and began maneuvering.

To Christofferson's amazement, he quickly found himself winning. Both pilots had turned level into each other, hoping to get an angle. But the senior's turn was wide and arcing, traversing a larger-than-needed amount of sky. He wasn't max performing his jet.

Christofferson was. Pulling six and a half G's, turning at something between 310 and 350 knots, whatever was the optimum, he cut inside the senior's turn, gaining on him. By the time they merged the second time, he had a whopping ninety-degree angle on the senior and was curling in to set up a shot on the senior's rear.

Recognizing his dilemma, the senior tried to match G's, pulling harder, sharpening his "corner." But it was too late.

Christofferson had him.

"Knock it off," said the senior in the traditional defeated exit.

Christofferson was elated. "I can remember thinking, Man oh man, I'm finally doing it here. . . . He's watching me . . . reacting. . . . I'm driving the fight."

The senior called for a second joust. He was a lot stronger this time and the two of them swirled "fairly neutral" for a couple of turns. Then Christofferson changed his game plan and went out-of-plane.

"It wasn't exactly vertical. More oblique."

The senior's counter was to continue turning in his roughly horizontal circle.

Christofferson, zooming above, reversed back. By this time, the senior had passed under him. Diving back, Christofferson again had the shot.

"Knock it off," called the senior a second time. He'd had enough. They went back to the ship.

"What a breath of fresh air," recalled Christofferson. "Rat had pushed me so much that all I knew was to fly my airplane to the max. . . . Now I'm flying against somebody who hasn't done that and I'm seeing positional advantage right away. . . . It really made me feel good because I realized what I'd learned."

The following summer, when the Bounty Hunters returned from cruise and got slots for Topgun students, Christofferson was chosen.

8

BRIAN FITZPATRICK BANKED the new F/A-18 Hornet back around. He was doing touch-and-go landings at the navy's Air Test Center, Patuxent River, Maryland, and feeling pretty cocky.

He had no way of knowing he was moments from nearly losing his life.

It was late 1980, and the young lieutenant who, a decade later, would lead a harrowing flight into Iraq in the first daylight navy raids of Desert Storm felt invincible.

"I was feeling my oats," he says. "I was having a great time."

Still a relatively junior officer, Fitzpatrick was among a select handful from the navy's elite test-and-evaluation squadron, VX-4, tasked with making sure the new McDonnell Douglas fighter-bomber was ready and rugged enough, in terms of operational ability, to join the fleet.

He'd been assigned to VX-4, in part, because of his performance in some top-secret flying at Nellis Air Force Base, Nevada. And since earning his wings in 1976, the Naval Academy graduate and veteran of two squadron cruises had already put in eleven hundred hours in the F-4 Phantom jet, the Vietnam-era bomber-interceptor the Hornet was designed to replace, and was in the midst of transitioning to the F-14 Tomcat, the fleet's main-stay fighter.

None of his colleagues had flown all three combat jets in such a short career span; he was the only lieutenant current and qualified in all three—a distinction he was quietly proud of.

Joining him in the evaluation were several academy classmates. It was a reunion of sorts, the flying basically unrestricted, which was a fighter pilot's dream. They could do just about anything they wanted when they wanted, and were having so much fun that all were voluntarily working six- and seven-day weeks, sometimes twelve to sixteen hours a day.

He touched down for probably the fifth time and lifted up, full throttle again.

The Hornet in his hands was touted as one of the hottest new jets around. The product of the navy's budgetary need to go back to dual-role combat planes—a need forced by mounting costs of increasingly sophisticated and complex aircraft—it was both a nimble dogfighter and a fast attack (bomber) jet, hence its "F/A" designation.

With its distinctly long, radar-filled nose, high angled twin tails for stability, and capelike leading edge extensions sweeping back along the front fuselage to the wings for extra lift, the Hornet had a quietly sinister look about it that appealed to the warrior in fighter pilots. It was the latest "electric jet," with "fly-by-wire" controls and inboard computers for automatic trimming and compensating.

You didn't have to fight with it, like you did the Phantom, although some veterans thought the computerized movements took some of the fun out of flying.

A "heads-up" display on the windshield gave the pilot eye-level target and flight information. He did not have to bring his eyes back into the cockpit in the middle of a dogfight or bombing run.

Fitzpatrick had been playing with earlier touch-and-goes. They were simulated to be like those on a carrier: full flaps for slowing; nose normally about fifteen degrees up when he lifted. He'd been raising the nose slightly higher than fifteen degrees, which allowed him to jerk the aircraft around. He was supposed to find out what it would do in unusual circumstances.

Now he decided to have some real fun.

He accelerated level and then lifted the nose much higher than the usual fifteen degrees. "I was hotdogging," he says; pushing the limits.

As expected, as the plane's angle of attack got steeper, its computer automatically raised his flaps from full down, which had slowed the plane on the landing, to only half down, giving him more speed. He planned to use the speed to raise the nose even higher, and started to feed in some left stick and rudder for a left turn to start coming around again.

But the combination of half flaps and rudder he was applying, they unfortunately had yet to discover, made the Hornet aerodynamically unstable. Its four-channel flight control computer didn't recognize what Fitzpatrick was doing as valid flight. It considered the inputs to be an error and "did what it was programmed to do. It shut off the primary mode of control," said Fitzpatrick.

At about eight hundred feet, the plane suddenly "departed," a major emergency, careening out of control.

"I'm trying to go left but I could feel it sliding to the right and starting to roll over."

Departure at thirty thousand feet is trouble enough. But at eight hundred feet and falling like a rock, it was tantamount to sudden death. The plane had lost its hold on the air and was no longer in controlled flight. It was skidding and pitching to the right—but with Fitzpatrick, because of the G forces, penned inside.

He had only a few seconds to "recover" the airplane or crash and die with it below.

In fact, approximately a month earlier, a similar emergency had occurred to Travis Brannon, another of the VX-4 "Evaluators." Falling in a less violent, pancaking flat spin that also involved a high angle of attack, he'd had fifteen thousand feet to try to start the airplane flying again, but still had not been able to recover because of a defect in the onboard computer, now corrected. He'd finally ejected at five thousand feet, the absolute minimum, and been lucky to come out with only minor injuries.

Chillingly, another problem they'd discovered with the airplane—but not yet corrected—was its parachute. It hadn't worked well in previous ejections, which caused a further increase of Fitzpatrick's "pucker factor," as some fighter pilots like to call the sudden realization of imminent danger.

He was now at approximately six hundred feet and had perhaps a second or two left to decide what he was going to do.

"I was thinking, Oh my God, I don't want to crash this thing for no reason. . . . At least Travis had a reason. I'm just fooling around . . . being a bozo doing Sierra Hotel [a navy expression for "shit hot"] touch-and-goes. . . . My career's over. . . ."

Not to mention possibly his life.

He really felt he had no choice but to eject. But as he forced his hands and feet, unnaturally weighted, from the stick and rudders and shoved his arms between his legs to grab the ejection handle, he realized that with the plane rolling right, he might be upside down when he was shot out.

Forget that the parachute was suspect. He would be rocketed into the rock-hard runway.

"I'm reaching for the handle, saying, No, man, I really don't want to do this. I want to save the airplane. If it rolls all the way through then I'll eject when it's upright. But if it doesn't roll through, I'd better go now."

His brain was slowed to a zillion calculations per nanosecond. He was "compartmentalizing" big time, focusing on the problem, eliminating distractions, which, in this case, included large assaults of fear and terror.

But at this precise nanosecond, he knew all he had were bad choices.

Then the plane suddenly righted itself.

It started flying again.

"By taking my hands and feet off the controls, I'd done exactly the right thing."

The plane had settled back. Its wings had caught new air, and the backup mode of its computer had taken over.

The Hornet, it turned out, was a "forgiving" airplane.

He grabbed the stick, easing back on the power, and "made a big, long, straight-in approach. Wide turns," he emphasized. "Let me tell you, not much angle of bank at all, and certainly no rudder."

He was being very careful.

Now was the time for, at least, weak knees. But Fitzpatrick said he wasn't so much scared as embarrassed when he landed and had to report what had happened. But, in fact, his job was to uncover just such characteristics in the new plane.

The company test pilot he reported to just shook his head. The problem that had caused the emergency was one more thing they'd have to correct.

Fitzpatrick filed a report and was back up flying the Hornet the next day.

Until the Hornet's departure, Fitzpatrick's scariest moment had been as a skinny little high school prodigy walking out on stage to play a trumpet solo at New York's Philharmonic Hall.

"I think I was a sophomore," he said. "This famous composer who used to fly back and forth between New York and Paris had written a song specifically for us. I was the soloist. I had to walk across the stage with a long trumpet with a flag draped on it. I remember I held it straight up and hit that first note."

Growing up just off the New Jersey Turnpike in Elizabeth, New Jersey, he had been so hyperactive that he'd studied music just to have something to do after sports and homework.

"We lived on a city block and we'd play stickball in the street," he remembers. "My parents told me I'd play with the kids until they got tired and went home and the next group would come out and I'd play with them until they got tired and went home. That was my life."

His parents worked hard to keep him and his brother in private school. Young-looking for his age, but with piercing blue eyes, he had assumed he would go to West Point until, sitting on the New York–West Point side during an early 1960s football game, he'd witnessed Roger Staubach destroy Army.

"I said, Gee, all those guys over there are having so much fun and we're sitting over here and nobody's having fun. I want to be with those guys. From that moment on, I knew I was going to the Naval Academy."

He set his mind to the goal, something he'd always been able to do, and his extra activities at school really paid off. In addition to good grades, the academy wanted well-rounded applicants. He did fine until his senior year, when he and some midshipmen buddies were caught sneaking beer and pizza into their rooms.

"It was a freezing January day and I came up with this brilliant idea. . . . Let's go have some fun. . . . I didn't know it was a dismissal offense. . . . [As punishment] they made us march every morning from five A.M. to six . . . bitter cold . . . inspections every other hour. This went on until we graduated, no liberty. No leave. . . . It was just unbearable."

He'd always gotten by on his wits and self-confidence, but did little studying. When he got to flight school, however, "I finally decided to apply myself. . . . You've got to understand that I always knew I had a home, was going to the Naval Academy, and that I'd have a job when I got out. . . . But the navy was shrinking after Vietnam. They had enough pilots. Competition was fierce. You had to have the best grades to get fighters. The very best."

He liked the challenge.

"I decided I was going to do it."

Joe Sweeney, a civilian test pilot now, was with Fitzpatrick at the academy. He remembers: "He was laid-back and broad-minded, into a lot of things, athletics and all, but didn't really put a lot of time into studies. I think he thought some of the things at the academy were silly. But then when he got out into the real world and saw why we were flying, to be combat ready, to be able to fly and fight and come back alive, he got serious."

The commitment to get fighters brought him his first real stress. He got sick each morning at basic flight. "It was like being pregnant . . . jump out of the rack, run to the head, throw up, go to work." But he studied every weekend, "didn't go out to the bars with the other guys." He'd gotten married right out of Annapolis, so his wife, Kathleen, had helped him. He had laid out an airfield diagram on the floor of their apartment and practiced procedures nonstop each night as she read from the manuals and graded his progress.

Succeeding, he graduated, and soon was flying an F-4 Phantom on the wing of Jim Ruliffson, one of the celebrated starters of Topgun in 1968.

"I remember when I first met Jim. I was still in the RAG [the Replacement Air Group, learning to fly the F-4]. We were going to have a hop [a practice flight]. The instructors said, Watch out, a Topgun instructor's coming down. I'd just arrived at Miramar, for Pete's sake. I didn't know what was going on. I said, What's this Topgun? Am I supposed to be afraid?

"Then this real nice guy came in and, you know, it wasn't any intimidating kind of thing. I just acted normal and said I'm here to learn. I think he kind of liked that attitude. I know I liked his."

143

Ruliffson remembers, "I couldn't believe he was an academy graduate. What was he? Twenty-four? Twenty-five? He looked thirteen." But he was "remarkably intense. Most RAG students aren't that intense. . . . Then he came to the squadron. One of the things I demanded of my JOs was that they really knew the F-4. . . . What were its idiosyncrasies? . . . How could you sweeten your opportunity for a shot? . . . You're not going to get many chances and it's gotta be right. He was the one who took my words to heart and hit the books the hardest."

Under Ruliffson's tutelage, he learned how to fight the Phantom, and in the process discovered a trait in himself that most good fighter pilots have.

"Jim took me under his wing and really spent a lot of time with me. I remember I went out against some other guy and lost and I truly hated myself for losing. . . . I'd finally realized that you don't get a second chance in this league. In combat, you either win or you're dead. I approached each training flight as if it were the real thing and it paid off. . . . You just finally say, I know I'm better than that guy over there, and when we go man-up, I'm going to beat him. That's all there is to it."

At the academy, Fitzpatrick had won some fights boxing for the brigade and was nicknamed "Rocky." Ruliffson tried to change it to "Rocky the flying squirrel," but it didn't stick.

Just "Rocky" became his call sign

"I have some reservations, sir."

It was June 14, 1983, and Fitzpatrick, now a lieutenant commander and the navy pilot with the most flight hours in the Hornet at that time, was cautiously volunteering his opinion before a Washington congressional appropriations subcommittee investigating problems in the F/A-18 program.

A committee member was asking if the Hornet was worth funding. And Fitzpatrick, outranked by most of the high-level officers there and almost silent until this point, had just heard his boss, Rear Admiral E. W. Carter III, as well as navy legend Rear Admiral John D. Bulkeley, recommend it.

Among other nicknames, the fearsome Bulkeley was known as "The Sea Wolf" and "Big Iron."

"Again, it was like walking out on that stage at Philharmonic

Hall and hitting that first note," recalls Fitzpatrick. "I knew what my answer was going to be, and it wasn't the navy answer."

Since tests on the Hornet had been completed, the new plane had been a source of major controversy. Evaluators like Fitzpatrick, civilian and military, had identified a multitude of technical and budgetary problems with the $22 million airplane, and the press and the legislators were questioning the wisdom of continuing to spend on such an expensive and seemingly problematic weapon.

In truth, most new fighters and bombers have controversial entrances into service, but the Hornet's entrance was especially so. Just a month earlier, a Defense Department audit had found that funds for another navy program had been surreptitiously shifted to the Hornet program in order to cover unexpected cost overruns. The shift wasn't illegal, but it nonetheless angered the congressmen.

Even McDonnell Douglas, the plane's manufacturer, was getting apprehensive. The day before the testimony, the company, dependent on congressional funding of the program and mindful that the hearings were being held, had purchased two full-page advertisements in the *Washington Post.* Across both read the headline: THE ONLY THING THAT CAN SHOOT DOWN THE F/A-18 NOW IS MISINFORMATION."

Chief among the airplane's operational deficiencies, according to its testers, was its comparative lack of range, or "radius," on a combat mission. It was said not to be able to fly as far, or with as many bombs, as the attack plane it was replacing, the Vietnam-era A-7 Corsair, a pure bomber with bigger gas tanks.

It also lacked an "electronic warfare system," which could jam enemy radar and warn the pilot of incoming missiles, and a safe parachute, which was still to be corrected. It needed a better radar and computer-flight-control system, as evidenced by the earlier crashes at Patuxent, and suffered from wing oscillation when overloaded. And there were many lesser problems.

But the Chief of Naval Operations (CNO), along with the Secretary of the Navy, had already decided to go ahead with the program, a fact that had been emphasized in prehearing briefings. And Admiral Bulkeley, hulking at a table in front of Fitzpatrick, worked directly for the CNO.

Fitzpatrick: "He was very impressive, a tremendous personality. . . . He only wore four medals—the Medal of Honor, Navy Cross, Silver Star, and the Distinguished Service Cross. I'm just an impressionable lieutenant commander. It's my first trip to Washington. He was Pug Henry [the hero officer of Herman Wouk's *Winds of War–War and Remembrance* sagas]."

Fitzpatrick wasn't far off with his comparison. Bulkeley, a motor torpedo boat skipper at that time, had won the Medal of Honor for single-handedly sneaking General Douglas MacArthur out of the Japanese-held Philippine Islands in 1942 and then returning to wage a guerrilla war against Japanese ships, planes, and troops until ordered out, according to the citation.

Commanding the U.S.S. *Endicott* and twenty-two torpedo boats during the invasion of Normandy, he had led a preinvasion diversionary action that had successfully helped deceive the Germans into thinking the 1944 invasion was hitting a different area. More recently, from 1963 through 1966, as commander of the U.S. naval base at Guantanamo Bay, Cuba, he'd outsmarted and backed down Cuban Premier Fidel Castro by building a desalinization plant on the base when Castro accused the United States of stealing his island's fresh water.

"As soon as I said I had some reservations," Fitzpatrick remembers, Bulkeley "turned deliberately and looked at me. He had this leathery skin, like he'd been soaked in salt water for forty years . . . piercing eyes . . . I remember my heart kind of jumped. I got really nervous and actually lost a little train of thought. . . . I didn't want to be canned."

Finishing the Hornet evaluation as the navy's chief test pilot, Fitzpatrick had just started refresher training in the F-14 Tomcat in preparation for joining VF-2, Joe Christofferson's squadron, as its maintenance officer, the number-three man. It was a necessary billet for promotion in any naval aviator's career.

"I was looking forward to joining the squadron, but I'm also a strong believer in the process and in the navy." He said he'd "seen people basically lying" about the Hornet's performance while he'd been an evaluator "in order to try and get it through. . . . Admiral Carter had told us to say what we believed, and I couldn't just sit there. . . . I had to at least try and tell them how, in my estimation, we were going backwards."

146

Fitzpatrick can't recall the exact wording, but he says he distinctly remembers Bulkeley at a pretestimony meeting saying something like, "I know I'm not an aviator, but the CNO wants this plane, and, by God, so do I."

He moved his eyes from Bulkeley and went on.

"I think that the range is a problem that is going to be very difficult to fix," the transcript shows him continuing. He believed the lack of range was the major problem with the aircraft, and cautioned about solutions given to the committee to solve it: Disposable fuel tanks would cause storage problems on the carrier and cost problems when they were discarded after each mission. Additional tanker aircraft would need even greater space and cost more money.

"We have worked all these years to get away from tankers," he said. "Now we are going to go back to them?" Buying the Hornet, in his opinion, was like "going back towards the F-4," which also had a range problem.

He fell silent.

It wasn't a very lengthy testimony, but it changed the tone of the hearing. Where before the thrust had been to correct the deficiencies and then buy the plane, objections from the other officers suddenly got stronger.

Captain Paul Hollandsworth, skipper of the attack evaluators, volunteered, "I would agree that the tanker problem—how we get fuel in the airplane—is a major concern. If we don't get some more [fuel] in there, we are stuck with what we have right now. We have been trying to get away from that."

Commander Roger Hull, also an attack evaluator, interjected that the range problem could leave the carriers vulnerable to attack by limiting the amount of fuel left in the tankers for the Tomcats. "If we have to take tankers away from the F-14s to supply the F/A-18s, while at the same time having lost our tanker-capable A-7s [which could be reconfigured as tankers], this involves a major rethinking in terms of battle group tactics. So [the decision to buy the Hornet] involves all aircraft."

He added that he felt the plane's lack of an electronic warfare system was also "critical." While the A-7, which he normally flew, could tell him "when someone is behind me. I cannot do that in the F/A-18." The Hornet's "EW suite," as its electronic warfare system was called, was ordered as part of the evaluator's recommendations, he noted, but it was two years away and untested. There were no guarantees.

Unfazed, Admiral Bulkeley said, "With the twenty-four deficiencies corrected ... we are going to have a pretty good airplane."

Many of the deficiencies were eventually corrected, or "worked around," notes Fitzpatrick, who now calls the plane "a beautiful machine," although range is still a source of controversy for it. But as he walked out of the hearing, proud for doing "what was expected of me in the position I held," he felt he might be in trouble. Admiral Carter complimented him, but he purposely avoided Bulkeley as the staff cars came to pick them up, and took the first plane he could out of Washington and back to Miramar.

If there were going to be any repercussions, he said, he wanted to be back on his home turf.

I don't think there are any real differences between navy and air force fighter pilots—especially at the top of the ladder—besides the navy's requirement that its pilots be able to land on and take off well from a carrier. Among the best of both services the pilots almost seem interchangeable—talented, dedicated, hardworking, a cut above.

But if there is a difference, in my opinion, it's the navy pilot's relative freedom. He seems more able to say and do what he wants. Not that the air force fighter pilot can't. He can—he just has to be more cautious about it. The air force seems more political, with more rules and regulations.

I think this is because of the relative sizes of the services. Naval aviation is smaller and thus has less resources. It therefore gives a larger rein to its aviators, enabling them to do more things with less. The larger air force is less individualistic in its approach. It has more bureaucracy, more policy makers, and hence more regulations.

I remember contacting a very well regarded air force fighter pilot and tactician on a rather innocuous matter. I wanted him simply to tell me about another fighter pilot he knew well—a friend as well as a well-regarded aviator. He declined, saying he'd like to help me but he was up for squadron commander and didn't want to jeopardize that promotion by saying something he shouldn't.

The navy pilots I dealt with never gave that a consideration.

As another pilot once commented, "We always said, in the air force, if it's not written down that you can do it, you can't do it. In the navy, if it's not written down that you can't do it, you can do it."

But the air force's largeness meant its fighter squadrons usually had more money for nonessentials like recreation rooms and such.

AS YOU ENTER the bar at the Nellis officers' club, there's a plaque to the right of the door with seventy-one names neatly enshrined. "Presented as a lasting tribute to the pilots of the 4477 TES Red Eagles," it says. "Check Six, 'The Fun Brothers.' "

The plaque is devoid of other information because it refers to one of the most secret programs run from Nellis in the 1980s. Code-named "Constant Peg," and ended in March 1988, the program was arguably the single most important air-to-air training aid to U.S. fighter pilots in the decade.

What it amounted to was a supersecret squadron of enemy fighters—MiG-17s, 21s, and 23s, if not 25s and higher, newer designations—housed at a guarded base in the remote Nevada desert. The MiGs were being flown by a group of select fighter pilots from each of the services against as many navy, air force, and Marine fighter pilots as could be cleared to participate.

The unit's name was the 4477th Test and Evaluation Squadron, or the "Red Eagles," as they were nicknamed, and its main purpose was "to take the gee-whiz out of seeing the enemy's fighters for the first time in combat," said one of its former pilots.

Studies of combat had shown that no matter how practiced and trained a U.S. fighter pilot was, seeing a no-kidding, for-real enemy fighter for the first time in an actual dogfight often caused "buck fever" in the perceiver. Adrenaline squirted, hands trembled, and the pilot, no matter how otherwise well trained, was prone to making deadly mistakes.

"The benefit," continued the former Red Eagle, "was that when you saw a bad guy, you didn't automatically think you were going to die . . . you didn't just fade and dissolve."

Experience had shown that even "I've-got-to-get-a-MiG-at-any-cost" pilots got this buck fever in first encounters.

At the program's height—in the mid-1980s—the MiGs were not only flown against good fleet and air force squadron pilots but entire Red Flag exercises, Topgun and Air Force Fighter Weapons School students, fleet and air force squadrons, even select National Guard fliers and reservists, who were often very good fighter pilots but who, for a variety of reasons—including family, money, dislike of desk jobs, and stymied advancement—had simply opted to retire and fly fighters on the weekends.

The only restrictions besides time and availability were that no foreign nationals got to see or fly against the MiGs.

Kept at a wilderness base on the Tonopah Test Range, thirty-two miles from the small former mining town of Tonopah, Nevada, which itself was two hundred miles north of Las Vegas, the squadron offered its pilots some of the best flying and fighting they'd ever experience, and the kind of freewheeling desert lifestyle formerly associated only with the Chuck Yeager test pilot days at Edwards Air Force Base, California.

"It was phenomenal," said another former Red Eagle about his time in the unit. "Some of the best sticks you've ever seen were there . . . best two years of my life in the [service]."

I first heard of the program while I was writing *Scream of Eagles*. Its forerunners, "Have Drill" and "Have Donut," were used during the Vietnam War. "Have Idea" had been its immediate predecessor. Acquiring enemy planes and flying them to reduce buck fever, discover attackable weaknesses, and pit them against our own fighters for valuable dogfight experience are old military secrets. We've done so since World War II, if not earlier, as have other countries.

But never to this degree.

At its height, according to sources, there were as many as fifteen MiGs in the squadron, giving first looks and multiple fights to more than a thousand air force, navy, and Marine Corps fighter pilots. And the program had relatively few accidents, which was a tribute to its maintenance crews and especially to its pilots, who usually never numbered more than eighteen at any one time.

They were, after all, air fighting in a no-holds-barred, take-chances arena. The point was to show our pilots exactly what it would be like when an enemy fighter or fighters came rocketing out of the opposing skies intent on killing them.

Although Constant Peg and the squadron were "deactivated due to budget cuts" in 1988 and 1990, respectively, according to an air force memo and other historical records I received from Nellis, the program remains classified, at least it was through early 1994. But that didn't mean it hadn't been publicized. Rumors of MiGs at Nellis have continually cropped up in the press since the 1960s.

One of the most circulated rumors occurred in May 1984, when Air Force Lieutenant General Robert M. Bond was killed in a mysterious crash on the Nellis range. The air force refused to give any details, causing *Time* magazine to speculate: "Bond was actually flying a Soviet-built MiG-23 Flogger. . . . That possibility drew attention to a little-known aspect of American military training. The U.S. has managed to assemble a minisquadron of between four and 15 Floggers, as well as at least a dozen of the easily obtainable MiG-21s. All of the MiG-23s, which the Soviets began producing in 1973, were purchased from Egypt."

Other sources say some have come from Israel, as well as from enemy pilot defections to the United States and other Western countries.

In 1981, *Aviation Week and Space Technology* ran an actual photograph of a MiG-21 with U.S. markings on it. It identified the MiG as "one of a squadron of 12 being flown by USAF pilots from a remote base in the Western U.S."

The shootdown of two more Libyan fighters by navy F-14 pilots in January 1989—sort of bookending the decade with navy-Libyan kills—prompted the most official acknowledgment of the MiGs. In a January 13, 1989, *New York Times* story, *Times* reporter Andrew Rosenthal wrote that Pentagon spokesman J. Daniel Howard had indicated at a press conference: "The American fighter crews that shot down two Libyan warplanes last week used tactics developed through mock combat exercises that include missions against Soviet-built warplanes . . . obtained by Western intelligence agencies."

Rosenthal specifically quoted Howard as saying, " 'For the most part, this training is conducted with U.S.-made aircraft. But we have some Soviet aircraft that we use for training.' "

Most former Red Eagle pilots will not talk about the MiGs or the program per se. But some will talk about their "time in the desert" or "the assets," occasionally referring to the MiGs by their code names, which was the officially sanctioned way they could speak about them back when they were in the program.

For instance, a MiG-17 was called an "A-4," a MiG-21 was called an "F-5," and a MiG-23 was called an "F-4." The code names were picked because the U.S. plane substitutions roughly matched the performance or size of the enemy planes. "We could talk about them on the phone and in the bars that way," said a source.

Although the navy and the Marines sent some of their best pilots to the program, Constant Peg was run by the air force. In the early days, the pilots lived in sparse trailers at the Tonopah base most of the week, flying the MiGs in the daytime and "relaxing with a few beers" or going into the town of Tonopah at night.

"There wasn't much to do at night," recalled one former Red Eagle, "so you could go into Bob's Barbecue, which was a house of ill repute there in Tonopah, get a beer, and say hello to the girls. Then put a little change into the machines at the Golden Nugget and go back out."

In spring 1993, I went to Tonopah. It's still a small western town. I couldn't find Bob's Barbecue, but the remains of Bobbie's Buckeye Bar, a former brothel, were still on the route to the test range. The highway back to the base was a meandering monster with long straightaways flanked by surreal dry lake and mountain vistas.

It reminded me of something from another planet.

Signs said LAST GAS and JOSHUA COUNTRY. My source said they called the beer from Bobs " 'Road Pop' . . . Get one and then go back to the trailer and go to bed. That was our lifestyle. I mean I didn't even care if I got a paycheck. All I wanted was enough money to buy my friends drinks. It was the greatest fighter pilot lifestyle in the world. It felt like Chuck Yeager and Pancho's. That's exactly what it was like."

And, in fact, he said, test pilots from those days in the 1950s, some of whom were by then working for defense corporations, used to fly into the range on business related to the MiGs and tell stories about the early rocket planes. Any unauthorized military pilots who had to land there for emergencies, which sometimes happened, were detained for hours for interrogation and then had to swear they would not tell what they had seen.

Before flying the MiGs against visiting pilots, said another Red Eagle, they'd "give the guys a two-hour lecture on each airplane ... elaborate on all the pros and cons and how the assets [MiGs] compared to the airplanes they were flying."

Then the MiG instructors would follow up with an inflight demonstration.

"This is what you can do," he said they'd tell the visiting pilots. "For example, on the MiG-21, put the flaps down and you can sit it there parked on its tail at eighty-five to ninety knots in full afterburner. Anything that comes near will overshoot and you can just gun it. Well, not quite that easy, but that's an example of why you'd tell them not to get in a slow-speed scissors with a MiG-21. The guy's going to flush you. An F-14 is physically incapable of control at that slow speed."

But the sleek 21 had poor radar and air-to-air missiles, and those were weaknesses that could be exploited, he said.

The "banana-winged" MiG-17 was "the greatest turning airplane any of us had ever seen," said another Red Eagle. "It just dazzled us. We couldn't believe that this guy Mikoyan [one half of the Mikoyan-Gurevich design team] had built such a great wing airplane. It was like a boomerang. . . . Shaking a MiG-17 off your six was like shaking gum off your shoe. . . . It made an A-4 laughable."

But the MiG-23 Flogger was a "pig, a piece of garbage."

With swing wings similar to those on the F-14s, and approaching F-4 performance, he said the MiG-23, a mainstay of most Third World air forces, had been built primarily as a supersonic interceptor that could take off and land on unprepared surfaces. As a consequence, it had heavy landing gear and poor maneuverability.

Fight a MiG-23, he said, and you can "call the press and get the blond dispenser. You're a hero. He's a dead man."

In general, said sources, the MiGs were not as well made as our airplanes, and, consequently, were more dangerous to fly. The pilots were especially leery of some of the ejection seats. They weren't sure they would work.

At least two Red Eagle pilots died in the project, sources confirm. A young air force pilot had a fire and tried to do a flameout approach back to the field but crashed a mile short. A navy pilot departed, got into a spin, and couldn't recover.

I didn't have time to check out these two deaths, or I'd have printed their names. It would have been a fight because of bureaucracy and red tape. But they deserve some recognition. That's the thing about military accomplishment. Some of it is never known because it's secret.

The MiGs were very hard to maintain because of the shortage or nonexistence of spare parts and repair manuals. That's where the project's maintenance crews deserved credit. Sometimes they had to repair or rebuild a part without any help or guidance except what had preceded them at Tonopah.

A typical sortie, said another source, would begin with the Red Eagle pilots meeting the visiting pilots at Nellis on the afternoon before the training fight.

"Maybe it's an F-15 squadron. We'd shake their hands, talk to them a bit, and then most of us would go back to Tonopah while one stayed to go over the mission and rules of engagement." Those rules, after safety restrictions, he said, basically boiled down to "I'm here to live in your behind, pal, and you're expected to try and do the same."

The visiting pilots would have already had the threat lecture and demonstration flights, so early the next morning, the Red Eagle pilots flying that day would have a brief at Tonopah during which the officer in charge would say, " 'Bullet' [not a real call sign], you'll be going in against Jerry Johnson, call sign 'Whopper' [again, not a real name or call sign]. His 'overhead time' in Range 71 is nine A.M. I write that down on my knee board card. That's all I need to know."

At about eight-thirty A.M., he said, he'd put on his G-suit and walk out to the " 'asset,' which the maintenance guy would have parked out in front. It's all set to go. You do a quick walk-around, climb up, strap it on. Before you start it up, you call the GCI [ground controlled intercept] officer and say, ' "Bullet's" up looking for "Whopper." ' He'd tell you ' "Whopper's" airborne out of

Nellis and should be in your area in about ten minutes.' Then he'd say, 'Press,' which means start up and take off."

This former Red Eagle said he often thought the best part to him was rolling down the runway and pulling up the landing gear after liftoff. "I always thought how neat it was to get airborne and be loving it. You say to yourself, It just doesn't get any better than this."

Flying to Range 71, he said the first task would be for the visiting pilot to do a radar intercept on the MiG, see how it looked in his scope, then they'd streak into the merge and a visual fight.

"We're maybe fifty miles apart and he's got to find me on his radar and intercept me. . . . So presumably he runs a nice intercept and then fights on. . . . Usually that means he's going to show me what he's got and I'm going to show him what I got. . . . He can go home, eject, whatever. I'm going to do my best energy-management turn for ninety degrees and watch how he reacts. . . . If he's defensive, I'll just come around and blow him away. If he goes pure vertical and into the sun or some other good move, then I know he knows what he's doing. . . . so I'm starting off assessing him."

He said he'd expect a two-circle fight from a good F-15 pilot. "In which case I'm in trouble, because at four hundred knots, I can do about four G's. He can do about six G's. If I stay in the horizontal circle, he's going to hurt me. So I may take it vertical, try to make it a one-circle fight, or I may go very nose low and do a split-S."

But if he gets aggressive, "I might just let him turn on me and then reverse quick and get him in a phone booth." Slow fight. Fangs out. "Okay, pal, you want guns? That's kind of what we call 'cautious aggressiveness.' I let him kick me across the tail and then I get behind his three-nine line [the area behind his wings] and keep him nervous until I can gun him or run him out of gas or I run out of bullets."

The 21's small size was an advantage, he said. Not only is it harder to see than the larger U.S. fighters, like the F-14 or F-15, but go low and "you'd disappear in the desert," while the F-14 and F-15 show large silhouettes. He would "bait" opponents to come close for shots, and then suddenly turn the 21's relatively large delta-wing surfaces so they looked like "knife edges."

Then he could either put the flaps out and slow it suddenly for an overshoot or loop over and end up on the surprised opponent's tail.

The "beauty," he said, was how the students learned from seeing such things. "You could just see their ability, enthusiasm, and confidence grow."

Later, he said, there would be a debrief over the phone when the visitors got back to Nellis. But the best debrief, because it was not hampered by phone security restrictions, occurred that weekend when the Red Eagles would come back to Nellis and hold session face-to-face in the o'club bar.

"The bottom line was that from the time we got back on Thursday until some time on Saturday it was just one big drunk. . . . You were a hero and you fought all these guys and you'd just overstress your hands for the next twenty-four hours."

As the program grew, conditions changed. For instance, the pilots got a couple of Mitsubishi commuter planes so those who wanted to go home each night could see their families. They started having catered meals at Tonopah, put in a mini-bar, video player, and pool table.

"The navy guys thought they were in heaven," joked a navy pilot.

Among the names I recognized on the Red Eagle plaque in the Nellis bar were Topgun CO Jim Robb, XO Stan O'Connor, and John "Black" Nathman, whom I eventually was able to contact in his new job as skipper of the *Nimitz*, one of America's newest "supercarriers."

Nathman—almost a "Clark Kent type," according to one pilot who flew with him: "unassuming, wears glasses"—was said by pilots to be a "mechanic" in the air. "He was a smart guy who would make a game plan based on numerical values he pulled from charts and stuff."

A graduate of Air Force Test Pilot School and a former Topgun instructor, he was a feared "energy" fighter, say his friends, who always knew the exact speed profile for whatever he was flying against whatever he was fighting.

Qualifying for the Red Eagles, said the pilot, Nathman got such a high score registering kills against air force F-5 pilots that the air force stopped making navy pilots with his background compete in that part of the qualification.

"It was unfair," said Nathman. "I'd just come from [Navy] Fighter Weapons School, where I'd been instructing in the F-5."

Another time, I was told, he was to fight an "unspecified" aircraft, which I assumed was a MiG, in a two-seat T-38 with an air force major in the back.

"He had this seven-and-a-half-G game plan," said the pilot relating the story. "He was going to go up to 430 knots and fly this seven-and-a-half-G profile. He was real intent on winning, but it took him three or four turns to gain an advantage and the guy in the backseat was just melting. I heard the tape, and Black's in there grunting through all this and finally the guy in the back pushes the stick forward, probably reducing the G, because he just said 'I give up. I give up.' We called it Black's '*pain* game plan.' "

But the Red Eagles, many of whom also worked at the fighter weapons schools or with other units on the base, weren't the only heroes at Nellis during this time.

The base was also home to the 64th and 65th Air Force "Aggressor" squadrons, which flew MiG-simulating F-5s against Red Flags and traveled to air force bases outside Nellis to do the same against operational squadrons.

Started back in 1972 as part of the air force's post-Vietnam upgrade in dogfight training, the Aggressors studied and taught Soviet tactics and rigidly flew them in the air so that air force squadrons would see what they really might face. They were relentless sticklers for pushing squadrons to the brink of air-to-air readiness, and sometimes got in trouble for it from more timid, safety-conscious commanders at other bases.

Rob Graeter had returned form his Korean Air Lines shootdown days at Kadena, Okinawa, to become an Aggressor at Nellis. The standard-bearer air force fighter weapons schools were there, as were numerous other air force and navy squadrons, continually coming in to participate in Red Flags, which were always huge, multiplane events simulating major bombing strikes like those used in Desert Storm.

Pilots like Joe Christofferson and Brian Fitzpatrick, who had become squadron mates in the VF-2 "Bounty Hunters," would make periodic trips to Nellis for training. Christofferson had done so well at Topgun as a student that he had been nominated for the American Fighter Aces Association's Fighter Pilot of the

Year Award. Fitzpatrick had not gotten in trouble for his testimony about the F/A-18 and was on his way to squadron command.

And there were other secret air-to-air programs on Nellis's vast ranges.

Each project, organization, and squadron had its own group of stars, a pecking order that was always present in some degree almost every night at the o'club bar—but especially on Friday nights, when almost all of them would crowd in to end the week raising drinks and flying hands.

"I think the best part was the notoriety," said one pilot. "When you drove through the Nellis gate with that yellow-and-black Aggressor scarf on, or the Red Eagle or weapons school patch, everybody knew you were somebody. You were one of the bros."

There even was an exclusive fraternity for fighter pilots. It was, and probably still is, called "Barstoolers." I never could find out much about it, but I was told it was started in the 1950s in England and was only for air force pilots. The Barstoolers liked to hold sessions in o'clubs to discuss tactics, flying, and topics of special interest to their members—like the time an airfight between two prominent Barstoolers ended with one of them ejecting supposedly rather than lose face.

"You need to know that it was a disgrace [just as it is today] to lose a fight in those days," said the pilot who told me the story. "The winner would go home first and alone, kind of a king-of-the-road-type thing. He didn't even want the loser on his wing.

"So these two golden arms were at the bar," he continued, "and arguing about flying. One said to the other, 'I'd eject before I'd let you gun me.' The next morning they go up to Caliente and do a one v one and [the pilot who said he'd eject] gets his brains gunned out. So the winner takes off for Nellis by himself and leaves [name deleted], who then reports an engine fire and ejects. He gets picked up by the helo, which brings him to the dispensary, which is right across the street from the o'club. He's fine, and a little while later shows up at the bar with something like the face curtain from the ejection seat in his hand—to prove that he had done it."

What the beaten pilot said to the others in the bar, according to my informant, was that he'd ejected *before* he'd been gunned—just like he'd pledged.

It was his word against the winner's—at least for the time being.

"There's this big uproar, real dramatic moment. This had never happened in the history of aviation, where a guy said he'd eject if he got gunned and then he does it. This was true Barstoolers honor—he actually did it. Of course, he's not telling (air force officials) that or he'd be in big trouble, so they had a Barstoolers meeting to (get at the truth)."

Apparently, the ejector was awarded free drinks for life—at least until the truth became known.

A Barstooler membership card I saw said, "The above named person having met prescribed requirements is hereby awarded an honorary command rating. The above named has barstool time of 3000 hours, 100 hours of which has been knee walking . . ."

In a broader vein, another pilot said, "Drug smokers don't know a real high. I was driving to work and saw this pickup truck with kids. They were smoking roaches with little pliers, the windows rolled up, music blasting. I'm thinking, Oh man, that's not it. They don't have a clue. In a few minutes I'm going to be flying a jet at five hundred miles per hour, turning faster than their little eyeballs were spiraling. That's arrogant, but that's how you thought. A real fighter pilot was consumed by the flying. Obsessed by it."

It was during this time that Jeremiah Weed first came to the base—and thus to the air force. It was brought there by one of the base's modern-day legends, Joe Bob Phillips, who'd "discovered" it at a small town bar when he'd been out looking for the remains of a midair crash.

"You can't talk about Nellis without talking about Joe Bob," said a 4477th pilot.

Mississippi-born, a Vietnam combat veteran, F-4 Fighter Weapons School instructor, and one of the original F-16 fighter pilots, Joe Bob—or "Clyde," as his close friends called him—was a two-fisted fighter marvel similar to the navy's Joe Satrapa, except he probably worked more within the system—a necessity in the political, rules-driven air force—and, judging from the barroom tales about him, he was probably better-looking.

"Real ladies' man," said a compatriot. "And arrogant. Thought he walked on water. He'd been divorced and was single, and I mean he had at least two girls—blondes—groupies—chasing him at all times. He had it all, so there was always a little bit of resentment and animosity . . . and the reason he got away with it was that he could back it up in the air. . . . He was well respected, so he could do just about anything he wanted."

One Aggressor told me Joe Bob had taught him everything he knew. A navy pilot said Joe Bob had showed him that the navy needed to put the "who" back into its ACM, meaning the fierce personal competition he was seeing at Nellis.

When he first came to Nellis, the pilot said, "We'd go out and fight and there'd be some kills called and some guys kicked out of the fight, and I just thought it was a good training session. Then we'd come back for the debrief, and one of the guys who lost [an air force pilot] throws his tape recorder across the room and it shatters. He grabs the video and unsplices it and starts tearing it with his teeth because he lost. I'm sitting there saying, Holy Toledo, these guys really take this stuff serious."

Pretty soon, he said, "I'd wake up in the morning, kiss the wife good-bye, and all I could think of was the fight with Joe Bob. I'm driving to the base and I'm thinking about it. I'm thinking about the gun camera film. . . . I not only want to make sure I gun him, but that I get it on record. I don't even see the traffic lights or hear the brief. I mean, I'm physically there, but all I want to do is get up there and kick his ass."

Joe Bob "never really acted real cocky," said another friend. "He just knew that he could fly very well and that he could teach. And everybody associated with him knew he was a no-nonsense type of guy. He lived on a boat out at Lake Mead [sixteen miles from Las Vegas]—until it sunk. Had a pickup truck and spent his weekends, like most of us, fishing or hunting."

I finally caught up with Joe Bob by telephone. He was a colonel in Alaska. Turned out Clyde was his real first name. He had recently returned from Desert Storm, where he had been instrumental in setting up an F-16 war-caused innovation that General Buster Glosson, one of the tactical planners in Riyadh, Saudi Arabia, said, "increased the effectiveness of the F-16 force . . . three or fourfold," according to an article in the April 1993 *Air Force Magazine.*

The innovation, borrowed from Joe Bob's Vietnam days, was the use of F-16s as "killer scouts" for other F-16s, on bombing missions, who were having a hard time distinguishing, as they dove on their Iraqi targets, real targets from trick or abandoned ones.

Air Intelligence was having the same problem, said Joe Bob.

The Iraqis were good at deception, he said. With the patrolling "scouts" regularly reconnoitering with binoculars and night-vision glasses, they could advise the bombers and planners what the true situation was. As a result, according to *Air Force,* Iraqi troop movements, storage deceptions, and surface-to-air shooting, which had taken an earlier toll, had been reduced to nearly nothing.

Joe Bob said he'd been brought up in the Far East. His father had been a navy pilot and later an international salesman for Goodrich. It had been his Vietnam experience, after graduating from the University of Mississippi, that had driven him to become what he was.

"We had just been MiG bait," he said of being a young lieutenant flying an air force Phantom in Vietnam. There had been individual achievement in Vietnam, like that of Steve Ritchie and Chuck DeBellevue, air force aces he had served with at Udorn, Thailand. But, in general, he said, air force fighter training for Vietnam had been a joke.

As a result, he said, he and a generation of young air force pilots had come out of Vietnam and set a course for "radical tactical changes." That had included going to Nellis when asked and helping to revamp the ailing F-4 Fighter Weapons School to a point, in the late 1970s, where headquarters, after several accidents, had begun telling them to "tone it down" for fear they were pushing the younger pilots too much.

The "low point" in his career came, he said, when one of the students he instructed at the FWS had gone back to his home base after graduation and within a week had "killed himself trying to show them how great he was." The new graduate had all the physical tools of a great pilot, he said, but not the judgment.

"We shouldn't have let him get through," he lamented.

When the F-16 was brand-new he had been one of the select pilots assigned to get the bugs out of it, which he'd done despite surprise departures (from controlled flight), which engineers had said couldn't happen because of the onboard computers and which were a real hazard in the early plane. He'd been flying it ever since, and had gone on to work on the new Advanced Tactical Fighter (ATF), which is supposed to take air force fighter pilots into the twenty-first century.

I asked him about a near fistfight he was said to have had in the old Nellis o'club bar, the one the current bar replaced.

Bud Taylor, a former Topgun CO—but an Aggressor at the time this happened—said he and Joe Bob were arguing about a no-holds-barred dogfight they'd had earlier when he'd insulted Joe Bob with "You're such a lousy gunner you ought to be a tailgunner in a B-52."

Joe Bob, already mad because of something that had happened in the dogfight, had retorted by throwing a glass of Jeremiah Weed into his face, said Taylor. But before any real punches could be thrown, "Buffalo" Burt Meyers, an F-15 FWS instructor who was about "as big as a door," according to Taylor, had stepped in and taken Joe Bob outside.

Meyers was a minor air force legend himself, having been one of the air force pilots picked to fly in the AIM-ACE air wars, and was frequently connected to secret programs at Nellis.

"I never went to the bar without my buddy Buffalo," said Taylor.

It's not clear what Buffalo and Joe Bob did outside, but when they returned, said witnesses, everything was straightened out, and Taylor said, "We all ordered another round of Weed. . . . The next day there were some hurt feelings but the camaraderie was stronger."

Joe Bob said, "I remember that because of Buffalo. He's a big dude. I've learned not to mess with big dudes. . . . It was just a difference of opinion between fighter pilots about the best way to do business. If you do that in the bar, what generally happens is it gets louder and louder and you get closer and closer. Soon, you're both calling each other a dumb shit. If you can't settle it that way, by God, then just step outside in the parking lot and we'll fix it right there.

"No big deal," he said. "It happened quite often, as a matter of fact."

I eventually got to have dinner with Joe Bob. It was at Luke Air Force Base, outside of Phoenix, where he'd come for some training.

He didn't look like I'd imagined after having listened to his deep southern drawl on the phone. He was tall, thin, and smoked a lot. With a full head of silver-blond hair, he had a kind of chiseled U-boat captain look, which was certainly part of what the girls must have found attractive.

He told me that the old Nellis o'club bar in the early 1980s had been a center of learning.

"I bet I learned more there than I did in the classroom," he said. It was a place, he said, where "you could open up your heart and say what you wouldn't say in the briefing or debrief. . . . We could mess it up and be nasty. . . . It was loud, noisy, nobody to bother us. . . . There were naked women dancing and women in there trying to get naked.

"Nobody exploited anybody. . . . It was just shoulder-to-shoulder in there with guys and girls. All the girls were in there for a reason . . . because there was something going on there that was absolutely real . . . guys poking each other's chests. Sometimes swinging at each other. I mean there was bullshit, but there was also real good stuff.

"And they liked it. . . . They weren't being abused. . . . Nobody forced them in. They came 'cause they wanted to. We had fun with them and they had fun with us. . . . I know today it's politically unacceptable, but I mean we'd take them behind the bar and . . . well, the statute of limitations hasn't expired yet so that's about all I can say.

"But they loved it and I know they loved it. . . . I mean the ladies' john was a replication of an F-4 cockpit. It had a rudder pedal . . . all kinds of things to play with. . . . You didn't talk about your career and shit like that in there. It was just women, whiskey, and fighter business, and that's all that went on."

When things got too wild, the base started clamping down and the fighter pilots just moved out of the o'club bar to a place called Sunrise Cedars, a dive right outside the base's main gate.

"It was a biker place," said a pilot, "little bitty redwood dump with a pool table and bar in the middle. Hundreds would crowd in there on Friday nights. It got famous. They sold Sunrise Cedars ball caps. You could wear what you wanted there, be loud, break bottles. If you did that at the club they'd have your ass in front of a general in no time."

Cedars got so popular that squadrons would hold their informal "dining ins" there. But base officials, unhappy with the image the bar portrayed, and the fact that it was siphoning revenue from the newly remodeled o'club bar, finally got it put off-limits, and when I went by to find it in 1993 it had been torn down or remodeled.

But it wasn't all fun and excitement at Nellis during those years.

"On a personal note," said an Aggressor about his experience there, "I learned that knowledge and courage overcome fear, and fear can be very paralyzing. You're always going to have a moment in what we do when you're absolutely scared out of your wits. And you don't like that. I don't mean the feeling, I mean you don't want to face the fact that you've been affected by fear.

"So you conjure up whatever it takes and get the job done. . . . One of the hypes [thrills] of fighter aviation is being right at the edge, I mean being so scared that you want to puke and run. But you don't do it because that's just not part of your lifestyle. . . . As [a commander once told him], when you get to the target you gotta do your job because we don't want to have to come back tomorrow and expose ourselves or our buddies to the same triple-A and SAMs. . . . Anyway, for most of us, I think it was important to overcome that fear."

It was a young man's job, the cutting-edge flying that was being done by fighter pilots such as those at Nellis. In fact, that Aggressor told me that as he got older, he began to lose the "fire": "You start losing your reflexes, eyesight, and reaction time. You're not so sure you want to put your finger in that fire again."

He was lucky. He was able to walk away and have no regrets or hunger for the lifestyle—at least not in the beginning. But for many, that's hard to do. For many, there will never be such an intense, rewarding time. And often, their home life goes with time, too. For the lifestyle and mind-set wreak havoc on some families, not just at Nellis but throughout the fighter community, even more so on the families of navy fighter pilots because of the at-sea separations.

I haven't met many fighter pilots over thirty-five who haven't been divorced. Not to put a stigma on that, for those things happen, and certainly can be for the best. But fighter pilots—especially those at the edge—are uniquely susceptible.

Some years ago, Captain Frank Dully, commander at that time of the Naval Aerospace Medical Institute, in Pensacola, gave a lecture to fighter pilots and their wives titled "Sex and the Naval Aviator." What he said, I think, applies to all fighter pilots, regardless of branch of service.

From a psychological viewpoint, he believed, fighter pilots are "overachievers" and "controllers" who generally had learned early in life—often from stern fathers whose praise some were, and still are, seeking—to stifle their emotions. They perceive emotions and attachments as signs of weakness. This enables them to function successfully in the often stressful and dangerous environment in which they perform.

Such a personality is great for the job, said Dully, but causes regimentation (everything, even lovemaking, must be done in a certain way, at a certain time and place) and distance (emotional) in relationships, which is one of the reasons why fighter pilots are so cool. The distance works well on the job, by keeping a pilot's mind focused on his work, and is even admired there. But at home, it's a wrecker. Intimacy is tough with someone who won't unwind. "If the controller can't control, he becomes irritable. . . . Feelings screw things up. . . . They interfere with missions. . . . On a mission, he's only to be thinking of safety, flying, and getting the job done."

Dully was the first I'd heard use the word *compartmentalize*, which is something, because of their training, they do, he said, from the moment they wake up: "Shit, shower, shave, dress. Then move to have breakfast with family. Aka 'Hold court.' Then drive to work, only the mission on his mind. He's not distracted by his wife's or kids' concerns. Only the mission."

Sounded a lot like the pilot driving to fight Joe Bob.

Dully's lecture was two hours long, so he hit a lot of other points in warning naval aviators to "take a look at yourselves" in regard to family life "before it's too late." The Aggressor confirmed that "you do tend to look at your wife and other women as just amplifications of your 'shithot' self." Such a view is not conducive to candlelight and flowers.

From my standpoint, it certainly is a macho society and I, personally, have no problem with that. I can't help admiring the level of courage, performance, dedication, and lack of phoniness such a society produces. These are mostly straightforward, honest men, albeit skeptical, who tell you right up front what they think, and who can be trusted—once you get to know them. And any time someone will die for another, or for a belief, or even rather than lose, something strong and powerful has been forged (nut groups notwithstanding).

But the courage these men show is physical, not the kind exhibited by those who bare their soul to a loved one, and the dedication is largely to the flying fraternity. So there's often a price to pay, be it loss of family, not really knowing your own kids or wife (or their not knowing you), or the major letdown and the depression that often follow one's severance from the edge-of-the-envelope life.

Such severance always happens relatively suddenly, either from inevitable retirement or from simply being bumped out of the cockpit and up into a largely desk-bound job. How are they ever going to regain the excitement and fulfillment of those crucial moments in combat and training, even just doing a job for something other than money?

In sales?

The greatest loss, I imagine—to those who do pay the price—is probably the later realization that they missed out on really knowing someone they loved.

Whatever, through much of the 1980s, Nellis was the center and flagship of U.S. fighter piloting, warts and all. It was a real gathering of eagles, which, in my judgment, would not be rivaled in the modern day until Desert Storm.

BOOK 3

SHIFTING SANDS

10

WHILE NELLIS WAS the epicenter of U.S. fighter activity in the 1980s, there were certainly other important centers.

For instance, the navy had Miramar on the West Coast and Oceana on the East Coast. Oceana was home to VF-43, an adversary squadron that came to be known as the "College of Spank"—*spank* meaning the initial humbling an adversary usually gave to fleet pilots, who were the primary recipients of adversary ACM instruction.

It was their job to keep the fleet pilots up to speed in dogfighting. They'd do so with the Fleet Fighter ACM Readiness Programs, or FFARPs, which were multiweek dogfighting practices that the adversaries brought to the fleet squadrons on a regular basis.

After the 1981 Libyan shootdown, Dale Snodgrass had joined VF-43 and become the "dean of spank," as they kiddingly called him. He had this phrase painted above his VF-43 office door. Others on the base at that time included former Key West Detachment instructor Roy Gordon, who had transitioned from the F-4 to an F-14 Tomcat, and Joe Satrapa, both of whom became "doctors of spank."

When Satrapa retired briefly in mid-decade, his "last" request, traditionally granted to favored sons of the Oceana air wars, was to have a final fight with Snodgrass. Guns only. Dress flight suits. Although the ACMR (air combat maneuvering range) monitoring room was overflowing with pilots and others who wanted to watch the classic match, the fight ended without resolution: Snodgrass said he let up at the last moment to allow his departing friend the victory, and Satrapa acknowledges that's probably true.

The navy also had a rejuvenated NAS Fallon, Nevada, by mid-decade. Fallon, adjacent to the Nellis ranges, was basically a bomber base, but one that would increasingly become important to navy fighters.

Following the December 1983 carrier bombing raid on Lebanon, in which a lot of things went wrong, including the downing of two navy attack planes, resulting in the death of one of the aviators, Secretary of the Navy John Lehman resolved to upgrade the navy's strike capability. As a consequence, the navy's Strike Warfare Center—"Strike U," as it's called—was created and moved from NAS Lemoore to Fallon, where it began conducting Red Flag–like exercises for carrier air wings.

The new upgraded exercises included much of the complex integration of fighters with the bombers seen in Nellis Red Flags. Fallon fighter commanders had an electrically monitored air fighting range so they could see precisely what they were doing right and wrong, and benefitted from on-the-spot experts like the Strike U instructors—among whom, eventually, was Joe Satrapa, who ended his last tour there after he reentered the navy at the special request of Secretary Lehman.

The result was that the study and development of navy fighter tactics, which were basically the same as air force tactics except for the differences between planes and their capabilities, became as centered at Fallon as they were at Topgun, VX-4 (the navy's operational test and evaluation squadron), and in the navy's adversary squadrons. (Eventually, Topgun was moved to Fallon.)

The 1983 raid on Lebanon was also notable for being the first time the United States bombed an Arab country—a trend that would increase.

For its part, the air force, in addition to Nellis, had strong fighter presence at Langley Air Force Base, near the nation's capital; at Eglin, Homestead, MacDill, and Tyndall, which were all in Florida; at Luke, Arizona; at Shaw, South Carolina; at George, California; and at overseas bases like Bitburg, Germany.

Marine fighter centers were mainly at Beaufort, South Carolina; El Toro, California; and Yuma, Arizona, where the Marines had an aggressor squadron and conducted their own Red Flag–type exercises.

(I'd wanted to visit some Marine fighter centers and profile some Marine fighter pilots. While at Topgun, Ice Ffield had told me that one of the best fighter pilots he'd ever fought was at Beaufort, and early on I'd been told about East German–born Manfred Reich, a Marine colonel who had been the first Marine to serve as a Topgun instructor. But he was over in the Gulf War when I tried to find him, and as a high-ranking officer would have been only a starting point anyway. Marine fighter pilots flew F-18 Hornets and AV-8 Harriers, the droopy-winged fighters that could hover like helicopters. But, ultimately, I just didn't have enough time or money to go to their bases and hunt them down.)

At each of these bases and more, American fighter culture thrived during the decade.

It also evolved.

As the 1980s matured, U.S. fighter tactics began a significant shift, evolving into what we would use to fight Desert Storm.

For years prior, especially in the early 1970s, right after the Vietnam War, pilots had been taught to concentrate primarily on getting to the merge with an opponent they could then visually identify, and to outmaneuver him in a close-in dogfight. This was in order to get on the opponent's stern, or tail—the best position from which to attack an opponent at that time.

But by the mid-1980s instructors were just as likely to emphasize shooting a missile at an opponent long before the visual dogfight began, and then defensing against a similar long-range shot by the opponent they'd shot at.

The close-in dogfight, although still very important—because there were ways to defense the long shot and thus get close in—became increasingly dangerous in combat. It was to be engaged in only when you couldn't or hadn't been able to destroy the opponent beyond visual range—BVR, as tacticians call it—and had been skilled enough or lucky enough, as the case might be, to get closer and avoid being killed yourself.

Such a tactical shift had been forecast by the secret AIMVAL-ACEVAL missile tests and simulated air wars of 1976 and 1977, and pilots since that time had been mindful of the BVR dangers, practicing appropriate beyond-visual-range offensive and defensive tactics in training, in case, in a real war, they encountered the threat. But as a practical matter, front-line pilots—those actually facing hostile fighters around the world—had not had to worry much about the long shot. The threat fighters and their missiles simply were not technologically advanced enough to pose such a danger.

The predominant threat, the MiG-21, was basically a close-in dogfighter armed with a stern-only Atoll missile and short-range guns. It had no BVR capability. The MiG-23 and MiG-25 had near "all-aspect" shoot-you-in-the-face missiles, but their poor radars couldn't spot low-flying targets (because of the indistinguishable radar returns, or "clutter," from the ground), and their missiles had very little BVR capability or maneuverability and, thus, were relatively easy to defense.

Good maneuvering and "disguise," which sought to deceive a BVR threat, plus releasing chaff to screw up a radar missile, or flares to attract a heat-seeker, were usually enough to defeat any of the three MiGs' shots—unless, of course, the shot or shooter was undetected, in which case it was a good bet he'd hand the unaware pilot his lunch.

So as long as U.S. fighter pilots were on their toes and vigilant, they could feel reasonably safe.

But then, around the mid-1980s, the situation changed.

First and foremost was the fact that the Soviet Union began fielding some very formidable air threats, especially the new MiG-29 Fulcrum and, later, the similar-looking but larger SU-27 Flanker. The Fulcrum, for instance, which entered operational Soviet squadrons around 1985, was comparable, as a fighter, to the F/A-18, the U.S.'s newest fighter, and so was also at least a match for America's older front-line fighters, the F-14, F-15, and the relatively new F-16, whose radar was best only close in.

The thin-winged, highly maneuverable 29 sported an unusual cobralike head (as did the 27) and, from all accounts, was just as lethal. Both it and the longer-range 27 could perform the quick-turn maneuver aptly dubbed the "Cobra," which the 27, even better at it, eventually made famous.

But beyond that, both had pulse-Doppler radar, believed stolen from the West, that for the first time in Soviet fighters had "look-down, shoot-down" capability, meaning they could pick out a moving target from ground clutter and lock it up for a missile shot. Against these two threats, American fighters couldn't go "down into the weeds" in order to evade detection—as they could, for instance, against a MiG-23 or MiG-25, which, although having the forward quarter missile, also had radars that could not distinguish a plane's radar return from ground emissions.

With twin vertical tail fins like those on the F-15 and F/A-18, both of which they resembled, and thrust-to-weight ratios better than any American fighters, the Fulcrum and Flanker were exceptional turners and climbers. So much so that Western intelligence analysts, who had first seen the MiG-29 flying in satellite photos in the early 1980s, were cautioning U.S. pilots not to dogfight with it unless they had to. It could accelerate straight up and pull up to nine-plus G's for superfast turns—if the pilot could stand it.

Their high-set cockpits gave the Fulcrum and Flanker drivers a better view of the surrounding sky than had the cockpits of the earlier MiGs, which were notorious for blind spots. And they had sights on their helmet visors that had only to be pointed in the direction of a visual target in order to aim and lock—a feature that gave the pilots a kind of "robo" capacity.

This meant that for the first time in a visual dogfight, a MiG driver didn't have to point his plane's nose—only his helmet—in the direction of the target in order to fire, although, at the speeds of modern jets, this feature was going to be hard to use in anything but a curling, slow fight.

But perhaps the scariest upgrades were the two planes' new missiles. The MiG-29 was the first Soviet fighter with all-aspect and BVR missiles that worked well. Its AA-10 Alamo radar missiles were said to have a range of approximately forty-three miles. This meant that without question the fight was now going to have to start way beyond visual range.

The F-16, which had a short-range radar and missile capability, would really have to be good at missile evasion tactics—which, in fact, it became, precisely because of the necessity.

For medium or close-in ranges, both threats had the AA-11 Archer heat-seeker, which had roughly the same all-aspect, face-and-side-shot capability that the current U.S. Sidewinders had. The MiG driver could now shoot from just about any position in the turning fight, just as the U.S. fighter pilot had been able to do for years. So that long-standing advantage was nullified—or, at least, greatly reduced—and the 29 and 27 pilots also had the added benefit of the helmet sight—if conditions were right for using it.

Secret details like these are hard to come by, but most insidious, at least in the 29, was its infrared search-and-track system, called "IRST." It allowed the MiG pilot to track a target without tripping the target's warning system, which all U.S. fighters had. He could do this at distances up to fifteen miles. This was another kind of "stealth." If the American pilot did not see the Fulcrum with his eyes or radar, or was otherwise not alerted, it could sneak up to within fifteen miles or closer and fire a shot without his knowing it.

No U.S. fighter yet had this ability.

And just about everything the Fulcrum could do, the Flanker could do better. The SU-27 had longer-range, greater on-the-edge maneuvering performance—enhanced by its fly-by-wire controls—and missiles that were deadly in the sixty-mile range. Even the most diehard U.S. dogfighters began to realize that the days of playing with an enemy fighter were coming to an end—at least until we got another huge advantage like we'd had in the 1970s.

If you did get into a visual fight—which was not the optimum situation—you were going to have to kill doubly fast, because if you didn't, your opponent certainly could.

Technologically, the playing fields were evening.

Additionally, beginning in the early 1980s, enemy pilots in the older MiG-21s and MiG-23s, if not the newer MiGs, began to indicate, by rote defensive moves they were making while sparring with U.S. fighters in the Mediterranean and elsewhere, that they knew the same counters—although they were not necessarily sure why they used them—that American pilots had devised in tests like AIM-ACE to use against the BVR all-aspect threat.

This meant that knowingly or unknowingly they were intruding on this advantage, too (although if they were using them only because they saw Americans using them, this could still work to our advantage).

Since the Soviets, at that time, had no real operational BVR capabilities that would have caused them to experiment and thus develop the tactics, their use suggested that the Soviets had acquired them probably through espionage. This suspicion was shown to be not as farfetched as intelligence analysts had first thought when, in the 1980s, the largest number of Cold War spies ever at one time in the American military were uncovered one after another.

Some of them, like former navy chief radioman John Walker and his ring, had been selling secrets since the Vietnam War.

"Walker gave our tactics to the Russians," Joe Satrapa told me when I first went to see him. "The fact that he sold top-secret VX-4 information about AIMVAL-ACEVAL is common knowledge."

To the military, maybe. But outside it, much of the Walker case is still secret, and I was never able to verify Satrapa's claim.

But it certainly seems plausible.

In 1982, Walker's son, an enlisted sailor, clerked for, and stole secrets from, the VF-102 "Diamondbacks," an F-14 fighter squadron based at Oceana. He then worked in the operations section of the nuclear carrier *Nimitz* and turned over sacks full of classified documents to his father, who sold them to the Russians.

Jerry Whitworth, another member of the ring, had worked in several key navy communication positions, including on the carriers *Enterprise* and *Constellation*, where he'd had access to untold numbers of classified messages regarding fighters and their tactics.

Satrapa himself had been at VX-4, the navy's air test and evaluation squadron, and said he had personal knowledge of the theft of the AIM-ACE papers, although he wouldn't elaborate.

It's also possible that they could have gotten these tactics through observance of American fighters with spy satellites.

Whatever, U.S. fighter pilots, by the second half of the decade, found themselves in a much more complicated and dangerous tactical situation than had existed when the decade had begun. Not only were airplanes and tactics being matched, but improved missile technology was being sold or given to potential enemies by foreign governments that were also developing better weapons.

Sounding the alarm in the April 1984 *Proceedings*, future navy Topgun instructor Lieutenant James A. Winnefeld, Jr., wrote: "There is an enormous difference between the tactics one must use against the old threat and (a threat) that can find you and 'shoot you in the face.' With the widespread export of French systems (such as [the] Matra all-aspect missile) and Soviet exports, we can no longer ignore the threat from the forward quarter, and we must train to defeat it."

(The Matra heat-seeker, or Magic 550, made by the Matra Company in France, was the missile Dale Snodgrass had worried about being on MiG-23s when he tangled with them off Libya in 1981.)

Similarly, aviation expert Dave Griffiths warned in the August 1987 *Air Force Magazine*: "The new threat of Soviet SU-27 Flankers, MiG-29 Fulcrums, and MiG-31 Foxhounds [more of a bomber than a fighter but with look-down shoot-down radar, terrific speed, and a highly touted BVR missile] means that aircrews must adapt their tactics to a new era of all-aspect missiles. Armed with infrared weapons that can be employed from any aspect, an enemy need not maneuver into a tail chase position to shoot. . . . Dealing with the head-on enemy is . . . the biggest change in fighter tactics in recent years."

Because of the issue's classified nature, there was a lot about it Winnefeld couldn't discuss in a public article, and Griffiths, a civilian, may not have known about it, or had chosen voluntarily not to include it. The BVR threat, for instance, was what worried most American fighter pilot instructors, although, as had been the case since World War I, they also believed that spirit and training always counted more toward winning a dogfight than technological superiority.

But the worrisome tactical shift Jim Robb had outlined for me during Desert Storm was beginning to take hold. The dogfight arena, as the United States moved unknowingly toward conflict with Iraq, was getting larger and more complex, its advanced technology forcing new tactics and countertactics.

And as tactics and technology changed, so did the fighter pilot. The navy, undermanned and increasingly concerned with the survivability of its carriers, required from its fighter pilots more emphasis on carrier operations and fleet defense, leaving less time and energy for basic ACM training, which was often left to the relatively short time between cruises.

Certainly there were fighter squadron skippers and members, even carrier captains (usually with Topgun background and inclination), who demanded air-to-air training of their charges whenever they could force it. There were the FFARPs, and Topguns too. But, overall, it was often a lesser priority for a navy fighter pilot to get dogfight training than it was for an air force fighter pilot.

(Ironically, this was the exact opposite of what had happened at the end of the Vietnam War, when the navy, realizing the seriousness of its low air-to-air kill ratios, began emphasizing close-in dogfight training in its fighter aviation, while the air force neglected it. The result was that the navy greatly improved its kill ratios at the end of the war, while the air force's ratios remained a dismal two to one.)

The combination of a more sophisticated threat, better long-range missiles on both sides, and a new fighter-bomber identity on the part of some of the F-18 and F-16 drivers caused a mind-set, especially among younger pilots, that turning with a foe—that is, dogfighting with him—was a last resort, to be engaged in only if the long-range missile failed to hit. And bombing was now viewed as just as important as dogfighting, as well it could be, depending on the situation. This was certainly the mind-set of those new F-16 and F/A-18 drivers, who thought of the ultimate mission as one in which they would not only kill a MiG but also drop their bombs squarely on a target.

The air force, however, unencumbered by the special demands of carrier defense and ship-bound flying, increased its emphasis on air-to-air training—at least in the mid-1980s—while, simultaneously, the entire U.S. fighter community, Marines included, girded for war in the Middle East.

Mark Fox was a Christian believer in the afterlife, so he was prepared to die—he just didn't know it was going to happen so soon.

The navy lieutenant in a half-inverted A-7 attack Corsair was hurtling toward a gray granite cliff wall deep in what U.S. pilots called "Star Wars Canyon"—a kind of miniature Grand Canyon in Oman where they challenged their skill and mettle—and had suddenly realized he was going too fast to avoid being smashed to bits.

He'd made a stupid, bravado mistake, and now he was going to pay the ultimate price for it.

No life story flashed before his eyes. There wasn't even time for remorse. Just a "cold, ammonialike" stab in his heart, he said, as he realized, "I'm going to die."

It was too bad, too, he might have thought if he wasn't so tensed for the impact, because everything had been going so good for him lately.

He'd recently been made a division (four planes) leader in his attack squadron, the VA-72 "Bluehawks," and was destined to join one of the new F/A-18 Hornet squadrons when this, his second cruise, ended, and he had a string of eight "OKs" on his carrier landings, which was the best grade you could get on recovery.

Heck, he was an academy grad, had a great wife. They were planning more children.

How had he gotten himself into this situation? he might also have wondered if he wasn't so wide-eyed with grim realization.

In a way, he couldn't be blamed. Flying "Star Wars" was becoming almost a must for American jet pilots operating in that remote part of the world. Its forty to fifty miles of steep ravined canyon meandering to the Indian Ocean offered some of the most challenging obstacle flying anywhere—and a pilot wouldn't be grounded for trying it, like he could in similar canyons in the United States.

Practically everybody in the air wing had flown it, although it usually took them a while to "get comfortable" and go low—if they took that step. Low was the real challenge.

Situated in the rugged coastal karst of southern Oman, Star Wars Canyon was roughly two thousand feet deep throughout most of its twisting length, and was comfortably wide at its top. But there was a great disparity between its top and its bottom. Down near the dry riverbed, the steep vertical walls were no more than two hundred feet apart, sometimes less. That didn't leave a plane like the A-7, which had a near-thirty-nine-foot wingspan, much room in which to maneuver.

And it wasn't just narrow down there.

The lower canyon was full of twists and tight turns, and the riverbed and low walls were strewn with giant boulders and other obstacles jutting up, or out into the canyon corridor itself, each demanding quick reflexes for instant negotiation. That was why it was so challenging. In fact, it had been a large "camel-back" rock in the middle of a series of quick turns, or "S-bends," in the riverbed that had put Fox in the desperate situation he was in now.

He probably wasn't the first to try the S-bends—but he was probably the fastest.

At this terrible second he was traveling nearly five hundred miles per hour.

Since the Iranian revolution, the United States had been look-ing for storage places and training facilities near the Persian Gulf. Saudi Arabia and bordering Oman, on the Indian Ocean side of the Arabian Peninsula, were among the few Arab countries to be receptive, and Oman was the only one to allow aerial training, al-though the arrangement was kept quiet.

Periodically, U.S. Air Force and Navy squadrons would con-duct secret exercises with the Omani air force, a group of largely British mercenaries flying Hawker Hunters and Jaguars. Many of the American visitors had "discovered" Star Wars during such exercises and looked forward to flying in it as they entered and exited training missions, or otherwise had the time and fuel to do so.

Fox had been participating in an exercise called "Beacon Flash," which included bomb dropping, and had flown the canyon's higher elevations several times before this fateful day. He'd noted the series of tight S-bends with the camelback and thought to himself, Hmmm, I can do that. Just the day before he'd made a trial run through the S-bends, noting the approaches and needed maneuvers.

"I wasn't trying to impress anyone," he said, "just trying to prove to myself that I could do it."

The series of S-bends were sort of like a snake's body in elec-tric high slither, which made the course hard enough. They would demand almost split-second reversals by the plane from one direction to the other—numerous times. And the camelback in the middle of them made it even harder to negotiate.

The easy way to get around the camelback was simply to go up and over it. But the real challenge was to zip down along one of its sides, dipping the wing toward the riverbed in a "knife edge," then jam in the reversal, dropping the other wing for the quick turn just ahead.

It was "one quick, right, ninety-degree, 'Reno-style,' yahoo pylon turn," he said, "followed by a quick, ninety-degree, 'Reno-style' yahoo left. Pretty exhilarating."

Following a successful bombing run, where he'd scored a direct hit on a truck target, and "feeling cocky," he'd exited from a mid-level flight through the canyon with two other A-7s, who had continued on, to fly lower and give the "Renos" a try. Only he "unconsciously accelerated" in anticipation, and once he got in the middle of the S-turn with the camelback, realized too late that he was not going the 350 knots of the previous day's reconnoiter.

He was about 100 knots faster!

"As soon as I'm committed," he said, "I realize, Uh oh, this isn't the same as yesterday. Faster speed means I've got a greater turn radius. I'm not going to be able to negotiate this turn anymore."

That's when the ammonia shot hit his heart.

"I realized that I was basically dead." The A-7, inching knife-edge through the camelback narrow at 450 knots, could not turn in the upcoming space provided. Nor could it right itself to go up and exit in enough time. It was hurtling uncontrollably toward the far wall beyond the camelback, and Fox, if he was lucky, had about a second before impact.

"I was gonna die. That was my conclusion," he said. He thought of ejecting, but in the plane's attitude, which was roughly parallel to the canyon's walls, he'd be rocketed into the granite. "That would be as fatal as flying into the wall."

So that option quickly dissipated.

It's hard to imagine what Fox confronted. The upcoming wall in front of his cockpit was exploding in his vision. Pulling on the stick as hard as he could, he was functioning on pure adrenaline. "The airplane shuddered in buffet," he remembered.

He steeled for impact.

Then, he said, a "miracle" occurred.

The granite wall flashed beneath—not into—the nose of the

A-7. The plane somehow turned. Unknown to him at the time, he'd pulled so hard on the stick that the A-7 had bled enough air-speed to reduce his turn radius. His effort—aided by God, he's sure—was probably analogous to the frail mother's being able to lift a car in order to save her baby.

Superhuman strength and a "forgiving" A-7.

He's not sure how close he came to impact. "I was exclusively focused on what was ahead of me," he said. But it couldn't have been much.

Still not out of trouble, he then had the reflexive moxie to re-verse in the next heartbeat into the hard turn immediately fol-lowing his miracle and zoom up in a shaken but thankful exit.

"I rejoined the flight (I'd left) after the other two had completed their trip through the canyon," he wrote years later in *Approach*, the Naval Aviation Safety Review. "My knees literally shook all the way back to the ship as I pondered how close I had come to killing myself. The only evidence would have been the shattered wreckage of what had once been a perfectly good A-7E, lying in a twisting river gorge in Oman."

Fox, who was later to become only one of two navy MiG killers in Desert Storm, was indicative of the new kind of fighter pilot increasing in the navy and air force in the 1980s—the dual fighter and bomber pilot.

Since military airplanes had split into fighters and bombers, there had always been a rivalry between the two communities. Bombing was rote, "air-to-mud" was the usual fighter pilot's take; while air-to-air took creativity. The bombers countered that fighter pilots were just glorified snobs who wasted gas much of the conflict while they, the attack pilots, did the hard work.

In truth, they worked hand in hand. Bomber aircraft needed fighters to keep the enemy off their backs. The fighters needed the bombers, or there wouldn't be much work. And, in fact, fight-ers had often been bombers, like the F-4 Phantom in the Vietnam War.

But after Vietnam, the trend had been back to the pure fighters, fleet and maneuverable air-to-air machines, like the F-14 and the F-15, which dominated the 1970s. But it's expensive to split up the functions and make a separate plane for each. And by the start of the 1980s, the new dual-role fighter-bombers, like the F-16 Viper and the F/A-18 Hornet, were appearing.

Fox came from the attack community, so his heart, so to speak, lay in the "mud." But he was a very good flier, as his Star Wars escape attests. He learned from that experience. "I reevaluated the faulty judgement that nearly cost my life," he wrote in *Approach*. "What I didn't consider was the consequence of changing just one of the variables—airspeed."

It was one of the "dumbest things I've ever done in my life," he later said to me.

Surviving a later near midair at night where the other A-7 came "so close I could see his cockpit lights go by," Fox transitioned to the Hornet in 1985, and in early 1986 found himself off Libya in an F/A-18 squadron skippered by John "Black" Nathman.

"Smart, motivated . . . a master tactician and flier," Fox said of Nathman. "The best commanding officer I've ever worked for."

While they weren't in the same unit, future Topgunner Ice Ffield, who had transitioned with Nathman but was in another new Hornet squadron, VFA-131, was there, as was Roy Gordon, who had left his "spank" activities at Oceana and was in Tomcat squadron VF-102, the same unit that, unknown to him, Walker's son had spied on.

This was the period culminating in the successful mid-April bombing of Libya by a joint air force and navy strike group. It had started the previous December when Libyan-supported terrorists had staged massacres in the Rome and Vienna airports.

Now, in early 1986, the navy had its new strike-fighter Hornets for the first time in a possible battle situation. As the United States cautiously inched toward the April 15 strike, the Hornets, as well as other U.S. fighters around Gadhafi's revived "Line of Death," began fencing with Libya's new Soviet-supplied fighters, including MiG-25s, which had much better forward quarter missile capability than when the two countries had clashed in 1981.

Nathman was "always thinking of a better way to do business," said Fox. For instance, on the way down to Libya, they had practice dogfights with Italian, French, British, and Greek fighters. Nathman posted a bounty of a "free soda on me" to any pilot with good gun camera kills.

"He wasn't talking about waving the pipper all over the place, or maybe getting something in the HUD for an instant," said Fox. "He meant, identifiably on the fucker's head. You need to be stable. So instead of just going out there and saying 'Fox one' and 'Fox two' [codes for shooting various missiles], the 'Privateers' were going out with knives in their teeth saying, 'We're going to get gun camera film and soda from the skipper.' "

The idea worked so well, said Fox, that one aviator embellished a collage of simulated kill film with rock music and a scene from the movie *Bridges of Toko-ri*. It had the carrier's captain marveling about his aviators, saying, "Where do we get such men who fly off pitching decks and go into combat?" Then the kill footage was spliced in.

But things weren't so upbeat as the fencing began with the Libyans.

Because navy adversary pilots are so good, said Fox, Nathman had always taught them in training to "take the shot you had" and then "blow through for another day." In other words: "You don't turn with them. You don't engage. They're too good. . . . It's just drilled into you from day one. If you turn at the merge without knowing where everybody is, somebody is going to nail you.

"Well prior to going out against the Libyans, [Nathman] says, 'I'm going to tell you something that may sound like heresy, but it's not. If you find yourself having to fight any Libyan, you turn with them until you kill them. First of all they're not that good. You're far superior in training. But most important, we cannot let them learn our tactics. They send out four airplanes, none of them must go back and say, Hey listen, here's [what the Americans] were doing. Don't give them a single learning curve. You find a way to kill every single guy that comes out [and engages you]. Then they'll never be able to figure out what happened, and that will make them more hesitant to come out the next time.' "

Fox said there were "hundreds" of intercepts during January and February, but the intercepts did not lead to threatening moves by the Libyans—and thus the shooting Nathman had advocated.

"It was clear they [the Libyans] were getting more out of it than we were," he said. "We had structured our tactics in intercepts in such a way as to never give them an opportunity to employ their forward quarter, all-aspect missiles, while optimizing our own ability to shoot them if we had to. They were watching what we were doing and were very benign and docile, with the exception of a few times where there was some aggressive maneuvering."

But as April approached, the situation started deteriorating.

First, the Libyans stopped "coming out to play." Then, early on the morning of March 23, in response to increased violation by the United States of their "Line of Death," they fired two Soviet-made SA-5 SAMs at Tomcats from the carrier *America*, one of which was piloted by Roy Gordon.

"We went into our plan of evasive maneuver," recalls Gordon. "It had to do with the curvature of the earth. . . . [They split-S'd down]. . . . We waited for the predicted time of flight of the missile to expire and popped back up. Turned out that the missiles impacted about a mile or so from where we had initially broken, so we were, said our watchers, in fact, targeted."

In retaliation for that and some more SAM firings that day, two A-6E attack jets from *America* sank a Libyan patrol boat and knocked out the SAM site. American ships aggressively moved into the gulf and defied Gadhafi to attack. But rather than take on the fleet, the Libyan leader preferred terrorism.

In early April, when bombs exploded on a Trans World Airways flight from Rome, killing four Americans, and another exploded in a West Berlin discotheque, killing and injuring many more, President Reagan ordered "Operation El Dorado Canyon," the April 15 night attack.

It was the biggest raid since Vietnam. Air force F-111 fighter-bombers flew nonstop all the way from England, aided only by tankers, but successfully rendezvoused with navy bombers from the carriers to hit a country that "had an air defense network much more complex and layered than North Vietnam's, the toughest the United States had ever faced until Desert Storm," according to Richard P. Hallion, a Smithsonian historian, in *Storm over Iraq*, a 1992 book about the U.S.–Iraq War.

Regardless, the air force and navy bombers proceeded to individually attack and destroy all their targets, including multiple SAM sites, a MiG shelter with at least five MiGs in it, and terrorist and Libyan army barracks and training facilities, if not some of Gadhafi's palace and family, as has been alleged by critics but denied by the United States.

Nathman and Gordon flew MIG CAP (combat air patrol) for the raid, although no MiGs came out. Ffield, still too junior to take part in the actual raid, flew CAP for his carrier the next day, which, again, was uneventful. And Fox, unable to go aloft because he'd been in the States for special training and returned too late, had been his squadron's representative down in the *Coral Sea*'s air operations room during the strike.

The successful attack marked a turning point in American bombing operations. Unlike the poor showing of 1983, this one was impressive for the following reasons: the distance the air force bombers had to travel without help from any allies, the precision of the bombing by both services, their participation in a joint task force, the integration of the fighter cover, and the high-tech, sophisticated nature of the weapons employed.

It was a foreshadowing of Desert Storm, which would be mainly an air force show, although Fox would emerge from it a navy fighter pilot hero.

KEITH BEAM WAS shocked. Humiliated, actually. A captain now, this was his first ride as a Nellis F-16 Fighter Weapons School student and he was getting creamed.

He'd thought he was prepared. He'd thought he was good.

"I'd be behind him ready to take a shot and suddenly I'm out in front," said Beam about the FWS instructor who was besting him. "The ride was like a blur . . . slow motion. . . . I was terrorized. I'd never seen anyone fly like that. It just seemed like he was doing things with his airplane that defied physics."

Such trauma was standard for weapons school students, especially in the beginning of their courses. They were dueling with experts—among the best at fighting airplanes. Their purpose was to teach. But Beam, four years removed from his training days vertigo and an accomplished F-16 demonstration pilot, didn't think he had that much to learn.

He had four years experience in the Viper—certainly enough to know how to fight. Before leaving for Nellis, he'd been coached by his squadron's weapons officers, graduates of the very school he was attending.

They'd made him think he was ready.

But now, disengaging from a slow fight high above the Nellis practice range on this winter day in early 1987, he was in danger of busting the ride (getting a failing grade).

He felt he couldn't let that happen. One of his goals at the school was not to fail a single ride. This was just the first of some thirty-five.

His pride and honor were at stake—at least that was the way he saw it.

Actually, Nellis was a homecoming of sorts for Beam.

After completing RTU (F-16 replacement training) in Utah in 1983, his first assignment had been to Nellis's 429th Tactical Fighter Squadron, the "Black Falcons." He'd spent two and a half years there. But that had been mostly as a wingman. His real growth had occurred in Korea flying with his second squadron, the 35th "Black Panthers"—or the "Black Pantons," as they were usually called. (This was a play on *tampons* that had been created by a rival squadron to ridicule but was brazenly adopted by the Panthers.)

Like West Germany in Europe, South Korea bordered on a belligerent—North Korea, a hostile country still threatening to reopen the 1950s Korean War. American units there were constantly on alert, and consequently had to be tactically ready and drilled to meet any sudden thrust by the enemy.

"A lot of times a commander's emphasis is on career progression," said Beam. That usually meant no tactically challenging flying because of the increased possibility of accidents. But not in Korea. "Everyone from the wing commander on down was tactically minded and focused on the mission."

They had to be.

Just how volatile a situation he was in became clear to Beam on his first semiannual squadron trip to the 38th parallel, the dividing line between North and South Korea.

The wing liked new pilots to know what they were up against.

"All along the line, we have looking posts," he said. Soldiers there scan the North Koreans through a neutral, demilitarized zone (DMZ). Back in the 1970s, one of the U.S. posts' view was blocked by a tree in the DMZ. A small contingent of American soldiers, lightly armed, went to chop it down. An argument en-

189

sued. Quickly, a truck full of North Korean regulars drove up and two of the outnumbered Americans were hacked to death with hatchets.

"They have pictures of the incident on the wall," said Beam. SAC (Strategic Air Command) went on alert, he said, and told the North Koreans: "We were going to chop down that tree and if they tried to stop us we'd go to war."

The Koreans backed down. Beam and the others were shown the tree stump and then taken to Panmunjom, the small village in the DMZ where the Korean War armistice was signed in 1953.

"There are some buildings there," Beam said. "North Koreans face-to-face with GIs. There's a lot of politics involved. We put our biggest army guys inside as guards. They put their biggest Koreans. They even put little heels on the Koreans' shoes to make them look taller. They just stare at each other for half an hour until they are relieved."

His was not a rest and relaxation tour.

His combat training included unrestricted flying near the border, including radar encounters with hostile MiGs and frequent trips to the Philippines for large, Red Flag–like air war games called "Cope Thunder" and "Cobra Gold." The exercises usually involved navy and Marine fighters, as well as friendly Asian air forces, such as those from Thailand, Indonesia, and Australia.

He'd loved the trips. But returning from one, he'd experienced what he said were his scariest moments ever in the air.

The fear wasn't for himself—it was for one of his buddies.

He and seven other Vipers were out over the ocean in the vast expanses off Southeast Asia, heading back to their base at Kunsan. They were taking turns on tankers when they entered a large area of bad weather. It was daylight, but the clouds and turbulence complicated the fueling, delaying it and making it much more dangerous.

Booms were popping out of the receptacles. It was hard to keep sight of the tankers and each other, a prerequisite for refueling.

Number eight, already dangerously low on gas, finally came up but kept missing the plug. He'd accelerate the plane and try to plug in and then slow down to retreat and try again. On one of the forward-back thrusts, the fuel line temporarily stuck in the restricted (or cutoff) mode, stopping the flow of gas to the F-16's lone engine, which then quit. Suddenly, the plane was falling into a remote, weather-churned sea from which it was doubtful he could be rescued.

Night was nearing, and the weather, they feared, would swallow him up.

"You'd think everybody would be screaming on the radio to relight [ignite the gas that eventually would be flowing back into the engine with a practiced procedure]," said Beam, "but the initial reaction is shut up, don't anybody bother him. Let him do his work."

A deathly hush took over the airwaves. Everybody silently waited.

The pilot had a mechanical device in the cockpit that could correct the problems and restart the engine. He had to dip down and get increased airflow into the engine.

But there was no guarantee.

They didn't hear anything for about a minute, then, to their great relief, he said he had a restart. But shortly, low and struggling behind them in the huge weather system, he announced he couldn't find them on his radar.

"We were all getting low on gas," said Beam, and "didn't want seven airplanes ditching while we're talking to him and trying to get his radar on us." In addition, some of the others were getting vertigo in the bad weather, and radio communication was being interfered with because of static discharge from the clouds.

They had to get back to the tankers.

The flight commander finally ordered Eight to try to find a certain divert base on the coast of Thailand, which he did, said Beam, "like an Iceman—no whining or complaining." But "about five minutes later—and I am the only guy that hears this call over all the static—I kind of hear Eight say, 'Eight lost his INS [Inertial Navigation System]. I don't know where I am.' "

Now Eight was nearly blind in the weather, having only a magnetic compass to navigate with. The flight commander "had to make an on-the-spot decision," said Beam, who, because he was the only one in communication with Eight, had to relay the messages. The flight commander ruled for the majority. "He just said, 'Well, all I can tell him is to keep heading west and climb and look for land.'

"When I heard that," said Beam, "all I could think was that [Eight] was toast. I mean, we're going to be hearing his beacon going off [automatically activated when the seat is ejected]. . . . He's got to be real low on gas, and even if he does find land, he doesn't know where the runway is. . . . We're probably never going to see him again. . . . That's all I can think about."

Beam said he was about to ask if he could go try to find Eight when an officer aboard one of the KC-10 tankers reminded them that the big plane had sophisticated navigational equipment that could probably locate Eight and enable them to talk him back.

It worked.

The radio static again complicated communications, but they finally contacted Eight, got him on the right heading and coming in.

But he was 180 miles away with very little gas.

"We got to make things happen real quick," said Beam. "The weather is still terrible and he has to be able to see us in order to tank."

What happened next, he said, was "like an act of God." A hole in the bad weather opened, Eight finally got them on his radar, and he was able to race up to the boom and get plugged.

He had six hundred pounds of gas, which was emergency level in the Viper.

But he'd survived.

What Beam liked most about the Korean tour, he said, was the camaraderie. "The families were back in the States, so the squadron was your family. You ate together, lived together. It was like being back in your college dorm or fraternity. Total dedication to flying."

Picked from the wing to be its aerial demonstration pilot, Beam had performed for, among others, the president of South Korea, and had been lauded by his wing commander, who had sent a letter to his parents about the "superb job" he had done.

In November 1986, he'd won the wing's quarterly "Top Gun" award with a perfect twelve-for twelve dive-bombing score. The score was remarkable, said the base newspaper, because of the relatively small size of the target (a truck) and the fact that he'd hit it each time from a half mile away—a distance that saw other pilots missing by as much as fifty yards.

He'd liked the tour so much that he had extended. But the honor of being selected for Fighter Weapons School had brought him willingly back to the States. Before he'd left, Charlie Lyon and Vince Bonasso, the squadron's weapons officers, had given him six preparatory rides, honing his BFM (basic fighter maneuvers), showing him techniques and Viper capabilities he'd not known.

"It had given me confidence," he said.

Maybe too much confidence.

Leaving the Pantons in late December, he'd gone home to Colorado to see his parents and pick up his white Mazda RX-7, and arrived at Nellis the Saturday before the school's early Monday morning start. Idle on Sunday, he and another Panton, Jim "Lips" Callahan, also selected for the course, had decided to go barhopping in Las Vegas.

Stumbling home at about 3:00 A.M., they'd both overslept the 7:30 A.M. start. Hearing Lips pounding on the door, he'd woken up in a stupor to see it was 7:35.

"I'm still in a daze. I'm running around. I hadn't shaved for a week because I was on leave. None of my stuff's unpacked yet. So I pull out an old wrinkled-up flight suit. I throw it on, run to the bathroom. I don't even have time to put any shaving cream on. I just slap on some cold water and start going at it with the razor."

Bleeding, toilet paper strips over the cuts, they raced out to the weapons school. They had expected the general and colonels to be welcoming the class, and were relieved to find only an instructor with the new group. But when they walked in, they "knew we'd taken the pressure off the others.... We were the screwups."

It had not been an auspicious beginning.

And now, after three days of near-dawn-to-night classes, vacillating between fear that he couldn't fly what they were preparing him for in the first lesson to certainty that he could, he was suddenly in the midst of a nightmare ride over which he seemingly had no control.

The ride had started off simply enough—or so he thought. It was an offensive exercise in which he was basically given his country-talking instructor's six o'clock. All he had to do—or so it had seemed—was dive into the IP's turn circle and finish him off.

But very quickly, he said, "I'm fighting for my life to stay behind him, and it was like he was just sitting over there smoking a cigarette. [The IP] came over the radio saying, 'Well, you got yourself into this mess. You going to be able to get yourself out of it?' "

It was very intimidating, said Beam. He had never flown against anybody so good.

"Every mistake I made, he capitalized on."

They did the setup several more times, then others from farther distances away, Beam still given the advantage. But he was unable to keep himself from being too aggressive. He would close too fast, not leave himself enough room to react to the IP's moves.

The instructor would call out his mistakes—embarrassing in its own right—then make him start over again.

Nearing "bingo" fuel, he felt he had failed the ride when the instructor asked if he had enough gas to do one more engagement. "I realized by his tone—just the way he said it," said Beam, "that if I could do it this last time, I might not bust the ride."

Disregarding his fuel situation, he quickly said yes.

It had been the right decision—at least as far as his passing or failing. He finally did the exercise to the instructor's satisfaction—although he wasn't told that until hours later, when the debriefing ended.

Flying back in silence with the instructor, he said, "I'm just going, Boy, what have I gotten myself into? I don't know if I can make it through this course. It was a rude awakening. Welcome to Fighter Weapons School."

Three weeks later, he did bust a ride—his first defensive lesson.

In the preflight brief, the IP had encouraged "separating," or leaving, the engagement if the student found himself at a disadvantage and had the chance. Better to come back and fight later with an advantage.

But Beam had thought that was "lip service," he said. "I didn't think they really wanted me to hike my skirt and run." So he'd fought as hard as he could, despite a disadvantage and numerous chances to exit.

The IP had gotten mad at him several times, and they'd not completed the exercise—a worrisome sign.

Returning for the debrief, he said, "I was real unsure whether I'd passed or not. We were standing up to leave and he still hadn't told me. Finally, he said, 'Oh, yeah, I guess you're wondering how you did.' He goes, 'Well, I think you're going to have to do this one over again.' "

The words struck like hammers, but "I didn't show it," he said. "I just kind of said, 'Yeah, you're right. I need to do that one better.' But deep down inside, I'd failed, which is a hard thing to swallow as a fighter pilot. For anybody it's hard to swallow, but in that competitive environment . . ."

He walked out. "I kept second-guessing. If only I'd done this. If only I'd done that. I was just making excuses for myself."

It was the low point for him in the four-month school. He couldn't adjust. "That night," he said, realizing the need for changing his attitude, "I finally had to tell myself to quit living in the past. It's behind you. Done. Grow up and press on."

He did—not that it made much of a difference.

"You're your own worst enemy at weapons school," he said. "You just want to prove to everybody that you've got what it takes."

Known for his ability to sleep anywhere at anytime, he'd already begun having trouble sleeping, especially on the nights before he was to lead a flight and had to give the brief.

"They're very picky about briefings and you want to be perfect," he said.

He'd work on it till late, try to get some sleep, but then find himself worrying. "Did I get everything I needed? Uh oh, I forgot this. Boom, the light comes on, you're out of bed and back working on it. Eventually you'd fall asleep from exhaustion."

But busting the ride was a turning point. In fact, he said, "thank God it happened," because, since the outcome of rides was withheld until the debrief's end, he'd been spending the two to three hours of postflight critiques largely worrying about his grade and not listening to the analysis.

"I hadn't been getting that much out of it before," he said. "Now it didn't matter if I busted a ride. My goal was unachievable. I could concentrate on what they were saying."

But the "brutal" pace continued. And there was no mercy, he said, because all the instructors had been through the same thing.

Not that the students wanted mercy. Most, like him, wanted to prove themselves.

They'd attend classes sometimes for twelve hours straight, and fly only every few days, although it seemed to him like much more. The work was master's and Ph.D. level, demanding study into the morning hours almost every night. When the workday was done, he'd grab a hamburger and fries at the Burger King and return to his BOQ room to start on the books.

If the workload got too large—as, for instance, when a student had a brief to give the next day in addition to his studying and he was also detained at a long flight debrief—other students would help by gathering information for the briefer, giving it to him when he finally arrived.

Such unsolicited help was a selflessness he came to respect in the others; it was prompted, he said, by the instructors' example.

Looking back, he said, "You can see how much they were doing and how much of their own time and effort they were giving."

He'd tried to continue working out the first few weeks, but had to stop for lack of time. He had little cognizance of how he was faring other than a feeling that some days were better than others. He didn't bust another ride—although multiple busts was average—but the only thing he was really sure of was that he'd "rather die than wash out."

He never doubted that he'd finish—just questioned the mechanics of how. "There were times when I really couldn't see my way through," he said.

Thank goodness, he said, they had weekends off.

Friday nights they'd go to the o'club and "get wasted . . . bitch and moan about our misery. Then it'd turn into funny stories about how we screwed things up and amazing feats that you saw out of the IPs." The joke was that the IPs had a magic switch in their jets that enabled them to perform as they did.

Another joke was about a mispronunciation. A student got so excited trying to radio "Cobra One. Tally two; engage [fighter shorthand for call sign 'Cobra One' sees two bandits and is going to engage them]," that it came out "Gazaba," he said, which thereafter became the class code word for such an engagement.

But by Sunday they were back at the books.

The first break in the pace came midway in the course when they went to Tyndall Air Force Base, near Panama City, Florida, to shoot a live missile and their guns at drones.

"It's two days of flying and then you have the rest of the week off," he said. "It's probably the first time that the IPs kind of let their hair down and get a little friendly."

He did pretty well in the shooting, he said, remembering his "adrenaline pumping" because he'd never fired a live missile before. The gunnery involved BFM with an F-86–towed "dart," a small, pilotless vehicle that the F-86 tried to maneuver. There wasn't enough money to do more than one exercise per student, so he'd spent most of his free time on the Florida beach, although he was supposed to have been working on a thesis-type paper that was to be delivered at the course's end.

His topic was an unclassified and rather dry one—"F-16 Fighter Weapons Instructor Course Syllabus Configurations," in which he urged that operational squadrons equip their F-16s with the same equipment FWS does in order to get more realistic training.

"Not being big on writing," he said, "I just took what was left over after everybody else had picked."

Back at Nellis, they began the bombing phase of the course, including flying three simulated nuclear bomb deliveries; "Surface Attack," where they had to plan missions and fly through to targets defended by adversaries and simulated threats like triple-A and SAMs; and "Close Air Support," in which they bombed under the direction of forward air controllers and flew night missions.

Then came what, in effect, was their final exam. Called "Weapons Phase," it was a Red Flag–like exercise in which the students had to put everything they had learned into several missions.

He almost died during it.

He and an IP had just delivered their bombs and were low above the desert, speeding south along a high ridgeline to their immediate west. Two F-15s above saw their shadows and started to dive on them. The IP called for a break right, which meant they would have to zoom over the ridge.

Just as he executed the right turn, Beam suddenly realized he hadn't armed his flares. "They'd told us not to get so wrapped up in the fight that we kill ourselves," he said, "but I'm thinking, Oh, my God, I forgot to arm. If this guy [the F-15] takes a shot and my IP doesn't see [in the shooter's HUD film] any flares coming out of my airplane [to divert heat-seekers], he's going to be a little upset."

He wrongly decided to go for the flares. The problem was that

197

the arming switch was down below the right side of his seat. The stick on the F-16 is on the right and he was flying with his right hand. Because of the G's in the turn, he didn't have enough leverage to reach over with his left, so he had to switch hands.

"So I'm making this right-hand turn, flying with my left hand, and basically putting my head down in the cockpit trying to find the switch," he said. He finally did and got the flares out. But "when I looked up, it basically scared the shit out of me because I'm almost about to plow into the ridge." The ridge was filling his windshield. "I made kind of a last-second save."

He missed the ridge by no more than a hundred feet, he said. "One of the stupider things I've ever done."

But the rest of the phase went well for him. And when the three weeks of it were completed—although they had one more phase, called "Mission Employment"—he knew that basically the IPs "considered that you'd earned the patch."

Although he still had to deliver his paper, he now knew he was in.

"When the debrief was finally done," he said, "all I wanted to do was go back to my room and sleep for about two days. I was totally exhausted."

He had just laid down when the phone rang and a girl he'd met called to find out how the day had gone. When he told her the good news, she asked if he wanted to celebrate. "This was like a Thursday and I wasn't doing anything the next day. So I said, well, what the heck."

Another student, who had also finished early, accompanied them. Starting off at Carlos Murphy's, a rowdy college bar adjacent to UNLV, they'd ended up drinking seven hundred dollars' worth of Dom Pérignon champagne at Botnay's, an expensive Las Vegas restaurant.

"It was a real dress-up place," he said. "I had on trashy shorts and thongs and my buddy looked like somebody from 'Miami Vice.' " Beam paid the maître d' forty dollars for the "best table in the house," and after being joined by some of the waitresses when their shifts had ended, he and his buddy had taken turns drinking the champagne out of the waitresses' shoes "and licking it off their legs. Everybody was looking at us but we didn't care."

They'd just become part of the fighter elite.

Several weeks later, Beam was voted by the instructors the class's outstanding graduate.

"Fighter Weapons School made me more knowledgeable," he said, "but it also humbled me a little bit. Because of the instructors and just their total quest for imparting their knowledge to you, it showed me that my job now, my responsibility, was to go back to my unit and do the same things for it."

In August 1989, he would return to F-16 FWS as an invited (by the other FWS instructors) instructor (the usual method)—the best of the best—and be in that position when the Gulf War started.

In early 1987, the United States, fearing loss of oil imports from the Persian Gulf and the possibility of increased Soviet influence there, decided to "reflag" Kuwaiti tankers (give them U.S. registrations so they could be under U.S. protection) and escort them as protection against Iran. The Iranian regime was in the seventh year of a stalemated war with Iraq and, in desperation, had been stepping up attacks against Iraqi supporters, including Kuwait.

If the United States didn't help, the Kuwaitis had said, the Soviets would.

What followed was an undeclared war as menacing as any the United States had fought in the decade. Almost daily, U.S. ships and planes would escort tankers through the narrow Strait of Hormuz, encountering mines, attackers in small boats launched from Iranian oil platforms (some of which the United States eventually destroyed), and hostile aircraft—one of which, on the night of May 17, fired two Exocet missiles into the U.S. frigate *Stark*, killing thirty-seven.

The pilot, an Iraqi in an F-1 Mirage firing beyond visual range, apparently mistook the American ship's radar signature for an Iranian one—at least that was the explanation given. The mistake certainly muddled the threats for the United States, but can now be seen as a prelude to what was coming: America's lightning war with Iraq, which would erupt in 1991.

But that was in the future.

As the most visible extension of America's carrier might, U.S. fighter pilots were, of course, sent into the reflagging fray.

Although the United States had kept a carrier presence near

the gulf since the Iran-Iraq War began, not since the 1980 Iranian hostage crises, when Tomcats had launched in anger from carriers in support of the ill-fated hostage rescue mission, had the Persian Gulf seen American fighter pilots above it with such resolve to shoot if given the opportunity.

One of those flying the reflagging missions was Joe Christofferson, who, since boltering through his first night carrier "quals" back in 1981, had graduated from Topgun, instructed several years at the F-14 RAG, and was, by this time, operations officer of VF-21 on the *Constellation*, where he was teaching young wingmen just as he'd been mentored by Rat Willard.

Reminiscing at Topgun, where he was a lieutenant commander instructor during the Gulf War when I talked with him, and later, when I met him and his wife in San Diego for lunch, he recounted that, in that reflagging action, he had come the closest in his career to shooting an enemy.

It was early summer, several months after the *Stark* disaster. He had arrived on the *Constellation* after it had taken up station at Gonzo in the North Arabian Sea. The carriers would not go into the gulf because the straits were too narrow and they'd be vulnerable. Instead, they'd stand off down south and send their planes north.

He and another F-14 were escorting a "high-value" P-3 surveillance plane. It was his first reflagging mission. They had rounded the straits and were going southwest near midday when what was later determined to be a pair of Iranian F-4s were detected on radar rising in the vicinity of Bandar Abbas, a relatively large Iranian port on the north side of the straits from which surface attacks were often launched.

It was not the first time during the reflagging that the Iranians had CAPed fighters, he said. They frequently did so when the convoys came by. But prior to his mission, he said, a similar encounter had caused tactical concern on the ship because a Tomcat had naively turned in front of an Iranian CAP, exposing its rear well within the Iranian's missile range.

The Iranians had not shot—but they could have.

"I didn't think they wanted to attack," he said about his own mission, "because they were already drained from the war and did not need to take on the United States. But if they could have gotten away with a sneak shot, they might have. So from that standpoint, I was concerned. I didn't want to do anything tactically stupid."

He was also concerned about the rules of engagement (ROE). Pilots had been ordered not to shoot unless threatened—which meant by any act that could be construed as overtly hostile, like pointing a nose and holding it—and definitely not to engage over Iran, which was territory they were to stay clear of.

He did not want to be the cause of starting a "declared" war, nor shoot a friendly.

They were to stay, basically, he said, twelve miles from the coasts, which meant, in the straits, flying roughly in the middle. From the 20,000-foot altitude at which they were, he said, "you could see both sides of the straits, which was nice. You knew exactly where you were. What made it dangerous was the close proximity to the threat."

They could always turn from their CAPs and be within quick range to shoot you.

Curling back in the normal flow of their racetrack, they started flying northeast toward the oncoming Phantoms, who themselves were over land and flying southwest in a leg of their own racetrack, approximately thirty to thirty-five miles ahead.

The Tomcats, not yet aware of the type of fighters they were facing, locked the bandits on radar.

As the two sides closed, said Christofferson, he started getting tense. Guarding the propeller-driven P-3, they were forced to fly slow, which left them little ability to maneuver.

The bandits, they were being advised, were streaking at four hundred knots.

Christofferson: "I remember thinking we're getting close to this guy and I'm two hundred knots. I can't maneuver if he shoots anything at me. But if I get speed on the airplane, I eat up all my intercept room, because it's such a short distance to the coastline."

Either way he was in trouble.

His backseater, Mike Galpin, an academy buddy just back from an instructor's tour at Topgun, doesn't remember such concern. He said he'd already been on several reflagging hops and did not consider the bandits a serious threat.

Not until it became clear the bandits were coming out over water would he have felt they were going to get in a fight, Galpin said.

But it was Christofferson's first such mission, and as the closure between the two sets of fighters rapidly decreased, he said he prepared to fire.

"If they're F-4s, like we suspect," he said, "they've got a forward quarter missile that can shoot us inside twenty miles. It's old, but it could hit us. . . . I'm thinking I'm going to shoot this guy. There's no doubt in my mind that as soon as somebody tells me, Hey, kill 'em, I'm going to go ahead and pull the trigger."

From a switches standpoint, he said, he'd armed the plane, made several selections he otherwise would not have: "I was basically ready to fire. I had Sparrow selected. I was in air-to-air [as opposed to air-to-ground, which was a bombing mode], which you have to be in to fire missiles. I had the master arm guard up which covers the switch. All I had to do was move that switch to the 'on' position and I'd get a firing light."

Galpin: "If they come feet wet and I'm beak to beak [as they were], then I'm blessed to shoot them. But I never felt that was going to happen."

Galpin was right.

Instead of continuing out over the water, the bandits, approaching the coast, veered left and south, as their CAP route would have taken them, and proceeded down the Iranian coast, paralleling the straits' eastern leg.

All Christofferson and his wingman could do under the circumstances was turn south themselves and mirror the Iranians' route, watching them. They did so until the bandits swerved back east into the Iranian interior, ending the threat.

Both Galpin and Christofferson said they were both "relieved" and "disappointed." But they differ as to just how close the Iranians got to them, Christofferson saying it was in the ten-to-twenty-mile range and he was a "nanosecond" away from firing, while Galpin insists the distance was more like thirty miles and he had no notion they were close to firing.

Galpin: "You can say they were in our weapons envelope, but they chose not to come out."

Christofferson: "I may be overstating, but he's understating."

Whatever, a month or two after that mission, two other VF-21 pilots did shoot missiles at Iranian fighters while CAPing above a reflagged convoy.

It was around August 8, according to Bill "Bear" Ferran, one of the two Tomcat pilots directly involved whom I was able to contact.

Ferran, a nugget at the time, was just out of the RAG, the wingman for an early morning mission with a more senior officer. He said they had just assumed their CAP roughly at the mouth of the entrance to the eastern leg of the straits when the E-2 radar plane advised that two bandits were rising out of Bandar Abbas and looking like they were coming for the P3, which was traveling south and thus had its back turned to the threats.

Although the P3 had an F-14 escort, those fighters were not to leave it. It was up to Ferran and his leader to intercept the Iranians.

They took off north.

In the days preceding Ferran's mission, the Iranian fighters had been getting bolder, seeming to test how far they could come toward the straits before turning back. Some had even ventured out over water before heeding American warnings to retreat.

These bandits did the same thing.

"This time they challenged all warnings and came feet wet," said Ferran. "They didn't turn around. Well, now you've got a high-value unit heading south as fast as he can go with his escort package and they're being chased. That becomes not a good situation."

Ferran and his leader rapidly closed the gap, locking the bandits. At about thirty-five miles, because Ferran had a better radar picture, the leader passed the lead to him and his backseater.

The bandits were coming in low, at about seven hundred feet. At twenty-eight miles, said Ferran, they zoomed to two thousand feet.

He tried to get a picture of them on his TV screen, but the sky was too hazy.

"He just keeps coming," said Ferran. "The range is decreasing. . . . It's not, well, frantic at this time, but just, people wanted to know, Hey, it looks like this is really going to happen. What do you want us to do?"

Their ROE said the oncoming bandits had to be within ten miles before they could shoot.

The fact that they were threatening was obvious.

"I pulled the trigger first," said Ferran. But the Sparrow didn't guide. "It just fell to the sea," he said. The other Tomcat then fired. It took off "real well, and we fired another. It followed his. Looked like two good guiders."

Ferran, who had never even shot a missile in practice before—let alone taken a hot vector on an enemy airplane—was later commended for having the moxie (sangfroid?) to shoot a second missile after his first had failed. But whether or not the missiles hit has never been officially determined.

The leader, then acting as Ferran's wingman, thought he saw his missile "fuse out" (explode), said Ferran, "and thinks he scored a kill and we're done." He called for a "break turn to get out of Dodge, and because of that we never actually got to see any wreckage, if there was any at all."

In effect, they'd turned with the enemy possibly still heading for them.

He would have rather gone on through the merge, said Ferran, but it wasn't his call.

"We go screaming down to the deck," he said, "and I'm, of course, looking behind me trying to find somebody and pumping out chaff and flares, and in that regard, it probably wasn't as successful a mission as it could have been." But "in the overall picture, our mission was to protect the high-value unit and we did that."

Perhaps the most telling part of the incidents is that in both engagements, neither sets of fighters ever visually saw each other, except on radars.

The respective distances between combatants in air-to-air fighting, brought on by the increasing range and quality of missiles and their attendant systems, including radars, were definitely growing.

The Persian Gulf actions continued more or less until midsummer 1988, when the United States guided-missile cruiser *Vincennes* mistakenly—and some officers say stupidly—shot down an Iranian airliner it mistook for a threat, killing 290 passengers.

A postscript: In 1994, shortly after being given his first squadron command, Joe Christofferson was relieved of that command for an affair he had with another officer's wife.

He had informed his wife, he told me, and had thought the matter private and ended (including the affair), when the offended officer informed his superiors about what had happened.

204

Such involvements certainly are not new or confined to fighter pilots. Nor had I ever heard of them leading to such action. What his involvement had to do with the performance of his job is hard to understand, although I was not privy to the details of the matter.

What I suspect is that while Christofferson is a respected fighter pilot—attested to by those who served with him—today's post-Tailhook navy demands he be a model of propriety as well.

Given that the navy's primary job is to protect the nation from its enemies—not its moral transgressions—the question is, will that action add to or detract from its war-fighting ability?

On the morning of January 4, 1989, the navy ended the decade of the 1980s on roughly the same note it had started it with—shooting down two Libyan fighters sent out by Muammar Gadhafi.

Most of the facts of the fight are well known because of a transcript of the crews' radio communications that was released to the press.

In summary, the continuing feud with Gadhafi had flared up again. The United States was accusing the Libyan leader of manufacturing chemical weapons at a plant he maintained was harmless. The issue came to a head after President Reagan said he was considering possible military action against the factory.

Holding exercises to demonstrate freedom of navigation in international waters off Libya, the carrier *Kennedy* was approached just before noon by two Libyan MiG-23s taking off from Bumbah Air Base, some seventy miles away.

The Floggers were fast and coming head-on. The carrier's CAP of two Tomcats was ordered to intercept. It did so, and watched on its radar as the two MiG-23s continually pointed at them as the Tomcats maneuvered away from the point five times.

Five times, according to the ROE, was all it took. With the Floggers approximately twelve miles away—just entering the distance within which they might be able to hit the F-14s with forward quarter missiles, the lead Tomcat fired two Sparrows, neither of which scored.

Why the Floggers didn't return fire, now that they had been fired at, has never been explained. But the Tomcats, unscathed, split as they had been taught, goading the Floggers to attack one of them. As the range decreased to only several miles—still head-on—the lead Tomcat, piloted by a squadron CO, fired another Sparrow, hitting the lead Flogger. Meanwhile, the "free" Tomcat, as the tactic had been practiced, reversed back into the Flogger wingman and shot him down with a rear-hitting Sidewinder at very close range.

There were charges by Libya that the Floggers were unarmed, to which the Pentagon produced blurry pictures of one of the Floggers from the rear purporting to show both Apex and Aphid air-to-air missiles on its wings. But regardless of whether the MiGs were armed or not, their hostile actions were enough to warrant attack.

By this time, U.S. fighter pilots no longer had to wait to be shot at—almost a suicide position—before shooting.

When I inquired about this incident, I was told by other fighter pilots that it might not be one that I should emphasize. The hints were that it wasn't a good shootdown to portray, not because anything illegal or wrong had been done but because the missed shots might point to bad "switchology" (the fighter pilot term for using the switches), and the Libyans possibly had been set up by the United States (as some fighter pilots I talked to inferred) or were so inept, or both, that the navy wasn't keen on celebrating the shootdowns.

Unable to get any after-action reports on the incident by a Freedom of Information Act request I filed, and thus feeling that I probably could not shed more light on the incident, I decided not to pursue it.

The Gulf War—the largest air-to-air battle America would fight since the Vietnam War—would be the air action to concentrate on.

12

LIEUTENANT COLONEL "PACO" Geisler was irritated.

It was the middle of the night—morning, actually—and he was being woken again by his immediate superior for one of those damned practice " 'Lightning' recalls." They'd already proved themselves, the commander of Eglin's 58th Tactical Fighter Squadron thought to himself.

Why do they keep wanting us to do the same thing over and over again?

But he shook off the sleep and complied with his DCO (the wing's deputy commander of operations), calling his own ops officer, who would in turn phone the others to get out of bed and report immediately to the squadron in preparation for launching the Eagles.

The 58th, nicknamed the "Gorillas," was one of the best-trained squadrons in the air force. Geisler, who'd spent the bulk of his fighter career at Nellis, was the primary reason. He'd taken his pilots out on training detachments, especially at Nellis, every chance he could get.

What he couldn't know on this pre–Gulf War night was that the squadron would more than reap the benefits of his strenuous regimen, becoming, stacked as it was with the stars he'd mostly recruited, a terror for Iraqi fighter pilots and almost single-handedly accounting for the resounding air-to-air victory in the Gulf War that U.S. fighters would win.

But that was in the future.

His major hope now was that the squadron would be ready for battle.

He got dressed, and was met in the 58th's parking lot, still dark in the early morning night, by Colonel Rich "Tuna" Hardy, the DCO who had woken him. "I told him that if this was another of these goddamn squadron exercises, it's really starting to piss me off," said Geisler.

But Hardy barely reacted. "Just come with me," Geisler says he retorted.

They walked to the Intelligence headquarters of the 33rd Tactical Fighter Wing, parent to two other F-15 squadrons besides the 58th, and into the building's weapons vault, a secure room where the wing's six-man battle staff was gathered and planning.

"That's when I found out," said Geisler, a Lake Wales, Florida, native with a heavy Southern accent. "Tuna closed the door and told me what we were really going to fly—cover in the invasion of Panama. 'Operation Just Cause.' They were treating it as a practice exercise because they didn't want the press or public to find out. We were going that night."

It was December 19, 1989, and Geisler had only about eighteen hours to prepare. To this day, few people know that an F-15 squadron guarded the invasion. There was little, if any, paperwork on the order.

"I think we were an afterthought," said Geisler, "because they'd been practicing this thing for months. Some general probably got presented the plan for the first time before they were going to leave and said, Who's going to protect you?"

Geisler, who hated his real first name, Francis, and thus used Paco, was to prepare eight Eagles and their pilots to launch in two four-ship waves. The first four-ship, which he would lead, would take off around midnight and CAP near Cuba, which was the closest threat to the huge air armada that would be forming from bases along the East and Gulf coasts and flying in a ghostly night procession south to the Panamanian isthmus.

The second four-ship would relieve the first in the early hours of the following morning.

Although Geisler, with dark brown hair and recruiting-poster looks, was as good a fighter squadron commander as there was in the air force, he had not been in actual combat since flying a "Fast-FAC (forward air control)" mission in an F-4 out of Korat, Thailand, for the rescue of the U.S. merchant ship *Mayaguez*." The ship had been seized by Cambodians when he was a lieutenant in 1975.

But, of course, he welcomed the challenge. Since earning his wings at Reese Air Force Base, Texas, where he'd been named an "outstanding graduate," he had successively been a Nellis Aggressor, an F-15 Fighter Weapons School instructor, and—since his name is on the Red Eagle wall plaque at the Nellis officers' club—he most probably flew real MiGs in "Constant Peg."

His official biography says he rose to operations officer in the 4477th, the secretive test-and-evaluation squadron that conducted "Constant Peg."

But what is not a secret is that he was picked as one of the select F-5 threat drivers in the pivotal AIMVAL-ACEVAL wargames in the late 1970s, won the Outstanding Flying Award as a student at the F-15 Fighter Weapons School in 1979, and was named Tactical Air Command F-15 Instructor of the Year in 1981.

Staying at Nellis through 1986, he had been at the forefront of the tactics creation there that some had loosely termed "Nellis Freestyle." These were the constantly evolving offensive and defensive tactics devised by crack pilots such as him, Joe Bob Phillips, "Buffalo" Meyers, and others for the new all-aspect, BVR missiles.

An air force fighter pilot couldn't fake better credentials.

Such background certainly added to his considerable leadership abilities.

"Probably the best leader I've ever been associated with as far as being able to keep his guys loose and on track," said Rob Graeter of Geisler, who recruited Graeter from the 65th Aggressor Squadron at Nellis when he took command of the 58th in 1989. "He leads by example because he flew such a good airplane. He's really good at letting you do your own thing, keeping you in line but not putting pressure on you. And at being one of the boys, which is real hard to do. There was also his reputation. He was known air force wide."

It was the reputation and notoriety that enabled him to get so much good training for his pilots. All he had to do was call a buddy at Nellis or elsewhere and they knew that, one, Geisler's squadron would be great to train against because he'd always have them ready, and, two, he was a guy they wanted to see again.

"He was charismatic, extremely colorful," said Jon Kelk, a Gorilla who would get the first fighter kill in the Gulf War. "Get him wound up and prepare to laugh. . . . He used his influence to get us training that other commanders couldn't. He had no-kidding, technical background that intimidated some people. He hadn't just been on some desk staff reading about tactics—he'd been creating them."

Squadron member Cesar "Rico" Rodriguez, who would get two kills in the Gulf War, said, "We must have gone to Red Flag a zillion times. We went to Green Flags [slanted toward the electronic gadgetry of war], Cold Lake [cold-weather Red Flag–type exercises]. We did AWACS [airborne warning and control system] training at Tinker, four v x's against the Guard at Gulfport. We went down to Key West and fought against the Navy's AMRAAM [new missile] upgrade program. It was about as tough a TDY [temporary duty] schedule as you could have in peacetime."

Geisler: "We probably spent more time at Nellis than any other squadron in the air force. . . . A lot of commanders are happy to keep their assets at home where they'll be safe and they can control what happens. Others think their job is to look pretty and buy new furniture. Mine was to spend my money on training."

One of the most important pre–Gulf War training trips they took was a six-week special Nellis exercise called "Triple ACT," an acronym for All-Aspect Adversary Counter Tactics.

The exercise, to be run by Nellis's elite 422 Test and Evaluation Squadron, was going to be a kind of mini–AIMVAL-ACEVAL, in which the air force hoped to quantify, in precise measurement and detail, the offensive and defensive moves, maneuvers, distances, and times needed to most effectively employ and defend against the latest all-aspect and BVR missiles, which were always being upgraded.

"In AIMVAL-ACEVAL we were concerned about a 1970s missile," said Geisler. "Now we were into the 1990s' generation missile. In AIMVAL, the threats only had an all-aspect heater. But now they have all-aspect radar missiles. So the F-15s had to learn how to defensively respond while being offensive."

Kelk: "The biggest threat we had to deal with in the early 1980s was the MiG-23. It had a limited forward radar and thus limited forward weapons threat. But the MiG-29 and SU-27 pose a considerably different [and better] head-on threat."

For instance, he said, "if somebody was locked on to him, the pilot generally knew he had to go to the 'beam' [move out laterally, or make a ninety-degree heading change relative to the threat, in order to break the radar's lock]. But what was absent was quantifying that. Exactly how long do I stay in the beam? Or at what range can you wait, and then go to the beam? Or what is the minimum range you can get from a threat and then turn around and run away and still be safely away?"

Geisler: "[It involves] natural timing. . . . At what range do I go into the beam if he's moving this fast? . . . Do I see him? No, I don't see him, so maybe he went somewhere else. Hell, if I don't see him then I'm not going to turn back in [after going into the beam], so I'll turn away. Just all kinds of things like that. By doing it over and over, your guys are learning it as a natural reaction."

When Geisler had gotten wind of the exercise, he'd also heard that the 422nd was short of F-15s with which to fly it. He called the CO, a friend of his, and volunteered Gorilla Eagles, the costs of which he'd pay from his own squadron budget—but there was a catch.

His pilots would have to fly them.

Money is often tight in any unit's budget. Geisler's proposal gave the 422nd a way to stretch theirs. The CO agreed and the 58th was off. Actually, they went up in groups, most for two weeks training; some, like Kelk, a 1987 F-15 FWS "distinguished" graduate, staying the entire month and a half.

"It was some of the better flying I'd ever been exposed to," said Kelk. "They (the 422nd) were mostly weapons school instructors. Very good. But we did every bit as well as they did, really held our own in the flying of the missions and as far as who got the most kills and who died the most."

It was also the first time an operational squadron had ever participated in such an important exercise. Usually, they were handled in-house at Nellis, where officials could count on having great talent.

211

Obviously, they thought Geisler could deliver.

"We had exposure to a lot of things other squadrons didn't," said Kelk—such as, probably, many of Nellis's secret programs. Sometimes this made other commanders mad. Geisler: "They'd complain to the [DCO], Hey, we want to go to Nellis, too. He [Geisler] gets to go all the time. And Tuna would say, Well, he's the one making the calls, or, He's coming up with the money for it."

He also had to contend with the pilots' wives, many of whom were not happy with their husbands away so much.

Geisler: "I told 'em, Look, all I'm trying to do is make your husbands the best so that if they ever have to go anywhere and fight they'll come home."

But his own home life suffered, which he refuses to discuss. "I blame a lot of it on myself," he said. "My whole life was the fighter community."

Authority didn't scare Geisler. He had a disdain for petty regulation, which endeared him to his men, whom he protected from higher-ups, as well as an affinity for practical jokes.

When he was an Aggressor, a general had thought his hair too long and ordered him to get a haircut. He went one better and got his head shaved, donned a bushy wig, and reported back. "The general had a hernia," said a pilot who knew him at the time. "Paco said, Don't worry, General, it's just a joke. He took off the wig. Bald as a cue ball."

He'd once rigged a sink faucet to spray an unsuspecting general in the crotch, and had taken part in a joke to greet an admiral visiting a secret project stark naked.

But sometimes, the joke was on him.

Like one Friday night after a lot of Jeremiah Weed when he accidentally locked himself in the kitchen of the cavernous BOQ apartment he was in and wasn't discovered until the following Monday morning.

Or out on the flight line, when he was so intent on not getting wet in a rainstorm that he jumped out of his jet and went running for cover and mistakenly left the jet's engine running.

He could get tough, too. Once at a Red Flag, he blew up over a lackadaisical attitude he saw in the squadron.

"Guys were laughing about getting shot," he recalled. "Their priority was Las Vegas. Hey, let's go gambling, stay out all night, have a good time, and show up tomorrow. They didn't have their minds on the job. I mean shit. We're professionals. We're F-15s from Eglin. We can't do that. Boy, pissed me off."

At first he was going to take his own Gorilla patch off "to show 'em I didn't want to be associated with them." But then he thought, Hey, this is *my* squadron. You guys take off the patches. I didn't talk to them. Wouldn't go to the club with 'em. They weren't good enough. Then they started flying, doing good, and I started approaching 'em one at a time, saying, You're out of uniform. Put your patch on. We did shit like that. I wanted 'em to be proud of that patch and who they were."

He always stressed safety, said Kelk. "He kind of reminded us that he's seen a lot of guys go down and just to remember that's nothing worth getting killed over," which was comforting to pilots whose job was so dangerous.

They got a chance to see he wasn't just talking when the squadron lost an airplane.

Accidents are career busters, and the CO usually takes the blame. But when one of his Eagles fighting an F-16 went out of control and crashed, the only thing Geisler got mad about was that the pilot who survived had ejected below the ten-thousand-foot minimum—in other words, not soon enough.

"The first thing Leo [the pilot] did when he got out of the rescue helicopter," said Geisler, "was say, I'm sorry, Paco. I ruined your career.' I gave him a hug and said, Leo, you didn't do anything except jump out of an airplane with something wrong with it. It wasn't your fault. He said, I tried my best to recover. I said, What altitude did you jump out? He said, Seven thousand. I said, You know what the book says; ten thousand feet. I always told 'em the most critical asset was themselves, not the plane."

Geisler gathered seven of his pilots into the squadron's intelligence room and told them about "Just Cause." "Their eyes got all big and stuff. We sat down for mission planning."

The seven comprised his "lightning team," a predetermined, rotating group on one-hour call for any contingency. He used it to reward periodic training accomplishments. This period it included: Kelk; Chuck "Sly" Magill, a Marine exchange pilot and graduate of navy Topgun; Scott Antolak, a young newcomer to the squadron; Bran McAllister, a veteran F-15 driver, weapons school graduate, and operations officer; and Al Cross, an experienced flight lead and flight commander to lead the mission's second element.

Graeter, not in the rotation that period, was, instead, the primary mission planner, and was already deep in the planning when the others entered. The problem was, they had hardly any pertinent information. "No altitudes, no codes, no [radio] frequencies, no routes, no resupply," said Geisler.

The dearth posed a variety of problems. For instance, they didn't have a tanker for gas, should they need it. They didn't know exactly where the armada would be passing. They didn't even have the time it would be leaving.

Cuba had MiG-21s and MiG-23s, and while they knew they couldn't count Castro out, they felt the distances involved for the MiGs to attack and return, given the general parameters they had, made an attack unlikely.

"My biggest worry was not running into a friendly," said Geisler. "I guess they [the planners] thought we were good enough to stay away."

Another problem was the ROE. "God forbid we'd pop some airliner, or one of our own planes."

First Graeter, and then the others, worked through the day trying to get radio frequencies and other details, all very important, needed on the mission. As those flying walked out to launch at around eleven P.M., Geisler said, " 'Guys were getting confused.' So I just told 'em, If I don't shoot, nobody can shoot. If I shoot, everybody can shoot."

That made it simple.

Besides himself, the first four-ship was comprised of Kelk, Magill, and Antolak.

Kelk, a captain who in 1986 had been on a similar mission in the Mediterranean to guard then–Secretary of State George Shultz, doesn't recall the specific ROE for the Panama mission except that "it was kind of a no-win situation. You could only shoot if attacked. Well, the optimum way to employ the F-15 is for you to shoot before he's even aware of you. If you let him get within range, then you are putting yourself on equal turf. That's not a good scenario."

Their final instruction, said Geisler, was "Take off, go three hundred miles south, and somebody will talk to you." The weather was "dogshit, lots of lightning and rain." All their divert bases (those they'd go to in case of an emergency) were closed, including Eglin after they left it. They weren't even sure where they were going, except that they were to CAP somewhere between Cuba and Cancún, off the Yucatán Peninsula.

But, sure enough, at the predesignated time, AWACS came up on their frequencies and started talking. Geisler: "They were using a lot of codes and stuff, which we didn't have. I said, Hey, slow down, we're new guys on the block. I remember asking Sly, You know what this guy's talking about? Sly said, Hell, I'm not leading this thing. You are."

They finally started communicating, got their exact designation and—a tanker.

"He was from somewhere in Texas," said Geisler. "Big ol' KC-10. He wanted to CAP like three hundred miles from where we were going to be, which meant I'd have to have two airplanes on him all the time while the other two were going back and forth. What a pain in the ass. So we asked, Hey, will you come with us? He said, Sure."

They went to their CAP.

"The tanker stayed up about thirty thousand feet and we'd go down under the weather and look around and then come back up for gas."

They hadn't been there very long when the armada started showing up on their radars.

Kelk: "We were five thousand feet above them. Unbelievable. It was the biggest stream I'd ever seen."

In fact, says the *Historical Dictionary of the U.S. Air Force*, "it was the biggest U.S. night airdrop in combat since Operation Overlord," the massive D-day invasion of Europe in World War II—111 aircraft, including 77 C-141 Starlifters, 22 C-130 Hercules, 12 massive C-5 Galaxies, and squadrons of tankers to feed them—the four lone Eagles of Eglin their only protectors.

But nothing happened.

No MiGs came up and the invasion proceeded without a hitch.

Eventually, the second four-ship arrived and Geisler and his birds started home—only there was nowhere to land. Every base between their CAP station and Eglin was socked in because of the weather. Geisler knew because he had the air defense controller at Miami checking all of them.

"The tanker had gone home and we were getting low on gas." Because he still didn't have the codes and official permissions to reenter U.S. defense zones, he had to convince the controller who he was.

"I said, Look, I'm four F-15s and I need a place to land. I've *got* to land; we're running out of gas. The controller said, Are you part of that mess that's going on down south? He said there was a small hole over MacDill [Air Force Base, Tampa], so we hauled ass there. That caused a little problem because it was about two A.M. and the airfield was closed and the tower controllers there were going, what the hell were we doing there? I didn't tell them anything except that we had live ordnance and needed a couple hours of sleep."

They eventually got back to Eglin and began a two-week, around-the-clock alert where they waited to go up again if any trouble came to the continued periodic airlift. But it never did.

The following April—three months before Desert Shield, and after lots more training—Geisler was reassigned to Keflavik Naval Air Station, Iceland, to be deputy commander for operations for the air force there.

He hadn't wanted to go, but if he was going to continue with his spiraling career, he needed another overseas tour, and he hadn't had one since Thailand as a junior officer.

"I'd rather stay here forever," he says he told his superiors. "They said, 'You can't stay here forever.' "

He had no inkling of what he was going to miss, or how much it was going to hurt.

All he knew was that the 58th was prepared.

Book 4

Victory in the Desert

13

THIRTY-ONE-YEAR-OLD CAPTAIN JON KELK knew what was coming as soon as he saw his CO's face.

Walking to debrief in their flight suits, he and Captain Rick Tollini, another of the 58th's most qualified combat pilots, had just returned from an all-night CAP on the Iraqi border, their mission being to guard against prewar incursion. It was approximately seven A.M. local time in Saudi Arabia, January 16, 1991.

The war, Kelk now realized, would definitely begin that night.

"He couldn't say anything," Kelk said of Lieutenant Colonel Bill Thiel, who had taken over the squadron when Paco Geisler had left. "We were still walking from the jets and it wasn't a secure area. But he just had this serious face, and I could tell, Okay, this is it. We're going."

Later, Kelk, a tall, blond, Wisconsin native would write home: "We were as aware of the January 15 [U.S. time] deadline as anyone, although we were skeptical [about whether] America had the will to start it."

Kelk, noticeably thin, was far from a warmonger. One of his most memorable times in an F-15 had not been fighting, or even training, but flying the "breathtaking" fjords of Norway, which he called a "mystical experience."

219

He would have preferred to go home.

But like so many other American soldiers in Saudi at the time, he was tired of the political maneuverings, the waiting and planning; of living in sparse quarters, air-conditioned as most of them were; of protecting a culture that, in certain ways, was distasteful to him; of so much effort for oil, which he questioned; and especially of being separated from his new fiancée, Michele, to whom he'd become engaged only a week and a half before he'd left.

The flight from the United States—fifteen hours nonstop in the rock-hard seat of an F-15, enduring vast stretches of stormy night loneliness above the harsh Atlantic, disorienting refuelings, Dexedrine "go pills" his most important sustenance—had been just the beginning.

Now, nearly four and a half months later, it was time to get on with it.

He was ready to fight.

Several days before, he'd phoned Michele to tell her how it would be.

"I told her, I don't really know what's going to happen but I read the news just like you. I said, If the fighting starts, you probably won't hear from me for a while because I want to be single-minded. I will need that tension and focus to do my job. I told her obviously I'll be thinking of her and that sort of thing. But I didn't want to have to talk or write until I could open up. I would just kind of shut down the personal aspect and not think of anything but what's at hand."

As squadron weapons officers, he and Tollini had been working on the 58th's part in the United States's first-night war plan—should that night ever come—since shortly after arriving in Tabuk, the isolated northwestern Saudi town where they were based.

The plan's essence—as far as the 58th was concerned—was that twenty F-15s, in a line of strategically positioned four-ships from several squadrons, were going to be the first air-to-air fighters to sweep across the Iraqi border after the Stealths, F-15E bombers, and Tomahawk missiles had made a surprise attack mostly on Baghdad's vital command and communications centers, hopefully knocking them out—and, with them, the country's air defenses.

Then, as the bombers, done with their surprise missions, sped back to safety south over the border, the Eagles, including two four-ships from the 58th headed by Tollini and Rob Graeter, would charge in over their top, engaging any enemy fighters that might be chasing and clearing a path for the waves of conventional, nonstealth bombers and other warplanes that would be following.

Tollini's four-ship, which would include Kelk as the other flight lead, would be code-named "Pennzoil." Graeter's was "Citgo." The eight pilots were considered the 58th's "varsity."

Although they felt they were better trained and had better jets, they were facing an Iraqi air force of what was believed to be around five hundred employable warplanes—a considerable weapon if massed for attack. These included dangerous MiG-29s and agile French Mirage F-1s, which were said to have the best pilots, honed, as most of the Iraqi pilots were, in years of fighting the Iranians.

With SAMs and triple-A factored in, air force computers were predicting 150 Allied planes would be lost the first night, according to "The Secret History of the War," a special report in *Newsweek* (March 18, 1991). The integrated Baghdad air defense was said to be one of the strongest in the non-Allied world.

"Of course there was anxiety," said Kelk. "More than anything else, I would say fear of the unknown. I had little doubt that I was much better trained than my opponents, but even if your training is better, you never know if you're going to be fighting their best guy. Also, the number of airplanes was a big anxiety factor for me. As we're crossing the border, how many will there really be?"

But now, in the early morning light, he was mostly tired walking to debrief. When they'd reached a secure area, Thiel told them what Kelk had already guessed. He and Tollini, probably others, including Rob Graeter, who was also going to be in the first wave, then went right to work on the final details of the plan. They didn't finish until around six P.M., so intent were they on getting everything just right. They went to get something to eat and then tried to get some rest until the ten P.M. brief.

Sleep was not easy. A lot was going to happen in the next few hours. They could fail. He could lose his life. His friends could die. He might never see his fiancée again. He didn't really think about getting a MiG. His primary concern was that the mission not fail.

"I'd been through a lot of exercises and a lot of scenarios," he said. "Now it was time to fall back on what I'd learned. I've always been a believer in the basics, the fundamental concepts of mutual support, two- and four-ship integrity, formation flying. If they'd worked in training, they were going to work in war. And I had my focus. You train hard and you fly with intensity. That's what you fall back on."

Kelk, the son of a car dealership owner and an accountant mother, had been interested in flying as long as he could remember. As a kid, he'd made his parents take him out to the small Eau Claire airport to watch the afternoon turboprop airliner come in.

He thinks it was a North Central Airlines plane.

In high school, he'd taken a job cleaning in a body shop so he could save money for flying lessons. The body shop owner had a private pilot's license and took him for his first flight. He'd gotten sick, but it had made no difference.

"Temporary setback. I knew what my vocation was."

By his senior year, he had saved enough to get his own license and solo, eventually working a deal with the Eau Claire airport manager to exchange work for flight time. At the University of Wisconsin, Eau Claire, he'd gotten his commercial license and worked part-time as an instructor. Graduating in accounting, he'd read in the *Wall Street Journal* that the air force needed pilots and had been accepted.

"No doubt my background factored in."

That was in 1980. By the end of flight training, he'd won the Flying Award and was a "Distinguished Graduate." They'd given him the only F-15 slot. His first squadron had been the 8th "Blacksheep" at Holloman Air Force Base, New Mexico, whose members included a "hard-ass MiG killer" from Vietnam.

He'd learned the rudiments of fighting.

"Like anything, you've got to earn your respect," he said. "But I usually met the challenge. There was a pretty good group of people there, and what I lacked on the court I made up at the club."

It was a fraternity, he'd learned, and he fit in.

After a month's deployment in Germany, he came back wanting to be there permanently. "It's beautiful there. Great beer, great food, great culture, interesting things to see and do. You can take off and go to Switzerland, Spain, Italy."

He heard that the 525th Bulldogs at Bitburg had an opening. He put in for it. Ten others did, too. He was the winner. He'd stay with the Bulldogs, a squadron that was part of our first line of defense against Eastern Europe, until 1988. During that time he'd made the memorable flight through the Norwegian fjords, guarded Secretary of State Shultz at the time of the Libya raid, but also lost a good friend.

"Craig Lovelady was his name. I'd been stationed at Holloman in F-15s with him. He was kind of a role model because he'd made it to weapons school on his first assignment, which is pretty rare. He was a hardworking, conscientious guy. Basically he was flying with a colonel who had misjudged their closure and ran into him.

"I remember waiting in the squadron bar, just waiting and waiting. Finally, about a quarter after five, I think it was the squadron commander who walked in and said, 'He's dead.' There wasn't a word said in that squadron bar for about ten to fifteen minutes. Not a word.

"It was a real impactual point for me, because I was a relatively new IP in the F-15, very aggressive, not dangerously so in my opinion, but it really made me stand back and think. This was someone who was much more conscientious than me. If it could happen to him, it certainly could happen to me."

In 1987, he'd been selected to go to FWS. Roughly a year later, he'd joined the 58th.

Just before they'd left for Saudi, another friend had died in an accident.

It was at Nellis.

"He'd gotten caught in an uncontrollable situation and couldn't get out. . . . Just another real good reminder of the lethality of our profession. I mean, carelessness wasn't even a factor in either of those [deaths]. But if there is any, even a smidgen of it, it's just a real wake-up call to what the consequences of error are."

Final brief was around ten P.M., lasting perhaps an hour. Before attending, Kelk paused and said a silent prayer.

"I'm a Midwestern Protestant, so I'm a regular churchgoer and

I think most guys who are regular church attendees did something like that. It was just basically, Well, this is it and Thy will be done. From that point on it's focus, intensity, win. Those kinds of buzzwords. There's no time left for second-guessing."

Intelligence's final estimates were that the Iraqis had between 350 and 375 fighters ready to fly and that they'd probably see 40 to 50 of them that night, said Captain Larry Pitts, who would fly as one of the wingmen in Kelk's four-ship. They expected to see MiG-25 interceptors high and fast, trying to get to the AWACS planes.

"They can get up to sixty to seventy thousand feet and do thirteen to fourteen hundred knots," said Pitts, "which makes it a very tough intercept. You need to start from maybe a hundred to a hundred and twenty miles away so you can get yourself up high and fast in order to help out your missiles. If they get by you, then the AWACS is pretty much unprotected."

The AWACS plane—flying airborne warning and control system—was a crucial part of the fighter's battle plan. The big Boeing E-3 Sentry, which is a version of the 707 airliner with a distinctive disk-shaped radar housing jutting up from its fuselage, is packed with sensors and electronics to detect enemy planes and direct friendly fighters to them.

The AWACS planes were also going to be the last word in distinguishing friendly aircraft from enemies. This was a crucial job, important to every Eagle pilot at the brief. They all dreaded shooting down an Allied airplane, but they knew that in the confusion of battle—especially the first battle—such a catastrophe was a real possibility.

Takeoff was at 0030, or 12:30 A.M., January 16, Saudi time. They were to meet tankers at the border at 2:00 A.M., refuel, and then wait there for their scheduled "push" over the Iraqi border in the wake of the returning Stealths and F-15E fighter-bombers at approximately 3:00 A.M.

Kelk felt "butterflies" in his stomach as he sat in his churning Eagle, waiting to take off with the others. But it was also "kind of nice because our training had been so realistic that it was just very easy to say, Okay, this is the way I did it every day and it's going to be just the same except this time I'm going to be shooting real missiles."

Waiting with Kelk and Tollini were Kelk's wingman, Captain

Mark Williams, a former OV-10 prop plane pilot who'd shown exceptional skill as a new F-15 driver; and Tollini's wingman, Pitts, who'd flown helicopters in the army as an enlisted aviator before switching to the air force and F-15s, and also showing promise as one of the squadron's best new members.

Taking off first was Graeter's four-ship. It included Lieutenant Scott Maw, another new addition to the squadron, whom Graeter had picked as his wingman; and Lieutenant Colonel Thiel and his wingman, Lieutenant Robert Brooks, a tall Alabama native, and a former college defensive back.

Somewhere in the night sky north of them, Stealths, F-15Es looking for Scud missiles, Tomahawk missiles, and army helicopters were already winging, or preparing to wing, to their assigned targets.

14

ONE OF THE MOST significant events in Air Force Captain Steve Tate's life was attending Marine Corps boot camp back in 1980.

"They tear you down," the F-15 flight leader said, "and then you have to find whatever you have inside to get back to the top. It teaches you extreme discipline and self-confidence, which you can [acquire] through motivation, aggressiveness, and desire. I worked real hard."

Tate, a short, blond recruit at the time, had grown up in tiny Watersmeet, Michigan, and didn't think he was academically prepared to go on to college, having graduated from a high school class of only thirteen students. Instead, he became a celebrated Marine private, winning the "Iron Grad" award at Paris Island and getting on one of the speediest noncommissioned promotion tracks in peacetime Marine history—from private to sergeant in only eighteen months.

Usually it took five years.

But he'd always wanted to fly. "I can remember as a little kid in elementary school pulling out the encyclopedia and writing a paper on becoming a pilot," he said. So while earning a college degree at night, getting a private pilot's license in his spare time, and running a survival equipment shop in a Marine helicopter squadron at Camp Pendleton, he qualified to try for an air force F-15 slot.

"The Marines and navy said they couldn't guarantee me fixed-wing. It depended on what was available," he recalls. "But the air force said if I graduated at the top of my classes, I'd get what I wanted."

He wanted an F-15.

"I can't remember why. It was just a beautiful airplane. I figured all I needed was an opportunity."

He'd been right.

As Graeter and Tollini led their Eagle four-ships from Tabuk, which was on the western, Red Sea, side of Saudi Arabia, Tate, a member of the 71st Tactical Fighter Squadron from Langley, Virginia, was preparing to do the same from Dhahran, some seven hundred miles east of Tabuk across the vast Arabian Desert on the Persian Gulf.

While Tate's four-ship was scheduled to be part of the five Eagle four-ships to simultaneously "push" across the Iraqi border at 3:00 A.M. that morning, his F-15s were closer to their tankers than the 58th's were to theirs. So Tate's four-ship would be taking off approximately 1:30 A.M., or roughly an hour and fifteen minutes later.

"You train as realistically as possible," he said about his feelings on that eve. "But you can never take away the no-kidding fear of getting shot at. It almost comes down to, you know, almost like a ball game where you practice and train as hard as you can and the whistle is about to blow. You're getting ready to put your life on the line, give your life for your country, if need be.

"But we were also hoping there would be a diplomatic or political solution, maybe the embargo or sanctions would work. In the back of your mind you realize a lot of death and destruction is about to take place. We didn't have any beef with the regular people out there, even the common foot soldier. But we certainly had a problem with Saddam and the top officials who supported him."

Closer to Allied headquarters at Riyadh than the 58th was at Tabuk, Tate and his squadron had learned of the war's starting in a personal visit that morning by Brigadier General Buster Glosson, commander of the staff that had prepared the Joint Strategic Air Campaign Plan, part of which they would be executing in a few hours.

Tate's wingman, Captain Bo Merlack, remembers: "We all knew what we had to do. I sat alone in my room by myself just going over it in my mind. You couldn't sleep. My hands were clammy and I couldn't stop thinking about it. It was one of those, you know, you're going to war and it could be the start of something very big scale."

A graduate of North Hills High School in a suburb of Pittsburgh, Pennsylvania, Merlack had wanted to be a professional baseball player, but his athletic dreams had ended at the semipro level. After graduation from Ohio State, where he'd joined ROTC, he'd been a navigator on an air force KC-135 for three years before being accepted for pilot training.

The 71st, which he'd joined in June 1989, was his first F-15 assignment.

Captain Rob Graeter's "Citgo" four-ship had left Tabuk fifteen minutes before Tollini's. That would have given them time to meet the tanker up toward the border, refuel, and be off it by the time Tollini and his Eagles arrived.

But he couldn't find their specific KC-135.

It wasn't where it was supposed to be, not in his radar beam or responding to electronic interrogation. And he didn't want to break radio silence.

Besides secrecy, the weather was the main problem.

It was "dogshit," said Pitts, Tollini's wingman, who was still en route, in perhaps the most succinct and vivid description. "Clouds and turbulence all the way up to thirty thousand feet."

The situation was a prime one for midair collisions, which the planners of the war, Graeter was reminded, were predicting would probably occur more than once in this first night of combat.

He didn't want to be the first.

It was a moonless, pitch-black night—purposely picked by the air war planners so their warplanes would be as invisible as possible. But stacked all around them up to 26,000 feet were other tankers flying fifteen-mile-long oval racetrack patterns, attending the many smaller warplanes they were gassing, or preparing to gas.

There were probably as many as fifty airplanes in their immediate vicinity—"clouds of iron" is the way one pilot described the scene. And because of the need for secrecy, all had only the

228

faintest of lights. All Graeter could see outside his cockpit was a streaking, ghostly goo with momentary breaks that sometimes revealed pinhole lights darting or lumbering by, depending on the size of the aircraft.

And the situation was getting worse.

Not only was visibility near zero, there was also violent turbulence and wind shear. Maw, Thiel, and Brooks were in various stages of vertigo, disoriented and dependent on him, their wing tips less than ten feet apart, their eyes glued to what they could see of the Eagle next to them, knowing it was their only salvation.

"They were just gritting their teeth and trying to hang with me," he said. "In fact, it would have been really dangerous if they'd lost me, because they would have been real disoriented with nobody to rely on."

But he knew Tollini would arrive soon and would be needing gas.

He had to do something.

They had entered the track of the tanker whose wingman was their designate and they were flying about a mile in a trail of the leader—precisely where they thought the designate should have been.

But there was still no sign of him—no identifying IFF "squawk," the electronic return in the "friend or foe" identification system, one of several methods the air force used to distinguish aircraft.

"I finally ended up having to call [the tanker in front of them]," said Graeter. "I didn't want to call. I wanted to keep it quiet . . . but [the situation] was starting to piss me off.

"So I am asking where his wingman is, and initially he says [the wingman] is in a trail a mile or so behind him. Now I'm really getting frustrated because that's where *I* am. Then our tanker finally comes up and says, Oh, you guys are about two miles in front of me. He'd gotten messed up in the bad weather, too."

Graeter had not thought to look that far behind.

It was welcome news but not the end of the danger.

The other three pilots in his four-ship were still very disoriented, and now they all had to make it back to the newly located tanker.

As they did, the track they were on took them out of the weather, and, for the first time, they could see their surroundings.

It didn't help.

"I mean everywhere I looked I could see a tanker," said Graeter. "They were all around me. That just added to the confusion."

They were going to have to be very careful going back to the designate.

But they finally made it and were coming up to within a thousand feet of their tanker when the track they were on took them back into the weather.

"I can't see him," said Graeter. "He's in and out of the weather and occasionally I'll pick up one of his little position lights." But the others were still so disoriented that "there was not enough of a hole to get them to transfer from me to the tanker without them losing their gyros," so to speak.

He waited.

"Even in peacetime," he said, "we've killed people in training, especially at night. So you want to be real careful with those guys, because in the darkness and with the G forces and the [intermittent] lights, it's very easy to get disoriented. The next thing you know, one of them is upside down and going straight down."

Finally the weather broke long enough "that I just told them to get up there now. They jumped real quick and were able to get to the tanker just as the weather closed back in." He said he had been "lucky that one of them didn't hit me. I was hyperventilating. I remember telling myself to calm down. It was about as tense as I've ever been."

As the leader, he got his gas first.

"The tanker guys are as white-knuckled as we are," he said, "but they did a great job and got us hooked up. Once you get the boom in it's actually much easier. You feel the pressure and the tanker's lights become more apparent."

He got his gas and they started the rotation, the next Eagle to be fueled coming down, while he swung up to take its place on the tanker's wing.

So far he'd eluded vertigo, concentrating as hard as he had been on guiding the others. But flying the tanker's wing, he suddenly became convinced a midair was hurtling up at him from below.

"I saw a tanker with two F-111s go beneath us," he said. "They were probably a thousand feet below, but in the clouds and gloom, the lights look real close. They were going to hit our tanker. I climbed up to get out of the way."

But then he realized that he'd misjudged the distances.

He settled back down.

Tollini's four-ship arrived. Since Graeter's four-ship wasn't through, they had to take a position about a mile in trail in the track and wait.

Graeter said that Tollini later told him he (Tollini) was so disoriented that it looked to him like the tanker and Graeter's Eagles were doing "aileron rolls."

Kelk remembers: "Scared hell out of me. Not so much the tanking. We'd been doing that for four months. But the weather [was so bad] and the tanker's track was so short that we were doing a lot of turning. Bouncing around. No visibility. Not the way to start off our mission."

But Graeter's four-ship finally got done and Tollini's "Pennzoil" took their place.

The original plan was for Graeter's four-ship to stick around, but he'd had enough of the rough weather and decided to go down low and about fifty miles south, where the weather was better.

He took the others in "Citgo" and left.

It was approximately 2:30 A.M. The Stealths, F-15E bombers, and Tomahawk missiles were close to their targets, if not coming right on them.

Desert Storm was still a complete surprise.

They were supposed to wait until the first wave of bombing was done—a little after 3:00 A.M.—and then speed in to challenge all comers.

But the inevitable confusion of war—especially at its beginning—was about to alter their plan.

15

THE LAST MAN to tank in Tollini's four-ship was still being refueled when the AWACS controllers began excitedly radioing that U.S. warplanes still bombing near Baghdad were in danger of being attacked by Iraqi warplanes.

The call was unexpected, but Tollini knew what he had to do.

Rather than wait for the bombers to exit, as had been planned, Tollini ordered, "Let's go." The tanker track was approximately fifty miles from the Iraqi border. "I remember thinking, It's show-time," said Kelk. "No time for thought now. Just action."

The Eagles zoomed up to thirty thousand feet, a predesignated ingress corridor, formed a wall, and sped north. AWACS hadn't told them how many Iraqi fighters were attacking, just where, said Kelk.

He was still worried about the numbers.

Graeter heard the call, too. But being fifty or more miles back, his four-ship had to follow in trail.

As a result, Tollini's "Pennzoil" was probably the first four-ship of pure fighters to cross the Iraqi border in the war.

"The Langley four-ship [Tate's] was supposed to be first," said Pitts, "but AWACS was screaming. We had no choice."

The five Eagle four-ships waiting to cover the bombers when

232

they exited were spread out—tanking, or orbiting, from one end of the southern Iraqi border to the other. Tate's and another from Langley's 1st Tactical Fighter Wing were on the eastern half. The 58th's two four-ships were on the western half, Graeter's "Citgo" the farthest west.

A four-ship from Bitburg was in the middle.

"Pennzoil's" early entry wasn't just a speeding up of the fighter sweep battle plan, it was a major problem. Because now, instead of being reasonably assured that everything in front of them was an enemy, Tollini's fighters would have lots of U.S. warplanes dotting their radar screens, putting doubt in their trigger fingers.

It was night. Although the weather was better farther north toward Baghdad, visual identification in total darkness would be nil.

Besides, they were looking for—and perhaps their lives depended on—the BVR kill.

None of them wanted to shoot a friendly.

Tollini's four-ship charged ahead, trying to maintain exact altitude and position for the wall but being forced to deviate as they got closer to Baghdad, where triple-A and SAM targeting caused them to jink and maneuver.

Each Eagle pilot had a forward chunk of airspace he was responsible for. Their inverted pyramid-shape radar beams covered the space, overlapping at the extremities.

As they got closer to Baghdad—somewhere within a hundred miles of the city—their radars began to pick up the bombers.

"There must have been fifty to sixty of them up there," said Pitts. "When we began checking IDs [electronically], the whole radar scope was filled with friendlies, so it was very hard to pick out something to shoot. In fact, when I saw that, I just felt there was no way I was going to shoot unless I was threatened or knew exactly what I was shooting at."

Perhaps fifty to sixty miles into Iraqi territory, still searching, both Tollini and Kelk got what appeared to be an enemy contact. It was between them and the gaggle of U.S. bombers. Tollini called it out, but the bogey was in Kelk's targeting space.

In addition, it was targeting Kelk.

"I'm spiked," Pitts remembers Kelk radioing.

"That was kind of scary," said Kelk, "because you don't expect to be the first guy he picks out."

The bogey was low, at about seven thousand feet, perhaps thirty-five miles ahead of them.

It was climbing toward them.

"I'm not sure if he'd just taken off or if he'd been flying for a while," said Kelk.

Within a matter of seconds, he had the bogey locked and targeted. But despite the fact that he was being targeted himself, he was hesitant to shoot. He knew it still could be a friendly whose IFF was malfunctioning and who thought he (Kelk) was an enemy—as remote as that possibility was.

"Because we'd been sent out early," he said, "and because the airplanes that were attacking Baghdad included Stealth, I wasn't completely sure what I had. . . . There was definitely a level of apprehension. I absolutely did not want to shoot one of our pilots. In fact, I would have rather been shot down myself."

But he was in danger of exactly that possibility. The bogey, which eventually would turn out to be a hostile MiG-29, could have already loosed a missile at him, in which case he had only seconds to react.

But he still held his fire.

What he wanted—but what wasn't required of him by the imposed ROE that night because of the F-15Cs' strong enemy identification systems—was AWACS confirmation that the BVR bogey indeed was a bandit.

AWACS had the best identification systems of all.

Pitts: "I hear him saying he's got something locked up and he's screaming at AWACS to try and help get an ID on this guy. But AWACS is seeing as many friendlies out there as we are so they are slow to confirm."

Pitts himself was tied up with defensive maneuvering because of SAMs and the possibility of being mistakenly shot by any of the nervous U.S. bombers, most of whom had air-to-air missiles.

Kelk: "There was so much radio [communication] going on that I could not get AWACS to respond. They were calling out different targets and people were talking to them. I just couldn't get a word in edgewise."

Meanwhile, he and the distant bogey were closing at approximately fourteen hundred miles per hour. There was very little time left. The closer the bogey got, the more lethality it posed. He either had to fire, and thus maintain a relative position to the target in order to enable his radar missile to track, or get the hell out.

Rapidly, he calculated the factors of firing at this target that he could not see with his own eyes and thus positively identify:

- It was not responding to his IFF interrogation.
- It was not at a steady, prebriefed friendly altitude, but climbing hostilely toward him.
- Most telling was that it was continuing to target Kelk.

The three factors together were suddenly enough.

He fired, closing his eyes. Never having shot a missile at night before, he feared its flash might mar his night vision just as a flashbulb would momentarily blind an onlooker.

Simultaneously, he wrenched the Eagle hard abeam (perpendicular to his line of flight) and down, releasing chaff, putting distance between himself and the just-loosed missile. The high-G turn and subsequent streak out from the bandit's radar beam was to try to break its lock. The chaff was to give the bandit's possible missile a false target—if such a missile was speeding toward him.

As he turned, he felt the missile "clunk" from its rail, as it presumably dropped and then rocketed out. But when he tried to jettison his external gas tanks in order to lighten the Eagle for more speed and maneuverability, he found that they'd stuck. Looking at his instruments, he discovered a more confounding problem: His armament status panel was showing that the Sparrow he thought he's just loosed was still on its rail.

"The panel kind of gives you a God's-eye view," he said. "It showed all four missiles still on the Eagle. That was a very confusing signal. It indicated I hadn't really fired. I wasn't expecting that. It was kind of like, Oh God, now what do I do?"

His mind raced for answers.

Should he turn back and try to shoot another missile, perhaps enabling the bandit's missile to hit him first?

Should he abort, run away, probably allowing the bandit to attack others?

Or should he stick with the course already chosen, dismissing the missile picture as a malfunction, which was his gut feeling?

Time seemed to stand still as he considered his options, racing out abeam, not totally turning away from his target, for his own missile—if it indeed had fired—needed at least a sixty-degree aspect on the rapidly advancing target in order to keep guiding.

"It seemed like an eternity," he said.

Finally, he went with his gut feeling. "It told me to disregard this confusing information and stick with my plan. I'd felt the clunk. The more you fight, the more you reinforce just going with your game plan, especially if it's well thought out and conceived."

He stayed the course, continuing his evasive maneuvers, his minimum aspect pointing.

It was the way he'd always done it in training.

And within a few more seconds he'd gone far enough out to break the bandit's lock, and was turning back to take another shot—still wondering if a sudden flash might be the last thing he would ever experience—when he saw a purplish-orange burst in the dark distance.

"It looked kind of like a big sparkler," he said.

It was coming from the general direction of where he expected the bandit to be, perhaps ten miles away.

"I knew it was one of three things," he said. "Either he was shooting another missile at me, dropping some kind of countermeasures, or I'd hit him."

Cockpit indications showed that he was no longer being targeted, and the bogey had disappeared from his radar screen.

But he was still not sure.

He'd never seen one of his missiles explode at night before.

"It lasted about three to five seconds, then it was dark again," he said.

Unknown to Kelk, he had just scored the first air-to-air kill of the war, later officially recorded as having occurred at 3:10 A.M. somewhere over the desert, approximately eighty miles southwest of Baghdad.

He blew through the area of the explosion, seeing nothing of the possible remains.

He looked for his wingman, who, unknown to him at that time, had received the same targeting indications he had and had been doing his own defensive maneuvering.

They had briefed what to do in this situation: Go to a predetermined position farther on their route and signal.

He sped there and flashed his lights.

Williams was right where he was supposed to be—about a mile and a half from Kelk's wing. He responded to the flashing with radio clicks.

"That was a good feeling," said Kelk.

Neither had the time or the inclination to discuss the possible kill. They were glad to be back together and were "concerned with what was up ahead," said Kelk.

They joined Pitts and Tollini, who had chased some other bandits but had not gotten a chance to fire, and sped onward.

Bob Graeter knew nothing of Kelk's kill.

At approximately the same time Kelk saw the "sparkler," Graeter and his three other Eagles were just crossing the Iraqi border, zooming to a deconflicted altitude (prearranged airspace for friendly travel) of 26,000 feet for their continued high-speed ingress.

Not only was there little chatter about Kelk's kill from "Pennzoil," but "Citgo's" radios were tuned at the time only to AWACS, or to needed communications between themselves.

They had not heard the first Allied air-to-air missile loosed.

Perhaps sixty to eighty miles west of Kelk, Graeter's "Citgo" was streaking almost due north, toward Mudaysis, a small forward Iraqi airfield that was part of Iraq's integrated air defense network. As the westernmost fourship, they were responsible not only for Mudaysis but for neutralizing the larger Iraqi airfields, "H-2" and "H-3," located in the extreme northwest, toward Jordan and Syria.

As the four-ship approached Mudaysis, perhaps fifty miles south of it, they could see on their radars—beyond the sparse field—a strike group of F-15E bombers egressing at high speed, MiG-29s in hostile pursuit.

"I was about to attack the MiG-29s," said Graeter, when both he and AWACS simultaneously saw bandits rising from Mudaysis. AWACS said there were three, although the numbers didn't quite register with Graeter because there was a lot of radio traffic going on about the F-15Es.

What Graeter is sure of is that the controller's "voice went up about two octaves and things got pretty hectic."

The Mudaysis bandits were closer than the MiG-29s, and the

F-15Es could probably outrun the MiGs anyway, so he turned to the closer targets and locked the first one taking off. It was a Mirage F-1, although all Graeter and his wingman, Maw, who also locked it up, knew was that the bandit had been called such by AWACS and wasn't returning the proper IFF signal.

But that was enough.

The F-1 was taking off toward the northwest, which was away from the incoming four-ship, but then making a climbing left turn back south, which would bring him back around to face Graeter. Since it wasn't targeting any of the Eagles—and, anyway, wasn't close enough yet to be a threat even if it was—Graeter had enough time to break lock on him for a few seconds in order to search the rest of the immediate area.

He wanted good SA (situational awareness).

He found the second bandit rising.

"If I just stay with one guy, I have no idea who else is out there," he explained.

Satisfied that he knew what was going on—although he'd missed the third bandit—he went back to the first, locked him up again, and radioed his intention to shoot the F-1 to Maw.

Hearing that his leader was going to take the same bandit that he had locked, Maw then switched his lock to the trailing bandit—the third F-1, just lifting off.

Graeter thought Maw had the second.

"The lead guy is now within eighteen miles of me," said Graeter, "so it's getting pretty close."

But instead of coming head-on to the four-ship, the Iraqi plane continued turning southeasterly in front of Graeter, toward the corridor to their east through which the F-15Es, getting closer now, would be exiting.

"I don't think they even knew we were there," said Graeter. "They were probably alert planes being vectored to the E-models by ground control."

Graeter was now about ten miles from the climbing first F-1, bearing down from 26,000 feet as the bandit crossed in front of and below him at about 3,000 feet, heading for the easterly corridor.

Behind the bandit, he could see the twinkling lights of the lone Mudaysis airstrip.

He fired an AIM-7 Sparrow and called out, "Fox One," code for a radar missile. The Sparrow guided several seconds and hit when Graeter was only four miles away, although considerably above.

"He pretty much took it in the face," said Graeter. "There was this huge fireball, almost a quarter-mile streak in the sky, sort of banana-shaped. He was full of fuel. It looked like a World War II flamethrower had been shot." The explosion lit the desert floor, and he could see "parts flying everywhere.

"I'd pretty much been calm up to that point. But then suddenly there were just a lot of emotions all mixed together. Awe. Maybe a little bit of fear. The one thing I'll never forget is the quiet. I'm in an airplane over a foreign country. It's dark and this guy blows up in front of me with no noise"—except what he normally had in the Eagle.

It was "horrific. . . . You just watch it. Very eerie," he said.

He suddenly had a strong sense of his own vulnerability. "Guys were dying," he said. But despite the "tenseness" and "excitement," the "adrenaline" and fast heartbeat, "you kind of drop into auto mode, where all the training you've done for so many years kicks in and you proceed almost subconsciously."

He'd descended to sixteen thousand feet in the attack, and his first thought as he jetted above the death scene was, Where's the other guy?

Instinctively, he switched his radar to "auto guns," a search mode in which anything found would be instantly targeted. But before the radar pinpointed a target, there was a sudden explosion below him.

It took him a few seconds to realize it was the remains of the bandit he'd just shot striking the ground.

"He was pretty low and had blown up again when he'd hit the dirt," said Graeter.

He went back to his radar, but then his peripheral vision picked up another explosion outside.

Again it was on the ground, but north and west of him, distinctly separated from the other.

"I thought, Holy shit, what was that?" he said. "I look and it looks like something out of a movie. There's an airplane tumbling across the ground. It had hit at a very low angle and was actually skipping in the fire."

What it was, was the second F-1, which he would eventually be credited with downing.

"As best as I can tell from piecing together what I saw on the radar, and [later] looking at AWACS tapes," he said, "it appears he took off and turned south, same as his leader. Then his leader blows up. He probably doesn't have any of his systems on and doesn't know where the threat is. He makes a hard right turn away from the fireball and he's low with no SA. With any descent rate at all, he hits the ground."

The official Saudi time was 3:24 A.M., fourteen minutes from the time Kelk had scored the first U.S. kill. Graeter had just recorded the second and third—because it was later determined that the second F-1 was reacting to his attack. But all that came to his mind was: "God, I'm here amongst all these [bandits], and I didn't even have this guy on radar. I need to get the hell out of here."

He was now a short distance west of Mudaysis, having flown by it in the preceding seconds. He called Maw for a status check.

The wingman, about seven miles southeast, radioed back that he was chasing a fleeing third F-1—confirmation that they were indeed in the midst of more bandits than he had at first understood.

Were there any more? he worried.

The F-1 was running so hard that he was already out of Maw's missile range and was not posing a threat to any Allied aircraft. Graeter, being upwind of the chase and therefore closer, figured he might be able to find the bandit and shoot him. But he had to consider whether sticking around to do so would be worth the risk.

"This was not a make-or-break situation," he said. "Not in this war, at this place."

They needed to go up to their designated CAP station between Mudaysis and H-2 and be available for the bigger picture.

Mudaysis, in effect, was defanged—at least for the time being.

They streaked upward in the darkness.

As Steve Tate, shortly after tanking and "pushing" a little after 3:00 A.M., led his easternmost four-ship almost due north over the Iraqi border on the hundred-mile trip toward Baghdad, he still held out hope that they might be called back.

"You just can't believe that in a very short while you're going to be wrapping it up with these guys," he said. "You think, Well, maybe we'll get a radio call and they'll say, Okay, it's been solved. But then you realize that's not going to happen. And I guess the aggressiveness that you've been trained to have starts coming out. You say, Okay, too bad for them, but here we go. Let's really do it."

Point for a strike force of thirty planes minutes behind him, including F-4G Wild Weasels and F-15E and F-111 bombers in a deconflicted path at thirty thousand feet, Tate had been struck by the almost idyllic evening light show below the four Eagles along the Tigris and Euphrates rivers.

"A lot of people live there and it's really very pretty," he said.

But now, having arrived near their CAP station southeast of Baghdad, the soaring vista resembled some kind of hellish phantasmagoria: multicolored bomb flashes splintering the inky blackness all the way to the western horizon, and the ancient city splayed out before them twinkling in desperation.

"City lights on the ground, and what looks like sparkling Christmas lights everywhere above them," he said. The two sides had begun furiously shooting at each other. His wingman, Merlack, described it as "the best Fourth of July fireworks display you've ever seen, magnified about a hundred times."

They were near the Al Jarrah airfield, where, Merlack wrote in his journal, "Mirage F-1s and MiG-29s were suspected to be located.

Lesser airfields were also nearby.

Tate split his four-ship into two counterrotating CAPs. Daman Harp and his wingman, Mark "Snake" Atwell, would stay high, orbiting one way; he and Merlack would go low, to ten thousand and eleven thousand feet, respectively, and orbit the opposite way, each two-ship thereby covering the other's rear as well as the arriving strike force.

"It put us [him and Merlack] down basically amongst the small and medium-sized triple-A," said Tate, "but there were just too many airplanes. I didn't feel I could adequately assess the risk with [all four Eagles] that high."

They hadn't been orbiting too long—one to three orbits, according to varying accounts by Tate and Merlack—when both of them got a suspicious contact on their radars running northeast toward the strikers.

The bogey was at eight thousand feet, which was not a

friendly, deconflicted altitude, said Merlack; but AWACS wasn't any help, said Tate.

They couldn't wait.

They both locked the bogey and exited the CAP for a run at him, Tate ordering that they jettison their wing tanks, which was something neither had ever done before.

"You drop tanks in peacetime and you're in big trouble unless it's an emergency," said Merlack.

He hesitated, but then flicked the switch.

Tate wanted the increased speed and maneuverability. "Man, things are really going to start hitting the fan now," he remembers thinking when he dropped his own tanks.

All around them were the starbursts and "snakes" of the furious aerial battle. Then suddenly the bogey returned a friendly signal through its IFF.

It was an F-111!

They had almost shot a friendly.

Turning back to return to their CAP, they got another suspicious contact.

AWACS called this one.

It was back in the direction of their CAP, coming toward them at an angle, several miles behind the unaware Daman Harp, although much lower, at the unfriendly eight thousand feet again.

Tate locked the fast-closing bogey at sixteen miles and excitedly radioed AWACS for confirmation.

"I was really worried about shooting a friendly now," said Tate, "especially after running on the F-111."

AWACS confirmed.

"The thing I remember," said Merlack, "was that we had a 'hot victor,' which meant he was coming at us."

It was an F-1, they would later find out. But because of the angle off, Tate decided he was not heading for Harp or them but for the strikers, although he couldn't be sure.

Merlack, three miles behind his leader, had the F-1 locked, too. But Tate told him to break lock and look for a possible trailer, which Merlack did.

Merlack got a quick contact but couldn't lock it, which could have been due either to a false target, which sometimes occurs, or to malfunction of his radar.

Meanwhile, down to just twelve miles closure with the bandit,

Tate, running out of time, fired, expecting, like Kelk, to get a blinding flash from the exiting AIM-7.

"I kind of dunked my head," he said, "to look at the radar scope and know in my heart that that's a no-kidding bad guy. But there wasn't any flash. It's more like a really large flare kind of thing that shoots out in front of the airplane. It started out slow and then really picked up speed [as the missile worked out a trajectory to its target], almost like a train."

He watched it a few seconds and then called, "Fox One."

Behind him—and before the Fox call—Merlack saw the same thing, but with a different interpretation.

"There was still a lot of triple-A around us," he said, "and what I saw looked like a missile coming at *me*. At night, aspect angles are very hard to tell, and so I thought this guy was shooting at Steve or me."

He broke hard, releasing chaff, time starting to slow down for him as he thought he might be the target. He didn't know if the shot was from the second contact or the first.

Just then Tate's missile hit the forward quarter of the F-1, exploding it into "an incredible fireball," said Tate, "lighting up the entire sky."

He was four miles away when the explosion occurred, and he had to pull as hard as he could to avoid flying into it.

"It was just a huge engulfing fire," spraying brilliance and airplane parts in every direction, he said.

His avoidance maneuvering made him fearful of a midair, knowing, as he did, that there were so many other planes around. Consequently, he didn't radio "Splash" (meaning he'd seen the target explode) for perhaps five seconds, thereby leaving Harp and Atwell, still back on CAP—but seeing the brilliant flash—guessing that long about what had happened.

"They thought I'd been shot down until they heard the call," said Tate.

For his part, Merlack was both relieved—because of the realization that the missile was Tate's—and awed by the explosion.

"It was just so amazing," he said, "a big white round thing, twenty-five or thirty feet across, little parts of airplane and I guess fuel that had blown up."

He watched it slam into the ground like a meteor. "It seemed like everything happened in slow motion."

But he quickly recovered.

"I remember saying, 'Tater! Where are you!' He [Tate] goes, 'I'm heading one-eight-zero.' "

That put his leader about nine miles away—and getting farther—a situation Merlack did not want.

"He's got to know I'm there," he said. "I quickly went into about a seven-G break turn to get back with him. I didn't want to lose him at that point because out in enemy territory at night by yourself is not good."

The air force officially recorded the time of the kill as 3:54 A.M. (although initially spokesmen had said it was earlier, possibly the first kill). This, then, was the fourth U.S. air-to-air kill of the fledgling war, as contrasted with none for the Iraqis. Rejoined again, however, Tate and Merlack were not concerned with times or records.

"The Iraqis have lots of airplanes that they can get airborne," said Tate, "and I am worried about my body and my three other guys and the entire package of strikers. So you don't have time to sit back and say, Hey, I just got a kill."

He radioed his wingman that they were speeding back to CAP.

Graeter's four-ship stayed on its CAP between H-2 and Mudaysis for perhaps fifteen minutes. At least one bandit appeared above H-2 in the distant west. But since the Iraqi plane was not immediately threatening, he decided that entering the airfield's dangerous SAM ring to engage it would not be worth the risk.

At approximately 3:40 A.M., he said, "Citgo" left in order to make room for the next wave of Allied attackers entering the western area, including a large navy strike force of mostly A-6 and A-7 bombers and F/A-18 fighter-bombers from the aircraft carrier *Saratoga*.

The big flattop, which had sped across the Atlantic in seven days to get to the war—the fastest such crossing since World War II—was launching from the Red Sea, the farthest operational war zone base from Baghdad. Thus, its planes, and the planes of the other carriers there—the *Kennedy*, the *Theodore Roosevelt*, and the *America*—had some of the longest times and distances to target to fly. This particular mission, which would set an ominous tone for the rest of the *Saratoga*'s Desert Storm operations, was no exception.

Leading it was Commander Mike "Spock" Anderson, a Hornet pilot and skipper of the VFA-81 "Sunliners," whose members also included Lieutenant Commander Mark Fox, who had transitioned to the F/A-18 after his "Star Wars Canyon" scare. But Fox was not with this strike. He was back on the *Saratoga* readying for its first daylight mission.

This mission was to suppress enemy air defenses.

The F/A-18s Anderson was leading were carrying High-Speed Anti-Radar Missiles (HARMs). The pilots behind him, who included squadron department heads Tony Albano and Albano's roommate, thirty-three-year-old Scott Speicher, both lieutenant commanders, would be firing their HARMs at enemy SAM launchers in support of the bombers behind them.

The HARMs, wickedly turning the enemy's destructive power on itself, guided at quick speed on the radar emissions the SAMs used for homing. But the enemy wasn't wise to this yet, and its SAM crews were eager to target any suspect plane within range.

Graeter thinks "Citgo," returning south, probably crossed near or directly over Anderson's group—like ships in the night—as the navy force headed northeast, its lights out, at thirty thousand feet toward its targets in the western Baghdad area. Each Hornet had several specific targets, such as the Al Taqaddum airfield near the Euphrates River, and a time to hit each.

Anderson's time-on-target was 4:00 A.M.

The group was about to lose Scott Speicher to what the Pentagon would later claim was a SAM. But available evidence tells a different story:

As they were approaching Baghdad—perhaps fifty miles away—Anderson said, "I got an immediate radar contact on an airborne target climbing out of an airfield near Baghdad. I immediately knew it was an enemy airplane because we have some technology [onboard the F/A-18]. I also knew by the indicated speed that it was not a U.S. airplane or a Coalition airplane."

The target was traveling at 1.4 Mach, he said, which means at approximately a thousand miles per hour, and climbing quickly, which was behavior common for a MiG-25 interceptor. Most telling was its exhaust. When it got closer, he said, "I could see the afterburner flame and it was an extremely long, yellow [flame] which I had seen before on a MiG-25. No question what you have in front of you when you see that."

The bandit appeared to Anderson to be trying to attack his group. "He obviously had a radar warning receiver in his airplane," said the leader, "because as soon as I took a radar lock on him, he turned to his right, and at that point I saw him start to go around me in a counterclockwise direction."

The strike leader responded by turning with the suspected Foxbat.

"I did a couple of circles with him," he said, "relaying all the information to AWACS and asking for permission to shoot." The lone Iraqi pilot—not only bold but apparently knowledgeable about U.S. weaponry—was just "trying to stay out of my firing envelope."

The particular AWACS controller he was talking to, however, did not see the MiG on his scope. "There were several other AWACS up there that night and the other ones did see him," he said he was later told, "but they were on a different frequency."

He could not get an authorization to fire.

"There are specific physical laws that could have prohibited that closest AWACS from seeing him," said Anderson. "Just the design of the radar. It has to do with Doppler." "Doppler" refers to the way the radar "sees" the target. Just as U.S. pilots go abeam (or perpendicular to the beams) of MiG radars in order to appear invisible to them, the bandit pilot could have knowingly or unknowingly done the same thing as he maneuvered to get out of Anderson's sights.

As Anderson was chasing the bandit, the other Hornets, getting close to their targets, apparently had begun dispersing to various areas of the western Baghdad night sky in order to get into the best firing positions they could. It was a large area of disbursement—perhaps fifty to sixty miles of sky, said Albano, who, located somewhere behind and south of Anderson, heard the leader's communications with AWACS.

"This guy [the bandit] is up there running around in afterburner probably just trying to lock up anything he could to fire at," said Albano, a 1979 graduate of the Citadel. "I was listening and frantically searching my radar trying to find the guy. But as fast as he was moving around, there are certain regimes of our radar that can't handle that type of changing environment. So now we got an [undefensed] bandit out there running around, and, you know, the skipper said, 'Well, that's it. I got to press on.' We all had time lines."

Anderson had chased the bandit until it had come out of afterburner, thereby rendering it invisible in the darkness. The bandit went behind him, "outside my radar picture. I lost sight of him," said Anderson.

Not being able to track the bandit, both he and Albano went on to their targets. Anderson was proceeding thus when shortly he saw a "flash" go off to his right at about the 4:30 clock position. At the time, there was a lot of triple-A around, and he didn't pay much attention, having his own immediate job to perform.

But later, after making an inflight roll call on the way home that revealed that Speicher was missing, he realized the flash had occurred in the specific area where Speicher should have been— to his right, south and behind him, perhaps three to five miles away. And in a subsequent debrief after landing, he said, "a couple pilots said they in fact saw an airplane blow up" in that area and "fall to the ground."

Eventually, despite the navy's quick and official declaration that Speicher was first missing, and then killed by a SAM, many of those involved as well as those who investigated the incident became convinced that it was the result of a MiG-25 shootdown.

Albano: "I pretty much traveled over the same piece of land that [Speicher] did, or that I assume he did, and I personally could see no surface-to-air missiles coming up in that vicinity. I mean, they were coming up, and there were a lot of them. But most of them were out to the east, and not directly under us."

Speicher's job, after all, was to be aware of SAMs and knock them out.

Anderson: "I can tell you that there is a significant amount of data, some of it extremely classified, that supports the belief that Scott Speicher was either killed by an air-to-air missile [fired] by a MiG-25 that I got tangled up with, or it was a midair collision with a MiG-25 I got tangled up with."

Personally, he said, he believes it was an air-to-air shootdown.

"It was a very intense electronic environment that night," he said. "There were a lot of things going on in the cockpit."

Speicher, some speculate, might have been concentrating on something other than Anderson's calls or indications of the bandit—perhaps a HARM shot—when the Iraqi might have seen the flash of that shot, thereby spotting a target in the dark night and, in any case, striking from behind, an unprotected area not covered by Speicher's radar.

Anderson was reportedly livid at AWACS when the full realization of what probably had happened became clear. But he denies that, and later said: "[The fact that AWACS was unwilling to let him shoot based solely on his determination] was probably the right ROE because we didn't shoot down any friendlies. . . . I remained a little dissatisfied with the fact we didn't put an effort into locating the wreckage and remains like we did with other casualties in the later parts of the war."

No trace of Speicher or his plane was ever found—or possibly even searched for—despite repeated requests by Anderson and others.

"It may have been because of the remoteness of the area [over which Speicher went down]," he said. "But I'm not sure the right information got passed to the right people. It's only my opinion, but there's evidence in my mind that perhaps [the requests] fell through the cracks, because as often as we inquired, we still got messages as late as two weeks after President Bush called it quits that, you know, is this guy [Speicher] still missing? Or, what's going on with him? They're asking me when in reality I'm supposed to be asking them."

An additional sad irony was that originally Speicher had not been scheduled to go on the first strike. Anderson had listed him only as a spare, an alternate who would step in only if a first designate couldn't go.

"A spare is a guy who has to know everybody's mission," said Anderson, "not just one. So I chose him because I had a lot of faith in him. But he insisted that he didn't want to be left out of the first strike. He needed to go on this one. And after about a day's thought on it, I honored his request and picked another spare and made him my number two. He was my number-two man."

Speicher's roommate, Albano, remembered that the night before they left, their air wing commander, a Vietnam combat veteran and a "great inspirational leader," had gathered the strike pilots below the flight deck and broke the news that they were going.

"He said, 'You probably saw the news reports [during the Vietnam War] about people protesting. You'll probably see some of those again. But I guarantee you there will also be people sitting in pubs and taverns in places like Pittsburgh, Pennsylvania, with a beer mug in their hand saying 'Here's one for the boys.' I'll tell you what, it got our hearts racing, the adrenaline flowing. We were psyched, both of us. Very apprehensive, but also very excited about going on the first strike."

Speicher was the war's first Allied casualty. But how he died was to remain a secret. The Pentagon didn't want anything to lift the spirits of the Iraqis, and factions in the navy—which, since Vietnam, had prided itself on its fighter prowess—apparently did not want it known that they had suffered what looked very much like the Coalition's first air-to-air kill.

The mission, itself, had been a success.

Following their engagements, in which they had become the first F-15 four-ships to shoot down enemy fighters, "Citgo" and "Pennzoil" joined south of Mudaysis and sped home together at forty thousand feet.

As soon as the eight-ship crossed back into Saudi, and consequently felt safe, Kelk, itching to know exactly what had happened with his missiles, turned on his outside lights and had his wingman, Williams, fly close underneath and take a look at how many remained.

"I couldn't stand it anymore," he said. "I told myself, 'I got to know. I got to know.'"

Williams moved close and looked up. "He goes, 'Uhhhh, you're missing one,'" said Kelk. "I keyed back on the microphone, 'This could be good.'"

It was the first jubilant reflection he'd allowed himself all night.

East of the eight-ship, Tate and Merlack, the last of their four-ship still on station, waited until the final bomber in their strike group had exited the Baghdad area and then climbed to the forty-thousand-foot safe altitude and began their streak south.

Merlack: "Tater goes to light his afterburner and had a blowout." The sudden explosion of injected gas "makes a big flash in the back and bumps the aircraft a little bit"—similar in effect to a loud backfire of a car. "He thought he was hit, and he screamed,

'Bo, I'm hit! I'm hit!' We were the last ones out and pretty excited at that point."

Merlack swung over but couldn't see any problem, which he told Tate.

"Oh . . . okay," he said Tate responded. "Yeah, I'm okay."

Tate: "It was a very long ride home. . . . You relive that [enemy shootdown] explosion over and over. . . . I'm obviously proud that I worked the radar like I should have, locked him up somehow. I mean, AWACS wasn't seeing him and they weren't providing any help for me so it was basically me or nothing [in the engagement that produced the fourth U.S. air-to-air kill of the war]. . . . I am proud that I did the job I was supposed to . . . that I was the fighter pilot, like, you know, every fighter pilot thinks he's the best in the world. . . ."

Most of all, he said, he was proud that they had not lost a single airplane.

As they sped on to a tanker, both of them said silent prayers of thanks.

But the fighting had only begun.

16

DALE SNODGRASS WAS still looking to bag a MiG. Nearly ten years had passed since he'd come so close to doing so while flying off Libya in 1981. But the chances just hadn't been as good in the interim.

Leaving the "College of Spank" at Oceana, he'd continued to distinguish himself in the Tomcat, winning Fighter Wing One's Fighter Pilot of the Year as a VF-143 department head and F-14 demonstration pilot. He also won Grumman Aircraft Corporation's "Top Cat" award, given annually to the F-14 pilot the company deemed best in the U.S. Navy.

A full commander now, he was advancing in his career and flying, too, which was hard to do.

In September 1989, after serving his time as an XO, he'd been given command of his own fighter squadron, the VF-33 Starfighters on the carrier *America*, and was in that job when *America* joined the *Kennedy* and the *Saratoga* in the Red Sea at the start of Desert Storm.

Because the *Kennedy* and the *Saratoga* had been in the Red Sea for nearly six months and had practiced the initial strikes many times, their planes were the first navy planes to go into Iraq when the shooting began. But Snodgrass had made sure he was up with the Tomcats flying CAP for the carriers when Anderson and the others left.

"Everybody was very tense," he said. "There was significant concern the Iraqis would make a Mirage/Exocet [missile] strike at the carriers. But the only inbound targets from Iraq were returning strikers from the *JFK* and *Saratoga*."

It was a familiar story for Snodgrass: no MiGs—although, in the large scheme, which he was certainly attuned to, that was the better situation. The carriers were in a vulnerable position in the relatively narrow Red Sea.

Just as well that he would have to wait until *America* took its turn in the combat rotation, which would be roughly thirty hours after the war's start. At that time, *Saratoga* would stand down for replenishment, and *America* would join *Kennedy* in launching its first strikes in what would develop into (roughly) two-days-on, and one-day-off carrier combat rotations.

He was slated at that time to lead the battle group's first fighter sweep—the tip of a large strike force going to downtown Baghdad.

Lieutenant Nick "Mongo" Mongillo was having a hard time sleeping.

The twenty-eight-year-old Hornet pilot from Stratford, Connecticut, had only joined the VFA-81 Sunliners a week before the squadron left for Desert Shield. Now he was scheduled to fly in *Saratoga*'s second strike, its first daylight raid, another large one with the *Kennedy*, which was launching in only a matter of hours.

"The execution order has been passed," Mongillo had written earlier that evening in his diary. "Tonight, the skipper, CDR Anderson, along with LCDR [Scott] Speicher . . . LCDR [Tony] Albano . . . [and others] put a [strike] package on Baghdad. . . . What started when I . . . received orders to VFA-81 for a supposed Love Boat Cruise . . . has come down to a strike . . . tomorrow afternoon.

"We will assault H3 [an enemy airfield]. It is heavily defended by 5 to 6 SA-6 [SAM] sites and possibly a HAWK [an American-built SAM] site. I am scared. I will go of course. It is my job and sworn duty. . . . I have no desire to hurt anyone. But I must do it. I fear for my life, my squadron mates, and mostly for my wife and daughter . . . born days before I departed the U.S. . . . I must be extra careful so she has a daddy to raise her. I long to see my wife . . . my dog . . . my parents. . . . We are doing the right thing."

He'd set his alarm for 6:30 A.M. in order to make an early morning brief. But the sounds of Anderson's strike group returning in the predawn darkness woke him early. He'd hurried down to the ready room to hear the "results and catch all the stories."

Mark Fox, a lieutenant commander now, and operations officer for the squadron as well as a spare for the next mission, was trying to sleep, too.

Earlier that night, he'd written in his journal: "[I've got] a variety of moods . . . and feelings. . . . Bravado, camaraderie, introspection, fatigue . . . relief that we are at last going to act—concern and fear of the unknown." That was his deepest fear—the unknown. He entered the names of his wife and four children— "Priscilla, William, Collin, Mason, and Abigail—what a cruel place this world can be. God protect them from the rancid and ugly evil that causes wars."

In the fevered pace of preparation that prestrike evening—aviators readying pistols, poring over maps—he'd planned to write his wife a good-bye letter, just in case.

"Some people look at you funny and say, Why are you doing that?" he said. "But if I were floating down in a parachute or trapped in a flaming plane, you know, my last conscious thought would be, Doggone it, I never said good-bye to the very people I care most about. . . ."

But then he put it off, "unwilling," he said, "to face the reality that we're really going to do this . . . that some of us might not return."

Down in the ready room, Mongillo, a 1984 computer science graduate of Western Connecticut State University, where he played linebacker on the football team, was paying close attention.

"You hear it was like the brightest fireworks show I'd ever seen," he said. "Spike [Speicher] didn't come back. . . . Somebody said he diverted to an airfield. That was the initial rumor. He just got low on fuel and had to land. So they're looking to see if he flew to any of the divert airfields. . . . I was scared."

Fox: "We still hoped that he'd diverted someplace, or had an airplane with a bad radio or something. But, obviously, there was a pretty tight-lipped, sober atmosphere about the whole thing."

253

Neither one of them was privy to Anderson's worst thoughts as, after debriefings with intelligence officers and others, the CO began to piece together what had happened and suspect that the squadron's administrative officer might have been shot down by the MiG-25.

Sometime that morning, Fox finally went back and wrote the good-bye letter to his wife, sealing it and putting it in his desk with instructions on the outside of the envelope to mail it if he didn't return.

"It was a hard thing to do," he said, "but, really, it frees you up."

They had breakfast and then went to the main brief, conducted by Commander Dennis "Dizzy" Gillespie, CO of VFA-83 and the overall strike lead. Their division—a four-ship of Hornets to be led by Commander Bill "Maggot" McKee, VFA-81's executive officer—would be in the front of the bombers, behind only the Tomcats that would sweep ahead of the strikers, confronting the many enemy planes they expected.

Mongillo was to be McKee's wingman.

Mongillo: "The briefs are three hours prior to take off. Very extensive, with all the flight elements and every pilot, co-pilot, NFO [naval flight officer, like an F-14 backseater] in one room and all the charts up. They'll hand you a four or five-page packet about frequencies, tanking, orders of battle. It has the entire plan and everything needed to execute it."

The target, H-3, so named by the British during their occupation in the 1920s, was an Iraqi stronghold, not only with airfields and strong defenses but also with Scud missile launchers, communications buildings, and storage facilities. H-3; H-2, a similar stronghold northeast of H-3; and smaller airfields nearby were all in extreme northwestern Iraq, near the Jordan and Syrian borders, and as such were the closest Iraqi threats to Israel, which was why the Coalition wanted them struck and destroyed.

Attacks on Israel, possibly causing Israeli retaliation, most certainly would destroy the largely Arab Coalition.

Seventy-two planes were scheduled in the strike. The plan was for the point F-14s to sweep up north and west of H-3, along the Jordanian border, flushing any airborne resistance. Then they would curl east around the stronghold, which would point them toward H-2, so they could counter anything coming out of that sector, and then continue on south around H-3 for their returning exit.

If the MiGs ran from the Tomcats, they'd be sandwiched by the incoming Hornets.

The strategy was like a football play, demanding precise timing. The hole, or flush of the MiGs, whether they were shot or chased away, would only open over the targets for a short period, probably only a matter of minutes. The strikers would have to do their work then and get out. The fighters couldn't guarantee elimination of the opposition any longer, although with luck they might extend the period.

Leading the point Tomcats was Brian Fitzpatrick, now a commander and executive officer of the VF-103 Sluggers. Since testifying about the F/A-18 before Congress, he'd been surprised at a lack of repercussions and had transitioned to F-14s smoothly, winning air-to-air gunnery and missile-shooting awards and, most recently, earning a master's degree in public administration as a navy selectee to the John F. Kennedy School of Government at Harvard.

He was slated to take over the Sluggers as skipper in the not-too-distant future, but, sitting in the briefing, he was as attentive as the rest—and worried. Not only had he "tossed and turned all night" with thoughts about the mission, but the maps he had been given were out of date. They had conflicting information. He was unclear about the extreme western Iraqi border along which he was leading the point fighters.

"I was uncertain whether one airfield [that he would fly over, and thus might have to attack] was in Jordan or Iraq," he said.

He'd tried to get better maps, but hadn't succeeded. Time had run out.

He would have to make do with what he had.

Mongillo had his own special worries.

While the Hornets and A-7s shooting HARMs at the Iraqi defenses, the jammers, and the other bombers in the strike package had remote control and/or guided weapons and bombs—and therefore could stand off from the heavy defenses to deliver their payloads—the four Hornets in his division had conventional iron bombs that had to be dropped in the old-fashioned "dive" style.

That meant they would be the only planes having to go "right into the teeth of the tiger," he said.

"This is the stuff going through your mind as the brief goes

255

on," said Mongillo. "They tell you which altitude you're going to take . . . what kind of threats are there waiting for you. Where before, in practice, you'd sort of say, Yeah, yeah, no problem, now you really take a look and say, God, I didn't know there were this many SAMs that can reach up and touch me this far out. . . . We were really scared that we were going to take some serious losses."

When the overall brief was over they broke into smaller, element groups, returning to squadron ready rooms, going over specifics for each element and airplane. Friends who weren't going were extra helpful. "They'd say, Hey, you want me to help you check out your gun?" said Mongillo. "Need any equipment? You could tell what was on their minds, like, I hope I see these guys again."

Then it was time for launch.

Fox wrote in his diary: "A distant sense of dread at losing a friend [Speicher]. Small things hit me as being suddenly presumptuous—putting my laundry out this morning, for example, presumes I'll be back to get it back. I am ever so aware—now more than ever—of my total dependence on God's grace. I am choosing to be strong and courageous. Into His hands I surrender myself."

Up on the deck, Mongillo had never seen the entire flight deck and its planes loaded with real bombs. "It was weird . . . nervous . . . 30-plus airplanes slung with ordnance . . . all the plane captains and the starting crews standing by. It was just like in the movies."

The bombs had messages painted on them like "This one's for you, Saddam" and "Mess with the best, die like the rest."

He stepped to his plane and thought of his newly born daughter again.

The navy armada droned east into Saudi Arabia, dropped off its fleet of tankers, and turned sharply north toward the western tip of Iraq, increasing speed as it crossed the border.

It was midday, skies clear and sunny.

Once into Iraq, they got almost immediate calls from E-2 Hawkeye navy controllers that bandits were circling above H-3. "At that time they were telling us four [bandits]," said Fitzpatrick. He formed the four Tomcats into a wall and they accelerated out in front of the main body, radars searching.

The sweep was beginning.

Perhaps forty miles from the target, they got word that the bandits were leaving H-3, heading northeast toward H-2, which would put them in the path of elements of the strike force, which, behind the sweeping Tomcats, had already begun to deploy to various routes, including heading for H-2, for their bomb runs.

"They were running from us," said Fitzpatrick, Lieutenant Commander Dana Dervey in his back seat.

It was just as well. One less enemy gaggle to worry about—at least for the time being.

But he was still concerned about the Iraqi-Jordanian border they were supposedly flying up. An outlying airfield was approaching on their left. The old maps indicated it was in Jordan, which meant it shouldn't be a threat. But if Iraq had occupied it, as they'd heard, the airfield might send bandits against them.

The maps did not have updates.

He watched it closely as they passed to the right.

Nothing happened.

Below and in front of them was only featureless desert—no landmarks to help them verify their position. He worried that perhaps he was off course, an unlikely possibility. But anything, he knew, could happen in war—especially on first combat missions, which, for him, this was.

One after the other, however, came clues. First a major highway to Jordan, known to be both a runway for enemy planes and a route for smugglers, came into view. Then, beyond it, in the distant northeast, he recognized outlying facilities attached to H-3.

"Okay, now I know we're exactly right on," he said he thought to himself. "Perfect timing."

Although they were keeping very quiet, he radioed the others so there would be no doubt.

They would now go into the riskiest region of their plan—the northern skirt of H-3, curling up and around its heavy defenses, to catch bandits who might flee the strike before completing the skirt and exiting back south.

"It was kind of aggressive," he said, "because if we had gotten heavily engaged up north we could very easily run out of fuel and still have to get back through the SAMs to get home [which would take a lot of maneuvering]. We had real concern about being trapped up there."

But if it worked, they'd have the sandwich.

It was approximately 2:00 P.M. Clear and sunny. The four pale blue Tomcats started their swing up and around H-3, curling toward H-2, perhaps seventy-five miles northeast. As they rounded the corner, putting an outlying auxiliary landing field for H-3 between themselves and the stronghold, they got four contacts, which they judged to be bandits, coming straight at them approximately sixty-five miles away, up by H-2.

They started sorting the contacts for shots, deciding which Tomcat would take which bandit—a preliminary to locking. Almost simultaneously, Fitzpatrick got spiked from his left rear, an indication that an enemy aircraft had locked its radar on *him* and was taking aim.

The targeting was coming from the west, back in the direction of the outlying auxiliary field they had just passed, which was nearly opposite the direction in which their radars were now pointing. Looking behind, they couldn't see the spiker with their eyes. "I wasn't sure whether it was valid or not," said Fitzpatrick.

He had to make a decision. Turn to the new threat, which would take time and possibly be unproductive, or continue with the four they were getting ready to lock—birds in the hand, so to speak.

He decided to continue forward. "I was scared," he said, "but we had such a good shot."

Still, he took the necessary precautions.

Telling his wingman to guard his rear, he popped chaff and maneuvered hard, watching for "smoke in the air or anything else" that would indicate a missile coming at him.

He didn't see any.

They went back to focusing on the four threats in front, which were now closer.

"We're beak to beak," he said of the targets. Under air force ROE, they still needed, after their own electronic indications, a "cleared to fire" call from the E-2 controller orbiting in Saudi Arabia. The Tomcat crews were all disciplined, having trained a long time for this kind of shot. They planned to fire eight long-range Phoenix missiles—two per bandit—"to ensure we get a kill on each and every one."

But the controller would not respond to their continued calls, said Fitzpatrick.

The distance between the two sets of fighters rapidly decreased as Dervey and Fitzpatrick tried in vain to contact the controller. At twenty miles from the bogeys and frustrated, they decided to visually identify the targets themselves. Tomcats have long-range television cameras on board for this purpose. The drawback was that by shifting their radar modes from "track while scan," which they were in, to "single target track," they risked, if the bogeys had radar warning receivers, alerting them to the fact that they were being targeted.

But they had to do something quick or lose the shots—or worse, possibly be shot themselves—although they were getting no indication of being targeted.

Sure enough, as the Tomcats went to single locks, the bandits apparently got indications they were "spiked," because they immediately broke hard to the north and dove to try to run away, causing the Tomcats to give chase.

Why they didn't get the clear to fire is a matter of controversy. E-2 later told him, said Fitzpatrick, that they had lost the ability to communicate with the Tomcats. Fitzpatrick said that his four-ship indeed had changed radio frequencies en route because one Tomcat was having trouble receiving the preferred one. But their calls on the new frequency to E-2 were heard by other fighters in the area, he said, and they themselves could hear the E-2—as is evidenced by what happened next.

As they started to chase the north-streaking Iraqi fighters, the E-2 began calling confirmed bandits to the south, back in the direction of H-3, including two, later identified as MiG-21s, "on the nose" of Hornets coming up from the south on the Iraqi airfield. That meant Fitzpatrick's Tomcats had the 21s between them and their route home.

Burning precious gas, still having to contend with H-3's defenses, especially the ring of SAMs around it, he broke off the chase of the north-fleeing bogeys and turned the flight back south.

"Our northern targets were no longer a threat to the bombers," he said. "But these new bandits were."

By now the strike on H-3 was commencing. As they turned back south, Fitzpatrick said, he was startled to see "about forty streaks of smoke coming right at him" as supposedly smokeless HARMs shot toward the airfield's radars, trails of smoke behind them.

But the sweep plan was about to come to fruition.

The bandits in the area would either engage his Tomcats or turn south toward the ingressing Hornets.

They turned south.

The Tomcats had forced the sandwich.

En route to the tankers, it had become obvious that Fox was going to go from spare to "go-bird." One of the Sunliners' scheduled strikers had experienced a systems failure and Fox had taken his place.

Other Hornets had gone down, too.

He wasn't a spare because of deficiency. In fact, as VFA-81's operations officer, he'd chosen the strike participants himself, taking the spare because it demanded a pilot who would know everyone else's assignment, "which was a pretty difficult task."

Having taken a "knife-in-the-teeth approach" to the preparation, he'd felt ready.

However, after they'd pushed from the tanker, one of the Hornets in their sister squadron, VFA-83, had developed pressurization problems. He'd had to take over that plane's slot—wingman to VFA-83's division leader, Lieutenant Commander Chuck "Bouncer" Osborne.

While he felt confident with the Sunliner targets, he had not briefed with VFA-83.

"Suddenly I become Bouncer's wingman and he's going after a completely different target. . . . It's not that I can't do it. The targets were nearby and there's no doubt in my mind that I can. . . . But I'm shifting more mental gears here. . . . This is the first day of the war . . . my main focus and concern [were] the very difficult SAM envelopes . . . the HARM and the jamming and everything else that we had to do. . . . It's just that I am spooled up for another target."

The mission, in other words, was not starting out well for him.

The four Hornets moved across the border in an offset box—Mongillo and McKee approximately a mile apart in the lead section, Fox and Osborne a mile behind them and offset in the slots to the right.

It was the best formation for mutual support and visual look-out.

"I was as psyched as I've ever been for a swim meet or football game," Fox later wrote. Mongillo said the same. "I must have done my combat checklist five times. You don't want to forget anything."

They were ingressing at upwards of thirty thousand feet and six hundred miles per hour, just below the altitude where their wing tips would make contrails so as not to draw attention. Ahead at H-3, the MiG-sweeping F-14s and other advance elements were already stirring things up. HARM shooters and Jammers were beginning their assaults. Radio calls of bogeys and bandits became more urgent and frequent.

He was scared, wrote Mongillo, mostly of "failing my duties as a wingman in combat . . . and I'm certain the others in the strike were scared too."

He was right.

Bombing was their primary mission and that's where their focus was, although their weapons switches, for the ingress, were set for air-to-air in case an enemy fighter slipped past the F-14s.

"We felt like we were going into the belly of the beast," Fox later told a newspaper reporter.

As they got closer, the four Hornets moved into a loose wall, side by side, and started to climb in order to get above the bursts and be able then to dodge them as they swooped down to deliver their ordnance. From left to right it was Mongillo, McKee, Fox, and Osborne. Their eyes were outside the cockpit, trying to keep good SA, but mostly scanning below, looking for SAM bursts.

They had intelligence on many of the SAM sites. It was the ones they didn't know about that worried them.

The closer they got, the more frequent became the radio calls. The battle was commencing. One aspect in particular was confusing. The navy controllers, by order of Coalition headquarters, were using an air force code word for the geographical reference point—in this case, a small airfield northwest of H-3—from which all targets were computed. The code word was "Manny." While the navy pilots had been given the code word, they had not practiced with it.

"It was pretty basic," said Mongillo about what was expected of them, "but the hardest thing for a fighter pilot to do in the midst of a fight is to try and figure out reciprocal heading. There were so many calls being made, bandits and bogeys, broken transmissions, people [talking over] each other on the radio."

He just tuned it out, he said, concentrating instead on "my main task of being a good wingman and putting my bombs on target."

So did Fox.

"I'm a relatively senior guy," he said, "almost three thousand hours in the airplane . . . four cruises . . . seven hundred traps. . . . I pride myself as a strike leader and being able to keep the big picture." But as so many in their first combat do, he got buck fever. "I was unable to keep the big picture on that first day's strike. It became easier later . . . [but] it was just hard for me to assimilate this 'Manny' business."

He'd written it down on his knee card, but "every fiber in my body was focused on finding the target and bombing it. . . . I mean, bottom line, I'm looking for SA-6s . . . I'm just not paying attention to the radio anymore. That's how spun up you are."

At about thirty-five miles from the target, both Fox and Mongillo—still tuning out the confusing calls—punched their weapons buttons back to air-to-ground. Although it was a little early for that, neither wanted to chance diving on their target with the wrong weapons setting.

They were just minutes from the bombing run.

It was approximately at this time—with their radios calling "Bandits!" and "Manny"—that Fitzpatrick's four Tomcats, somewhere in the process of rounding H-3's northeastern corner, were forcing the two MiG-21s to head south—right into the searching radars of McKee's four northbound Hornets.

But the Hornet pilots hadn't yet detected them.

Fox suspects this was because they were all still looking for SAMs. E-2 controllers, tapes later showed, he said, were trying to alert them, calling the two 21s in relation to "Manny." But none of them heard it, he said. Then, he said, an E-2 controller pointedly called McKee's mission call sign "Four hundred" with "Bandits on your nose, fifteen [miles]."

Mongillo: "Right away I'm like, Holy cow, what did he say? Did I hear that right? 'Bandits on our nose at fifteen! How can that be? There's F-14s out there [who should have taken care of that]. But as I'm thinking that, I'm switching back to air-to-air real quick. Just a flick of the button and I'm a fighter again. That's what's amazing about the Hornet."

Apparently only he and Fox heard the four hundred "bandit" call (Fox only later remembering hearing it, but acting accordingly anyway). McKee, he said, did not. The leader had mistakenly heard "bogeys"—not yet confirmed enemies. All he knew, therefore, was that the BVR contacts were not returning the proper electronic signals—an indication, but not a confirmation, that they were bandits. (Fox said the "bandit" call was almost subliminal in his mind, and he later realized that he heard "Four hundred" as "Hornet," which was testament perhaps to how unconsciously tuned in to the situation—since the two words are phonetically similar—he really was.)

In any case, he, too, flicked his weapons switches back to air-to-air missiles.

The two enemy flights were now closing toward each other at over a thousand miles per hour, the MiGs climbing from below, afterburners in full blast.

What happened next occurred rapidly.

All four Hornets initiated independent locks, Fox on the lead 21, Mongillo on the trailer. But, because everything was happening so fast, no one knew what the other was doing.

From an ROE standpoint, Mongillo said he definitely had heard the call "Bandit" from the controller. In addition, both he and Fox knew that the MiGs were not returning the proper electronic signals, so both of them, with the E-2 bandit call, felt they had satisfied the ROE requirement of two independent confirmations.

They were both ready to fire.

But McKee, having only the single electronic indication, felt he needed a second confirmation, and so—in spite of the danger to himself posed by the rapidly closing MiGs, both of which could have forward quarter missiles—he called that he was moving out ahead of the division to get a confirming VID.

But the 21s had now closed to less than ten miles away, and Fox, actually finally seeing them with his own eyes, said he became certain they were not friendlies. "They were just specks," he said, "little pinpricks—certainly too small to be F-14s. . . . It was just a process of elimination. . . . There was just no doubt in my mind that something that small was a MiG-21."

He fired the Sidewinder, but it was smokeless, and he lost sight of it as he concentrated on the target. Thinking then that the Sidewinder had malfunctioned and been lost, he quickly fired a second missile, a Sparrow. "I said, Okay, I wasted the first one but that guy's not going to get away."

Not more than a few seconds later, however, his first missile, the Sidewinder, hit the targeted MiG with a "bright flash," causing it to erupt in fire and black smoke. But because he thought it had gone stupid, he assumed the hit was someone else's.

His Sparrow then impacted the MiG, which he could now see was tan, increasing the fire and damage.

He recorded the hits at 14:05:00 (2:05 P.M.) and 14:05:05, respectively—roughly five seconds apart—thinking that, at best, he was sharing the kill.

Meanwhile, Mongillo was afraid that the MiGs might be 29s, in which case they definitely were in range to shoot the Hornets in the face. But he was also grappling with what McKee had told him in the morning brief: Shoot a friendly and don't return.

He didn't want to make a mistake.

"They've told me he's bad," he said he was thinking at the time. "But what did the XO say? All these things are racing in my mind. Finally, I just couldn't take it anymore."

He fired his Sparrow with the trailing MiG only two and a half miles from the Hornet's nose—a hair away from minimum range.

"[The missile] pulled lead to the right as soon as it came off the rail," he later wrote, "so much so that I thought it had gone stupid." But then it corrected itself and zipped to a "spectacular direct hit," almost right in front of him, causing the 21 "to disintegrate in a sheet of yellow flame," which passed beneath him.

His Sparrow had impacted only seconds after Fox's missiles had hit their target. But Mongillo had been so concentrated on his own shot that he was unaware of the other shootdown.

He made the first victory call: "Mongo. Splash one."

Hearing the call, and watching the wounded lead MiG go blazing beneath him, Fox figured it was Mongillo who had beat him to the leader, and Osborne, who quickly called an acknowledging "Splash two," who had gotten the second kill.

"I figured the best I'd get would be a RBI [run batted in]," he said, "and rocked up on my left wing and watched [the MiG] go under. I could see a glint of sun on the canopy . . . the delta wing with a huge plume of flame." It surprised him that the MiG was still intact. "I guess I got that from watching movies like *Top Gun* where they just explode."

Hearing Osborne's call, Mongillo turned and realized what had happened behind him—at least to the extent that there had been a second kill.

The two Hornet drivers had just scored the fifth and sixth air-to-air kills of Desert Storm, incidentally becoming the first single-seat navy fighter pilots to down MiGs since September 1968, when an F-8 Crusader pilot had last done it during the Vietnam War.

But only Mongillo was sure he was a MiG killer. And no one in the advancing Hornets had any time to reflect.

No sooner had Mongillo looked back from "the unbelievable scene," he said, than "bammo, Bouncer gets a lock on somebody twenty to twenty-five miles on our nose. I'm thinking, Uh oh, there's still more after us."

The bogeys were dead ahead and rising from the H-3 area. But they weren't as fast as the previous two and cockpit indications did not identify them as friend or foe. In fact, later, their tapes showed that E-2 controllers had again been calling the targets as "bandits," with coordinates from "Manny." And again, it appears, the Hornets had been tuning them out.

All but McKee got locks and the four shot straight for the bogeys to make a VID, Mongillo calling closure distances as they sped closer.

Because the contacts were high and slow, Fox worried that they might be bait for a trap that the Iraqis were known to have used against Iranian F-4s in their war. But the bogeys ran, and while they debated a few seconds about whether to chase them or not—because the Hornets were certainly close enough to have fired valid shots, and thus might have killed more—the mission won out.

They were by that time almost at their time-over-target, and bombing was the reason they were on the strike.

Still cautious in case the bandits returned, they banked from them in preparation for delivering their bombs.

Fitzpatrick watched the two MiG-21s die as his Tomcats rounded H-3 and started exiting south. "We were probably fifteen to twenty miles away. I could look over to my right and see these guys blowing up."

He'd heard Vietnam War strike tapes and they always had "chatter." But the Hornet pilots were "real casual. . . . The fellow in the lead bomber [presumably Fox's leader, McKee] just said, 'All right, we got a contact here. I'll go down and take a look' . . . I mean, great voice . . . no emotion whatsoever . . . then boom. The MiGs got it."

It was time for Fitzpatrick's division to exit—all part of the plan.

A raging battle surrounded them as they gunned it back toward the Iraqi border—warplanes bombing, firing HARMs, or "jamming" enemy radars with special standoff electronic equipment; other fighters chasing bandits within sight of them. They still had E-2 communications problems. So once they had reached a "certain safe point," said Fitzpatrick, they switched their radios over to air force E-3 AWACS controllers and learned that two bandits were on their tails approximately twenty miles back.

It was decision time again.

Shooting a MiG was what he had "worked so hard all these years [to do]," Fitzpatrick later said. But by the time he could turn and try to engage—because he had to put his radar beam on them before he could get a lock and launch—the bandits could have already gotten him in range and fired a missile and then he'd be in trouble.

He'd not only be jeopardizing himself but his wingman—if not all four planes.

They were low on fuel, already well on their way home, the bandits not an immediate threat.

What he reluctantly decided to do was vector another fighter that was in a better position to challenge. "It was my MiG," he later said, "but it was the right thing to do."

In his cockpit was new software for a "data link" that aided SA. It showed him where other navy fighters were. He saw that Chuck Wyatt, leader of two Tomcats protecting an EA-6B Prowler, was streaking under him with his wingman, heading north—which was toward the pursuing bandits.

Wyatt, a VF-74 pilot, wouldn't have to turn around. He was already in a firing position, nose to nose with the enemy planes.

Fitzpatrick radioed Wyatt.

As it turned out, Wyatt had already been alerted to the ban-dits—later identified as F-1s—which was why he was flying where he was. He was so tensed up and concentrated because of the threats to the Prowler and himself that he never heard Fitz-patrick's call until he replayed his tape in the debrief.

"I was just trying to go moment to moment," he said. "Your brain feels the size of a pea. I mean, add six and six. What's six and six? It gets that bad."

His not hearing Fitzpatrick, however, didn't really matter. The F-1s soon turned and fled rather than fight. Later, Fitzpatrick, who was already much farther south by that time, lamented not getting a MiG, not so much one of the F-1s, because he still rea-soned he had been right not to have turned on them, but one of the earlier bandits they had targeted and locked north of H-3.

"Flubbed at the last second because of a lousy radio or lousy controller," he said, "I don't know which. . . . It just kills me. . . . You wonder what might have been. . . . A day doesn't go by that I don't think about it."

McKee's Hornets took forty-five-degree angles from as high as thirty thousand feet and dove on their targets, which were differ-ent and dispersed.

Fox was the only one who could not quickly find his pri-mary—a product of his having been switched at the last mo-ment—and so chose a secondary: a large, white, concrete hangar that was easy to see.

"It was related to supporting airplanes or something that we want to cripple straightaway," he said, "and I've got the ord-nance to do it."

They were each carrying four Mark 84 two-thousand-pounders.

At about seventeen thousand feet, Fox started pulling up, which, in effect, would "dive-toss" the bombs. A plot line that he flew on his HUD told him exactly when and where to do it, but he had to enter the appropriate math, correct for high winds, and fly the line correctly.

Nothing was assured, and he wanted to do well.

"You just feel, Gosh, am I going to screw this up? What if the bombs don't come off or something else stupid happens? You really don't want to come all the way and then screw up the bomb run."

It wasn't just a simple dive.

Fox was roaring down into the heart of H-3s defenses, its triple-A, which he could see firing up at him, peppering the air with the gray "popcorn" bursts, so-called because they flashed yellow before spewing the deadly flak.

But as they'd planned, he'd been able to elude the flak. And, as he started pulling up, feeling the sudden "thud" and the lightening of the Hornet as the bombs were loosed, he'd "rocked" up a wing for a quick look on the other side, which was not standard procedure, as speeding away was.

"But I hadn't come all this way not to see the results," Fox said.

So, as he was supposed to, Fox jinked and released chaff along with taking his look. What he saw brought his first "elation" that day—his four Mark 84s were "flying formation together," headed straight for the top of the hangar.

But he also saw closer triple-A flashes, and the corkscrew tails of several hand-held SAMs spiraling up toward him.

Fox jinked again, fighting to regain speed and altitude, "madly pumping out chaff and unconsciously doing just a whole lot of other things."

Still jinking—the SAMs missed him—he "rocked" a wing up again to grab a final look "just in time to see the four Mark 84s walk right through the hangar"—four direct hits in rapid-fire succession. "I'm exhilarated," he said.

Fox still thought he'd been beaten to the MiG kill by Osborne, and "the bottom line was that we had briefed to go in there and drop bombs."

He'd just done that about as well as he could.

But they still had to get out.

Suddenly worried about bandits again, still jostling violently, striving to get higher faster, Fox anxiously looked for the other Hornets. About seven miles away, toward the east, he finally saw McKee and Mongo in combat spread. He sped over and "snuggled up between them."

He felt safe again.

Osborne joined them and they started back south toward the border and a tanker, where they would replenish for the long flight back to the Red Sea.

As they exited the area, they flew east of the downed MiGs,

two columns of black smoke rising above their desert wreck-ages—a sight he said he will remember forever.

McKee was big on radio silence so they didn't talk except for essential communication. But Fox got a chance to see that Osborne and McKee still had all their missiles, and Mongo had lost only one.

It began to dawn on him that "Hmmmm, just maybe that Sidewinder had worked."

Maybe the first MiG was his.

But he wouldn't let himself dwell on that—not yet.

They still had to get home.

Only after he'd pulled beneath the tanker, safely across the border, and the boom operator kept excitedly gesturing to his wing tip did he finally let himself go.

"The Hornet's got the Sidewinders on the wing tips," he said, "and the little guy was grinning and giving me a thumbs-up."

Emotion suddenly flooded him. He started to choke up.

Fox had made it through alive. His buddies were alive, too. They'd done what they'd set out to do, and he'd become a MiG killer as well.

"I can't describe the feeling of accomplishment and relief," he said.

They had survived and triumphed.

But the euphoria was short-lived. He was to be back in harm's way that night.

17

KELK AND GRAETER had returned to Tabuk before sunrise that first mission and therefore had not flown victory rolls before landing. It was still dark. No one would have seen them.

However, the celebration on the ground was just as heartfelt.

"The crew chiefs are just jumping up and down," said Graeter. "It was their first chance to do their jobs in a combat environment and they were barely able to control themselves."

But the Tarmac backslaps were cut short because "we didn't know at that point if we were going to be targeted by Scuds," he said.

The war was still only hours old.

Graeter was leading a strike the next evening—the night of the seventeenth, Saudi time. He had time to sleep maybe six hours before preparing—if the adrenaline would let him. But Kelk and the others in the "Pennzoil" four-ship—Tollini, Pitts, and Williams—were scheduled to take off again at 11:30 A.M., only a few hours away.

"I went back to my room and pretty much tossed and turned," said Kelk. Finally, he fell asleep for perhaps the last thirty minutes. But they all had the Dexedrine "go pills" if they needed them. And when he went into the early morning brief, an intelligence officer told him that his kill had been confirmed.

There was little time for reflection except for a sense of accomplishment at having survived. As far as killing the enemy pilot—if, in fact, that had happened—he had no problem about it whatsoever, a determination that echoed the feelings of most of the Americans who had downed Iraqi planes so far.

"It was honest combat," he said. "He was trying to get me and we were definitely in conflict. He wasn't a guy just tooling around minding his own business."

The mission they were going on that afternoon was an eight-ship MiG sweep in advance of a large strike force going up to bomb Al Taqaddum, a weapons and industrial center about twenty miles west of Baghdad.

Although this was hundreds of miles east of H-2 and H-3, they'd be arriving on target about the time the tail end of the navy strike from *Saratoga* and *Kennedy*—which had included Fitzpatrick, Fox, and Mongillo—was exiting from H-2.

Leading the sweep was Captain Chuck "Sly" Magill, the Marine exchange pilot who had flown with Paco Geisler on the Panama CAP. A graduate not only of navy Topgun but the Corps's Topgun-like course at Yuma, Arizona, Magill, a former F-18 pilot in the Corps, was one of the 58th Tactical Fighter Squadron's four weapons experts—along with Graeter, Tollini, and Kelk—usually entrusted with the squadron's most important tactical missions.

"We were leading thirty-two F-16s with two-thousand-pounders . . . four Wild Weasels, four EF-111s, another eight F-15s from Langley that were flying support," said the Arizona State graduate, "probably about fifty airplanes."

It was the 58th's first daylight mission, and the Coalition's first attack against Al Taqaddum airfield, which had as many as seventy fighters, according to intelligence estimates. About thirty miles west of Al Taqaddum was Al Asad airfield, which had a concentration of MiG-29s and also had not been hit.

If the Iraqis marshaled strong resistance from the two airfields—and the 58th couldn't repel it—the strike group couldn't go in.

It was Magill's job to see that didn't happen.

In addition, on the first leg of the sweep, they were going to have to fly past Mudaysis—the small airstrip near where Kelk and Graeter had recently gotten their kills—to make sure it was still neutralized.

They would need all eight Eagles.

Flying in Magill's four-ship, call-signed "Zerex," were his young wingman, First Lieutenant Mark Arriola, whom Magill had been flying with throughout Desert Shield, and with whom he'd forged a special bond based on their shared experiences and Arriola's wingmanship; the other flight lead, thirty-three-year-old Captain Rhory "Hoser" Draeger, a Wausau, Wisconsin, native temporarily assigned to the 58th from another squadron because of his experience; and Draeger's wingman, thirty-year-old Captain Tony Schiavi, a former football player from Assumption College in Worcester, Massachusetts, who had been married only two weeks before leaving for Saudi.

The other four-ship was Rick Tollini's "Citgo."

"We knew they didn't fly much at night," said Schiavi, "but we didn't know what to expect in the day." Tension about the mission had kept him from getting any sleep the night before, "but it's amazing what the human body can do on adrenaline," he said.

They took off at 11:14 A.M., according to Schiavi's log, and ran into a problem tanking just below the Iraqi border.

Although mission particulars like tanking were supposed to be precoordinated by headquarters long before takeoff—which Magill thought had been done—he could not get one of two scheduled tankers to the eight-ship's tanking point because it was considerably west of the normal tanking tracks.

"You're so nervous about the overall mission," he said, "tanking is not where you want it to break down."

Eventually, however—borrowing another squadron's tanker—everyone got gas.

Even as they tanked, AWACS controllers were already alerting them to bandits.

"AWACS is calling two MiG-29s near the target," said Schiavi. At the same time, he said, Draeger's radar was malfunctioning, and Schiavi therefore thought that since his was working he'd get a chance at one of the MiGs, an opportunity he was itching for. But "by some miraculous act, right at push time, his radar comes back up and we start heading north."

The sweep was on.

272

Leaving the strikers back with the tankers, they ingressed at approximately twenty-eight thousand feet, the clear day giving them almost unlimited visibility. They were in a semi-tiered wall, Magill's "Zerex" on the western flank, Tollini's "Citgo" about ten miles back and to the east.

"It was a beautiful sight," said Magill, "eight Eagles crossing the border together." He later said he felt proud and honored that the air force had allowed him—a Marine—to lead.

They roared due north—Mudaysis beyond the horizon, dead ahead.

"We didn't know if they still had fighters that were flyable there," said Magill. The Fulcrums being called by AWACS were up by the targets near Baghdad—perhaps a hundred miles farther north and east. "But if I had gone straight for them and the Iraqis had launched from Mudaysis, then we could have been in a sandwich."

He was worried about a trap, wondering if the two 29s were just bait to get them up where they could be overwhelmed by a massive launch.

He didn't want to get suckered.

With their radars, they scanned the airspace over and around Mudaysis, but found nothing threatening. Still, Magill didn't want to "wake up some guy out there sunbathing or something," he said. And so, about twenty miles before overflying the small airstrip, he veered the sweep northeast, out of sight of Mudaysis and into their route's second leg—toward the Al Asad and Al Taqaddum airfields and the CAPing 29s, which were roughly between and a little south of the two bases.

They were now on a diagonal leading straight toward the bandits. Tollini wanted to take his four-ship north toward Al Asad. He expected to find a lot of enemy planes there. But Magill was still worried about a trap and wanted Tollini's Eagles to stay with him for the added firepower.

Finally, at about forty miles from the CAPing MiG-29s, Magill felt secure enough to let Tollini go. The two four-ships crossed one below the other, Tollini's "Citgo" streaking forward north, Magill's "Zerex" coming from the western flank to flow northeast toward the protecting MiGs.

The first task was to get a second identification on the BVR MiGs with their radars, which they started doing.

Almost immediately, they ran into SAMs.

"Everybody's headset started giving alarm," said Magill. The tones went from steady beeping (for being targeted) to high-pitched screams (for lock). Schiavi called out that he saw the smoke of at least one of the missiles, meaning it was already on its way.

Magill did not. But there was no time for him to search—only act.

"Our hearts were really pumping," he later said.

They were still in a wall, at around twenty-eight thousand feet. He ordered immediate countermeasures, including a fast break. Almost simultaneously, the four Eagles released their auxiliary gas tanks for easier maneuvering and sliced downward, dropping chaff; Magill and Arriola breaking right, Draeger and Schiavi to the left.

"Mark Arriola will tell you it looked like a World War II movie," said Magill, "four fighters flying together and all of a sudden eight tanks come off at the exact same time."

But the SAM attack was just the kind of threat that could screw up their mission.

"Your wingman can lose sight of you," said Magill. "You can lose your situational awareness of where the threat is."

Prior to the SAM breaks, they had been tracking the MiG-29s on their radars, getting ready to get second confirmations that they were not friendlies. But after diving nearly ten thousand feet, racing out independently from the SAM sites to break the missiles' locks, they all—incredibly—recovered back together.

"I look out and I've got my wingman," he said, "Rhory Draeger's got his. We're three to five miles apart, Rhory's got the contacts back on the radar, and we haven't lost anything."

He credited their constant training, at such exercises as Red Flag, for smooth regroup.

They pressed on, the SAM site alarms retreating in their headsets, the CAPing MiGs regaining their focus.

"We're about thirty to thirty-five miles away now," he said. "I'm locking them up, but it's a real quick sample just to find out their [direction], range, and altitude."

Locking any longer would have alerted the bandits that they were being targeted and they might have run away.

On the other hand, the information he was getting from the

quick locks was surprising, making him worry again that perhaps the MiGs were indeed setting a trap. At fifteen hundred feet altitude and 360 knots, the two Fulcrums were both low and slow, and seemed to have no clue that there was any danger. Then, as they watched them on the radar, the bandits made a casual turn in their CAPing oval—from coming south toward the Eagles to go back north—literally offering "Zerex" their tails.

"That to me was such an invitation," said Magill about the classic mistake.

He wondered if they weren't just making it too easy and now suddenly heading back toward their base so the larger MiG force could swoop in. Further radar sweeps disclosed no ambushers, but if they had missed anything, they could be in trouble.

"The blood's really pumping now," he said, "and I say, 'Push it up! Push it up!' " He was asking for more speed from the others so they could run the MiGs down before they landed, shoot them and get out.

The MiGs were still beyond shooting range.

"Zerex" descended, closing quickly as it dropped.

Then, at about twenty miles away, the MiGs suddenly turned again—this time in a more aggressive manner—back south, toward the onrushing Eagles.

"Their speed goes from 350 to 550," said Magill. "They're after something. They're not coming right at me. They're offset a little bit, so I don't know if they're trying to end-run us like standard Soviet doctrine would do or they're chasing somebody else."

Later, after conferring with *Kennedy* F-14 crew members from the strike to H-2 who had come east and said they were being targeted, he became convinced that the MiGs were going after F-14s.

But at this moment, he didn't know that.

The sudden turn back now meant that the closure rates had heightened dramatically. The MiGs were rapidly coming into range.

It was now or never.

By prearrangement, Magill and Draeger would do the shooting. Arriola and Schiavi would "sanitize"—search the surrounding skies for other bandits; deal with them if necessary.

The kills would take teamwork. Each of them knew that.

The two MiGs were in a formation their Russian instructors

called "Echelon Bearing"—the wingman a mile behind his leader, swinging in a rough sixty-degree cone. The fluid movement made him more flexible, and it gave Magill and Draeger trouble locking the bandit each wanted.

But they finally did.

The MiGs were now less than fourteen miles away, approaching the Eagles' firing ranges. The four-ship sped closer, descending farther as it did. It was at a slight angle to the closing MiGs, who were still looking like they were trying to make an end run.

Draeger shot first—a Sparrow—because, considering the angle at which they were approaching, the wingman's rear swinging made him closer than the leader at the moment the MiGs came into range.

Magill shot a Sparrow a moment later.

As the missiles left their airplanes, both pilots radioed "Fox One"—as was their habit in training—and immediately began turning to the outside in case they themselves had been targeted. The approximately sixty-degree offset moves would also enable them to come back, should they need to shoot again.

But as Magill did this, everything seemed to slow down.

"The AIM-7 is a fairly fast missile," he said, "but this thing comes off at almost slow motion and I could see the yellow band on it and the brown band which means it's a [live] missile, and not a training missile. . . . It just hung out there . . . seemed like a bloody eternity."

In Vietnam, the same phenomenon occurred to even the most seasoned veterans when they finally shot in a real life-or-death dogfight.

But this was Iraq, 1991.

As Magill watched the Sparrow, it dipped nearly straight down, and although the MiGs were considerably below them, the missile didn't seem to him to be functioning correctly. "So I immediately come back, center the dot, and take another shot," he said.

By now the low-flying MiGs were close enough to be seen with their eyes. "They were beautiful brand-new gray-and-blue camouflage," said Magill, "just an amazing sight."

The Fulcrums had shot out from some low-lying clouds and were barely two miles away when Draeger's missile hit the wingman "dead center, right in the nose," said Magill. It made a red-orange "flash," he said, as metal shards exploded out of the war-head at thousands of feet per second.

Seconds later, Magill's Sparrow—the one he thought had gone stupid—hit the leader in the right wing root, his second missile impacting the resultant fireball, which he thought would have been bigger in both MiGs had they had more gas.

"But they'd been CAPing a long while," he said.

The MiGs were only five hundred feet above the desert and seemed to crash right away. But Magill was already too far offset to look at them, and even if he had not been he wouldn't have stuck around.

"Any decent guy in fighters will tell you you can't hang around to see what you shot," he said. "You want to get away from there as quickly as possible because you shoot the first two, and there's usually someone behind them who will gun your brains out."

He was "overwhelmed" by what had happened, he said. "I mean, we've just busted through SAMs and shot two Fulcrums which I thought was one of the best airplanes in the world . . . [but] we're also a hundred and sixty miles north of the border and you don't want to let up."

Pouring on the speed, quickly setting his radar to "auto guns," which would automatically target anything up to ten miles in front of him, Magill charged the four-ship through the area and ahead, perhaps five miles, until sand below them began to sprout vegetation. That meant they were coming up on the Euphrates River and thus nearing downtown Baghdad, which, because of its heavy defenses, was "a place we didn't want to be in."

He decided it was time to go home.

But which way?

If they went back the way they'd come—from the west—it would take more gas and expose them to the SAMs.

"I had already expended two missiles," he said. "We only had one external gas tank left on the airplanes. I elected to go back south."

It was the shortest route.

The four-ship sliced back hard right. As it did, the pilots heard strikers over the radios cheering what they'd just done.

"It made you feel good," he said.

But they were not out of the fight yet.

Tollini's four-ship had not encountered any MiGs and was already exiting to the west.

"Zerex" would go home alone.

Knowing the strikers were now streaming in, Magill zoomed the four-ship up. "I climbed a little bit higher than I wanted to," he said, to approximately twenty thousand feet, where he felt he didn't have to worry about "fratricide" from the incoming strikers, whom he knew, after the radio show they'd just given them, "would be itching to shoot."

But the higher altitude made it easier for the Baghdad SAMs, which, in this case, turned out not to be as sophisticated as the previous ones—but were just as scary.

"I get aural warnings," he said. "I look on my radar warning receiver and it tells me they're locked on me from my nine o'clock."

He looked left and, sure enough, saw at least three "giant telephone poles" lifting toward him. They were the old SA-2 SAMs of Vietnam War vintage. "It was the strangest thing, like watching mini space shuttles. You can see the booster and the sustain phase."

The rockets would roar up above them, then turn back and relentlessly dog.

"The first one was easy," said Magill. "It was the second and third you had to watch out for. They're coming from all angles. We had to jettison our last tanks and do more evasive maneuvering."

He broke several locks and was finally able to defeat the tenacious missiles. But suddenly his gas gauge was on empty, and "Bitchin' Betty," the computer voice in his cockpit, started "yelling 'Bingo, bingo,' and then 'Fuel low, fuel low,' " he said.

He was low in the sky and very fast, and the noise inside the Eagle cockpit in those conditions sounded like a "freight train," he said. "So I've got screaming in my headset. SAMs are going off. It got real chaotic. I'm thinking, Geez, man, maybe I got hit?"

It was pucker time again. He'd survived all this only to go down because of a fuel problem?

Magill had Arriola swing in and take a look. In the meantime, he checked with Draeger about Draeger's fuel supply. Arriola couldn't find any visible problem and Draeger said he still had seven thousand pounds.

"I'd been doing the same things Draeger had been doing," he concluded, "so it had to be a gauge problem."

Twenty miles farther and the danger seemed behind them. They streaked to the border, and after tanking, the pressure slowly lifting, he and Draeger decided to do victory rolls when they got to Tabuk—something that might get them in trouble, "but I was a Marine and probably could get away with it," he said.

They arrived in a battle box—two in front, two behind.

It was a beautiful, clear afternoon.

"We're five hundred and fifty knots into the overhead. Then we broke. Number two [Arriola] and number four [Schiavi] landed. I go around full AB [afterburner], do a snap roll, and land. Rhory does the same. You wouldn't believe the troops. I mean, the whole base was out there. They were going nuts, almost crying."

The war was only approximately twelve hours long and the 58th already had five of the eight Allied air-to-air kills.

The next day Magill got word that his wife, Lisa, had just given birth to their first baby, a girl named Caitlin.

18

BAGGING A MIG WAS IMPORTANT, but this—at least officially—was even bigger.

It was January 19, the dawning of the third day of the war, and despite the fact that Tollini's four-ship pilots had gotten little sleep since the shooting started, his Eagles were positioned for what their commanding officers hoped would be a major coup, maybe even a war breaker.

Intelligence believed that Saddam Hussein might, sometime this first light, try to escape Iraq. In the tradition of the famous World War II mission to kill Japanese Admiral Isoroku Yamamoto, "Citgo" had been ordered to shoot down the Iraqi leader at all costs.

"It was a big deal," said Pitts about the spur-of-the-moment mission, which had Tollini, him, Kelk, and Williams waiting anxiously on a tanker up near the border as the sun rose over the desert horizon.

"Somebody thought he was going to jump in one of his military transports and try to leave the country," he said. "We called it the 'Buster Mission,' because it was invented by General Buster Glosson. He actually came to our wing and promised us, stood there right in front of us and promised that if we had to run out of gas to shoot that airplane down he'd make sure we were picked up. We knew, as did General Glosson, that we could save a lot of lives if we were successful."

They had very little information other than that AWACS would direct them to the plane, and that by flying in a military plane, the Iraqi leader would be a legal military target.

But the vector never came.

The sun rose higher.

"After six hours, he hadn't launched," said Pitts, "so they sent us home." No sooner had they landed, he said, than "the ops officer said, 'As quick as you can get gas, they need you to take off and do a sweep.' "

A squadron that was scheduled couldn't make it. Schedulers knew they could count on the 58th because its pilots were taking everything they could get.

More chance of getting a kill.

It was "go pill" time, early afternoon. They would be on the ground for roughly forty-five minutes and take off again.

They did not know it but they were on their way to taking part in some of the scariest daylight air-to-air combat of the war—the last time the Iraqis would really try to fight in the air.

Flying and fighter piloting hadn't come easy to Cesar "Rico" Rodriguez.

"I wasn't what you consider your 'golden hands' kind of boy," he said. "I always had to work harder, be as dedicated and driven as possible, because I didn't have the natural gifts some of the others had."

There had been a time during his initial flight training in 1982 at Vance Air Force Base, Oklahoma, when Rodriguez thought he might wash out. "I said, Shit, I guess I might as well go to navigator's school so I could keep flying and try again later."

But he'd "always been able to count on my attitude," he said, "giving it more than just a [75 to 100] percent effort. And when you see someone who's giving it an effort, they give you the benefit of the doubt."

Still, in his early thirties and a captain, he'd come up the hard way. No glamorous F-15 or F-16 right out of basic. He'd gotten an A-10, a Warthog, then instructed in AT-38 trainers before getting assigned to Eagles in 1988.

But Paco Geisler liked the bull-chested Texas native who called Puerto Rico, where his parents live, home, and recruited him into the 58th.

Geisler: "I thought he had potential. He was always so reserved and he was an A-10 guy and, of course, the guys in the squadron went holy shit. But I said, No. He can do all right. . . . He had a hard time at Eglin. There were times when I said, Rico, you're not hacking it, buddy, and he buckled down hard. He never gave up."

His father had been a U.S. Army colonel, and he had moved around a lot as a kid, graduating from the Citadel in 1981. He worked out with weights and carried a concealed .38-caliber pistol under his arm when he flew in Desert Storm in case he got shot down—and a hundred-dollar bill in his wallet for a bribe in case he couldn't use the gun.

He wasn't on the "varsity" like Tollini, Kelk, Graeter, Magill, or Pitts. So on January 19—as Tollini's four-ship waited to shoot Saddam—he and his wingman, Craig Underhill, a former C-130 navigator from Midland, Michigan, who had also been flying the Eagle for only a few years, were being paired for the first time to help guard an AWACS control plane just south of the Iraqi border.

It wasn't one of the plum sweeps—a mission with the best chance of engaging MiGs. It was hanging back on the Saudi side of the border, flying racetracks, knowing the real action was up north, because the Iraqi fighters had not been coming that far south.

But they were happy to be going out. Underhill was a little disappointed because he'd been scheduled to go on the sweep and then had been pulled at the last moment. But they both knew that at this early stage in the war anything could happen.

Tollini's four-ship got gas and started to form up for the sweep, which was scheduled to take them north up central Iraq in advance of an F-16 strike on Al Qaim, a gas and germ warfare center northwest of Al Asad.

"As soon as we came off the tanker," said Pitts, "AWACS started calling MiGs close to the border."

The MiGs were in two groups. One was directly in front of them. Two MiG-25 Foxbats, perhaps fifty miles away. They were at ten thousand feet, coming fast. The other group was roughly the same distance away but northeast, toward Baghdad—a pair of MiG-29s.

Tollini's "Citgo" shot north and started searching with their radars.

They got blips from both groups at about forty miles. Since the Eagles had already gotten confirmation of "bandit" status from AWACS, and their cockpit indications were the same, they prepared for relatively easy BVR shots—right to the faces of the oncoming enemy planes. Being on the eastern flank of the advancing four-ship, Pitts thought he might get a shot at one of the easterly Fulcrums, but they suddenly turned back north.

Either they were racetracking on a CAP or trying to "bait" the Eagles. In any case, they were "no longer threats"—at least for the time being.

"We were kind of stiff-arming them," said Pitts.

They turned attention solely to the Foxbats, which had now closed to around twenty miles. Both groups were at ten thousand feet, still head-on with each other. Sorting and targeting, Tollini and Kelk prepared to shoot when the Foxbats came into range, Tollini actually locking one of them. Pitts and Williams searched the surrounding skies on their radars for other possible bandits.

Suddenly, the Foxbats turned ninety degrees and executed a "beam" maneuver, heading west and perpendicular to the Eagles' line of flight. As it was supposed to, the tactic banished the Foxbats from the four Eagle radars and broke Tollini's lock.

Now the Eagles were in trouble, because two MiGs were presumably in range of shooting them and unseen—until, luckily, at about five miles in front of them and very low, approximately five hundred feet from the desert floor—they picked up the radar blip of one of the Foxbats rocketing in front of them, from west to east, at seven hundred knots.

It was another "beam" maneuver, said Pitts, but this time it was being executed too close to the Eagles to work. "Since I was on the east side, it was easiest for me to engage him," he said.

He radioed Tollini his intention and dove after the MiG as it passed below.

As he did so, the MiG began a wide, 270-degree arcing turn beneath him, back south, west, and eventually north. The large oval and resultant loss of speed by the 25 enabled Pitts, who had visually acquired the MiG as he'd converted on it, to cut across the Iraqi's turn circle and rendezvous on his tail.

"I'm able to roll in a mile and half behind him and start shooting," he aid.

The next sequence of events happened very fast.

Pitts was so close to the MiG's exhaust that his first shot was a heat-seeking Sidewinder. But the Iraqi decoyed it with flares.

Gaining on the Iraqi, he fired a Sparrow, but it didn't explode. The Iraqi didn't try any evasive maneuvers. He just kept running straight and level north—still very low, his exhaust still beckoning.

Pitts shot another Sidewinder. The Iraqi decoyed it with flares again. Pitts was getting frustrated. Any closer and he'd be out of missile envelope and have to go to guns.

He fired a fourth missile, another Sparrow.

Meanwhile, up above, Tollini, now functioning as Pitts's wingman, had been watching and decided he'd better jump in and help. He dove toward the fight and fired a Sidewinder of his own at the fleeing Foxbat. But before it got there, Pitt's final Sparrow either went up the Foxbat's tailpipe or right near it, and exploded, causing a small fireball.

"It was like a sparkler," he said.

Tollini's missile than impacted the fireball.

The MiG stayed relatively intact but went down into clouds. Pitts saw the canopy come off and the "explosion" as the pilot's ejection seat fired out. But he didn't see a parachute because "I know the second guy is still out there and I immediately start looking for him."

Both he and Tollini blew through the merge, Pitts being lowest and suddenly realizing he was too low—three hundred feet on his altimeter. "I actually sink into the clouds a bit as I'm climbing out. That scared me. I got so wrapped up in shooting him I forgot how low we were. I could have very easily hit the ground."

Coming back up, pointing west, he spotted the second Foxbat. It was coming east, about five miles in front of them, going belly up as it tried to turn north in front of them and run, Pitts speculated.

Kelk and Williams, low on fuel, had already left. Tollini, who had his radar on "auto guns" now, didn't visually see the bandit until Pitts called him out, but the "auto guns" setting would have automatically locked the Iraqi anyway.

First, Tollini fired a Sidewinder. It was decoyed with flares.

Chasing in afterburner, he fired a Sparrow. The radar missile hit, disintegrating the MiG-25.

These were the ninth and tenth Allied air-to-air kills of the war.

"It wasn't what you'd call pretty," said Pitts about the botched BVR, the well-executed "beam" defense that could have been a deathly problem had the Iraqi pilots been well trained. "We let them get too close."

But they'd won—which was the only viable outcome in wartime air-to-air competition. As dogfight instructors like to say, there are no points for second place.

After the war, Pitts, reflecting, also said he hoped the Iraqi pilot he'd shot had not been killed. "I'll tell you why," he said. "We spent a lot of time up there watching airplanes run away from us. I felt like these two Foxbats actually tried to engage us. I've got to give them credit for that. At least these two actually tried to protect their homeland."

But now, right after the fight, running so long on afterburner, they were both nearly out of gas, alone in hostile airspace with at least two MiG-29s in the area and their tankers way south of the border.

Even if they got to the border—which, given the circumstances, was by no means a given—they would still have a long way to go.

When Tollini's four-ship had been tanking earlier, he had called Rodriguez, who was on his AWACS protective CAP, and asked if he and Underhill would cover them when they came out.

"Citgo's" radars would be pointed back toward the south as they egressed. They needed Rodriguez and Underhill to sweep their tails to make sure no one snuck up on them.

So when Rodriguez heard "Citgo" was engaging, and Kelk and Williams were already leaving, he and Underhill sped north.

They crossed the border at approximately twenty-five thousand feet and picked up two bandits roughly sixty miles northeast. The bandits appeared to be threatening "Citgo." Rodriguez and Underhill started after them.

At first they ran into an unexpected problem.

Locking the bandits up at around forty miles, they started getting "friendly" returns on their IFF receivers behind the bandits.

The returns confused them.

Were they mistakenly targeting Coalition airplanes?

Unknown to them, the replies were from a navy strike group egressing back across northern Iraq after a raid in the east. For whatever reason, the fact of the navy's presence had not been relayed to the central sector AWACS with which Rodriguez and Underhill were in contact.

In any case, before the bandits came into range, they suddenly turned back in the direction they'd come from and retreated into a SAM belt. Rodriguez knew that they were no longer a threat to "Citgo" and decided not to pursue them into the dangerous area.

Almost at the same time they broke their locks on the bandits, AWACS radioed, "Contact 330 13," said Underhill. The call meant that probable new bandits were bearing in on them from the left, roughly perpendicular to their course—and just thirteen miles away!

At that distance, depending on the type and capability of aircraft, the contacts could have already shot missiles at the Eagles.

"They were real close and dangerous," said Underhill, who, like Rodriguez, was not only startled and apprehensive to hear the call but angry that it had come so late.

The Eagles dumped their auxiliary tanks and made hard, multi-G left turns into the bogeys. Because of their relative positions, as they straightened out, Rodriguez ended up in front, Underhill a mile or two behind him.

The minute he straightened out, Rodriguez got a lock at eight miles, but he could not get AWACS to confirm that the contact was a bandit.

He was closing fast, trying to get a visual identification. His warning gear wasn't indicating that the bogey had shot a missile at him, but, given the shock of the engagement, he didn't trust it. He wrenched a "beaming" maneuver out left and started streaking perpendicular to both lines of flight (theirs and the bogeys'), hoping to break the lock of any oncoming missile.

"Almost simultaneously," said Underhill, AWACS finally identified the contact as "hostile."

Later, piecing everything together with Tollini's four-ship, they decided that these were the same two MiG-29s that "Citgo" had chased and then "stiff-armed" earlier. Apparently—because their line of flight would have taken them eventually to the rear of the retreating "Citgo"—the Fulcrums were returning for a sneak shot.

But all Underhill knew at this second was that he had a bad guy bearing down on him and time was running out.

"Almost before AWACS had the word *hostile* out, I fired," he said.

The Sparrow went right over the beaming Rodriguez—which scared Underhill, because they'd never had to shoot in such close proximity in practice. But he immediately turned his eyes away to find and reposition with Rodriguez—as was his job as wingman—and missed the missile's impact.

Rodriguez, still running perpendicular, saw the fireball. But by the time Underhill turned back for a glimpse—perhaps ten seconds later—all he saw was a "brown cloud. No large pieces. It had just disintegrated. I expected to see like half of an airplane spiraling down."

Rodriguez also saw a parachute, according to Underhill, but neither of them had time to look further because AWACS immediately called the second bandit.

He was back in the direction of the disintegrated leader.

Both of them, now at the extension of Rodriguez's ninety-degree "beam" maneuver, pitched back to face the trailer.

"I pick him up visually," said Rodriguez. "He's about a seven- or eight-mile 'tallyho' [visual sighting]."

They spread out, bracketing the bandit, putting him in a kind of pincer, both coming head-on, trying to get a visual identification, preparing to shoot, but ready to turn should the onrushing bandit try a defensive maneuver or shoot first.

Underhill was locked, ready to fire at the sunlighted silhouette rocketing toward them, but suddenly thought it was an F-15.

"I'm five miles away and I get a little friendly return on my air-to-air interrogator," he said. He was never able to figure out why, but "as similar as the airplanes look, I just was not confident enough to shoot the guy."

But as they blew through the merge—the bandit being closer to Rodriguez than Underhill, and not obstructed by light from the sun—Rodriguez positively identified it as a MiG-29 and called that he would engage.

Behind them now, the MiG sliced downward, starting a turn circle parallel with the horizon. Rodriguez pitched back by initially going up and then slicing back down beneath the bandit's turn circle—getting in a position to cut the angle on him.

Underhill zoomed up to support Rodriguez.

In effect, they again had the MiG bracketed—Underhill high, Rodriguez low—both chasing him.

The MiG dove in his turn circle. Rodriguez dove with him, slicing corners, pulling to within three thousand feet. At one point, he got so close that he felt he could see the Iraqi pilot's face as the Iraqi fleetingly looked back.

"You know what he's thinking because you've been there before," he said. "He's looking over his shoulder and he sees us both and he knows that whichever way he goes, one of us is going to get him."

The MiG was now at the bottom of its first turn circle, at only two thousand feet altitude, Rodriguez, at about the same altitude, pressing. The Fulcrum pilot rolled inverted in preparation for pulling downward into another turn circle that he hoped would allow him to exit the opposite way.

The maneuver is called a split-S, and Rodriguez, recognizing it, knew the bandit didn't have enough altitude left to complete it.

Rodriguez went up. If the Iraqi was faking, and was going to right himself and try something else, Rodriguez or Underhill would be waiting for him.

But he wasn't faking. He pulled through, curling downward and smashing into the desert.

Same as a shootdown.

It was the only true turning fight of the war, and it left Rodriguez a MiG killer—he and Underhill notching approximately, if not precisely, the thirteenth and fourteenth Coalition air-to-air victories of the war.

But neither was gloating. They were in trouble. The fight had taken almost all their gas, and AWACS was again calling bandits heading for them—the same two they'd chased into the SAM belt earlier.

Like Tollini's "Citgo" before them, they were far from the tankers. They dropped low—five hundred feet—in order to present confusing "ground clutter" for any enemy radars trying to target them and started streaking south in afterburner, broadcasting what they were doing.

Because they weren't coming out at the normal high, safe (deconflicted) altitudes, they wanted all friendlies to know they weren't enemy.

But Saudi F-15s were also in the area, and they "didn't have the capabilities we have to interrogate friendlies," said Rodriguez. "They're in their CAP and they are actually spiking [Underhill]. . . . I keep telling AWACS to tell those guys to get away from us."

"Citgo" was lucky.

Hearing the four-ship's calls for gas, several tanker commanders decided to take a chance. Although they were unarmed, they gunned their ships north to meet Tollini's Eagles almost at the border.

"They did a great job," said Pitts. "At that point in the war it was pretty scary for them to get that close."

Keeping as quiet on their radios as they could, the four-ship started mating. Still excited from the fight, Pitts said he "was shaking so bad I couldn't even stay on the boom of the tanker on the first try."

But he finally made it and began taking the needed gas.

Then, out of the silence, came Rodriguez's and Underhill's calls.

They were even lower on fuel than "Citgo."

Pitts had his radio on a different frequency, so he didn't know what was happening, but all of a sudden his tanker started "trying to shake me," he said. "I couldn't figure out why."

He got bumped as Underhill jumped on with barely fifteen hundred pounds—five to ten minutes before flameout.

They'd finally all made it, although each one of them counted himself lucky.

"If they had known what they were doing," said Rodriguez of the two Iraqis he and his wingman had shot down, "they could have had our asses real easy."

Coming in from the side like they did, the Iraqis could have shot them BVR. "We had our radars pointed forward and had no SA on them."

Later, he confronted the AWACS controller for not letting them know sooner. "He knew who I was when he saw me walk into the office," he said. "Probably from his standpoint, he was eating inside a lot more than I was, knowing one day I'd walk through that door."

The controller wasn't as experienced as some of the others, said Rodriguez, and told Rodriguez, in effect, that he'd made a mistake. After a "lengthy discussion on how, when he sits up there a hundred miles away from everything, fat, dumb, and happy, [he should never] take his eyes off the scope," Rodriguez said he considered it over.

That night, according to an observer, they closed the doors of their quarters and celebrated "with a little bit of bootleg Jack Daniels."

19

BY THE FOURTH DAY of Desert Storm, some say sooner, the battle for the Iraqi skies—the fighter air war—had largely been won.

There would be more engagements, but they were basically turkey shoots—Allied Fighters chasing fleeing Iraqi fighters and missiling the ones they caught.

Iraqi pilots did not challenge again.

"I think the first two days did it," Graeter told me. "The F-1s were supposed to carry their top pilots. I think a combination of launching the F-1s and MiG-29s, and having only half of them come back, pretty much put them in a mind-set that they didn't want to mess with us."

Other pilots said the same thing.

The war's initial engagements, of which the 58th had over half, turned the tide.

And winning control of the skies basically meant winning the war, because with the ability to fly and bomb wherever and whenever they wanted, the Allies dominated. Allied forces—air, sea, and land—were free from aerial harassment. The Iraqis had no effective counterpunch to the bombing or troop movements, no ability to repel a strong, smart, and relentless attacker.

Victory, although still to be hard fought, was just a matter of time.

But that didn't mean continuing to fly in the war wasn't dangerous. In fact, the scariest moments for many fighter pilots were still ahead.

Snodgrass, for instance, lost an engine on his Tomcat during a January 21 night sweep in support of a strike near Baghdad.

It started with a SAM bursting out of the clouds right below him. He turned hard into it and beat the missile, which exploded behind and above him. But the sudden, high-G, wrenching turn caused the Tomcat to depart controlled flight, which was followed quickly by a flameout (or stoppage) of his left engine, which would leave him only the right engine and, consequently, underpowered.

Suddenly, he was in trouble.

The departure was something he'd almost expected, given the sudden wrenching turn. By releasing the stick, he was able to neutralize the instability and get the Tomcat flying again. But relighting the dead engine normally required a lengthy dive to get air flowing back through it, and as they dove uncontrollably into the same cloud the SAM had come out of, he realized they were heading straight for a wall of triple-A.

"I saw some stuff that was blowing up," he said. "It was barrage fire, not guided. But it was just glowing all over down there, and then the clouds at night, the depth perception is very difficult. It might have been a half mile away, but it looked like it was right on my wing tip."

It was an artillery maelstrom he and his backseater, Kenny Floyd, were diving toward, and the thought of colliding with it was as unsettling to him as any thought he'd ever had in the air.

Rather than continue to try to restart the engine in the dive, he wrenched the crippled F-14 almost ninety degrees, to level flight, losing considerable speed in the process, and therefore becoming vulnerable to Iraqi fighters—one of which, according th their initial cockpit indications, was now on their nose and threatening.

They had dived from a relatively safe thirty thousand feet to seventeen thousand feet, and gone from 600 knots to a creeping 230. They were more accessible not only to any MiGs, but also to more SAMs and readjusting triple-A.

"That's when I really got antsy," he said.

He wanted to speed out as soon as possible, but with only the one engine he didn't want to ignite afterburner because it might make him look like a single-engine Iraqi F-1. AWACS was calling bandits, and other Coalition fighters in the area might mistakenly shoot him.

And then there was the bandit stalking them.

"I wasn't so threatened by that," he said. In fact, this was the chance to get the MiG that had always eluded him. "What I didn't want to do was have to go all the way home on one engine, you know, two hundred and fifty knots."

They'd completed the sweep and he'd be the lone straggler.

He went to minimum burner and crept out, trying to refire the engine and preparing to shoot at the bandit when it came into range. It turned out, however, that the bandit was a friendly, and on the fourth relight try the second engine ignited.

They zoomed away.

Back on the *Saratoga*, Nick Mongillo, although now a MiG killer, struggled with "strange feelings" he had about the war.

"I'm in a situation where I could die very quickly," he wrote in his journal on January 23. "I could be shot down by SAMs or bogeys. Killed or interned as a POW. With all this, I still welcome the flights, the challenge, the chance to shoot down another bogey. I'm not sadistic but why do I want to go. . . . It's almost scary. . . . I have a family yet I'm laying it on the line and at times enjoying the risk. Crazy!!"

He thought of Scott Speicher—"his friendly joking manner. A young father who has two kids—children who will probably be fatherless. I fear the worst but still hope. How can I look forward to the challenge in such a light? I wish it would all end tomorrow. I wonder if we are really hurting Iraq. Are our raids successful?"

Fighter pilots in the Vietnam War had had the same feelings. For some, the challenge—putting themselves in harm's way to see how they would perform—was at the heart of their desire to fly fighters.

To a few in Vietnam, testing themselves, feeling the thrills of that testing, had become almost a lust.

On January 26, Draeger and Rodriguez got their second kills; Schiavi his first. It was a textbook offensive mission incorporating BVR kills, and probably will be taught as such at Nellis, Topgun, and elsewhere for years to come.

Draeger led it. They were guarding an AWACS plane, but the air threat had so diminished by then that AWACS officials felt secure in letting the Eagles go north to try to shoot some bandits AWACS had detected when Draeger requested it.

The bandits were nearly 120 miles north of the four-ship, lifting off from H-2 and trying to flee east, presumably to Iran. Since the bandits' route would take them across Iraq's northern portions, Draeger knew it would be hard to catch them, but his four-ship had already been CAPing for several hours and nothing else in Iraq was flying.

"It was the only game in town," he is quoted by the air force as saying, "so I figured we might as well go find it."

That was the first plus. Like Rodriguez on the day of his first kill, Draeger was looking for opportunities. He could have stayed in the CAP, but he took a mission that others might have disregarded, or might not even have recognized as an opportunity.

The fleeing bandits proved too fast and far.

They escaped.

But as the four-ship turned back, AWACS called four more bandits rising from H-2, and this time the four-ship was between Iran and the bandits taking off, almost parallel with H-2. And once they'd turned west toward the bandits, who were coming east, right at them, they were close enough—about eighty miles away—to start targeting.

Now for the prosecution.

The bandits were low in two groups, one group roughly behind the other, flying fast. The Eagles formed a wall and started sorting as to who would shoot whom. In order not to alert the Iraqis to their presence—in case they didn't know already—Draeger, as they got closer, had his Eagles lock only fleetingly. The bandits didn't appear to have a clue about what was happening.

The weather that midday was extremely cloudy, so the Eagles didn't figure to ever get a look at their prey. The shooting would be BVR.

Radar would be their eyes.

At about forty miles, one of the bandits turned around and went back to H-2.

That left three.

At thirty miles, the Eagles dropped their tanks in unison, started bearing in so fast that Rodriguez remembers the condensation trails streaking off their wings.

"It was a pretty awesome sight," he said.

The low-flying Iraqi pilots were following a highway out of H-2 that ran roughly northeast over Baghdad and into Iran. They never gave indications they knew anything was about to happen.

Draeger shot at the lead bandit from fifteen miles away; Schiavi, Rodriguez, and Bruce Till, the fourth pilot in the four-ship, shot from approximately thirteen miles away.

Everybody knew whom to hit and when.

As they were waiting for cockpit indications of success, a hole in the weather opened and, ahead and below, at about seven miles, they suddenly saw the bandits—three brown-and-green-camouflaged MiG-23s racing forward, the missiles the Eagles had shot rocketing toward their noses.

Till's was the last to reach one of the fireballs, so he wasn't credited.

"I remember this [kill] in extreme detail," said Rodriguez, "because I had the patience and . . . my heart rate wasn't as high as on the first. . . . Everybody saw the same picture on the radar. Everybody sanitized their areas of responsibility, melded their radars at the right time . . . then it was just a matter of whether they knew we were there, if they were going to do any kind of reactions, and whether the missiles worked properly."

They did, and the relieved four-ship left three smoking crashes in the desert sand—none of the Iraqi pilots, to their knowledge, getting out alive.

Moving from the "fog of war" of the first days, the 58th's Eagles were now more seasoned and performing with professional precision—a "ballet of destruction," one pilot called it.

Back on the *Saratoga*, the twenty-sixth was a "no fly day in Gas Alley," wrote Mongillo. "[Lieutenant Commander] Beamer, XO of [Topgun], came down. . . . He interviewed me and [Fox] on our MiG kills and viewed our [HUD] tapes. . . . Strike is coming up tomorrow. . . . I'd love to get more kills but really doubt it. One's much better than none and—I should have two but missed radio calls on the first day."

On the twenty-seventh, two F-15 pilots from Bitburg—Captains

Jay "Opie" Denney and Ben "Coma" Powell of the 53rd Squadron—
chased and shot down four fleeing Iraqi fighters; three MiG-23s
and an F-1. Bitburg had gotten two other kills on January 19
when Lieutenant David Svenden, Jr., and Captain David Prather
had each downed an F-1.

With the exception of Tate's one kill the first night, and the
navy's two kills the first day, Bitburg Eagle pilots were the only
U.S. fighter pilots to have shot down enemy planes up to the
twenty-seventh.

On the twenty-eighth, another Bitburg Eagle pilot, Captain
Donald Watrous of the 32nd Squadron, downed a MiG-23.

But on the twenty-ninth, a 58th pilot got still another.

Captain Dave Rose, a Texas A&M graduate, was actually a
member of the 60th Tactical Fighter Squadron, which was in the
same wing, the 33rd, as the 58th. But because of his experience,
which included fourteen hundred Eagle hours and two years of
flying at Bitburg, he was substituted for a newly arrived pilot
when the 58th went to Saudi.

A ringer, one might say.

Rose's kill was notable for its location—in the extreme northeast of Iraq above Baghdad, far from the southern border and its
support—and for the fact that he chose to visually identify his
target before shooting it, although he could have taken the safer
BVR shot.

With virtual rule of the skies, it was the first time a 58th four-
ship had gone that far north. Upon arrival, because it was such a
long trip, the four-ship split up, two F-15s performing "roving
CAPs," which were loose, nonorbit routes, and the other two going back to the border for more gas.

It was the turn of Rose and his wingman, Captain Kevin Gallager, to rove. Gallager got a radar contact some sixty miles away,
which Rose, leading the two-ship, quickly found, too.

They started the intercept.

Because the AWACS plane was so far away—down south, on
the Kuwait-Iraq border—it could not confirm the bandit status
that both Gallager and Rose were getting from their cockpit electronics, which probably included IFF, NCTR (a noncooperative
method reading the target's jet engine revolutions), and, perhaps,
a third, classified method. Rose already had enough confirmation
(the exact nature of which is still classified) to shoot BVR, but

"we hadn't had a friendly shootdown yet," he said, and decided to visually identify the target in order to be sure.

The two F-15s streaked closer to the lone target.

It was a good thing they had not shot. Midway in the intercept, Rose and Gallager had been startled to pick up several Bitburg Eagles on their radars whom they had not been told would be operating in the area.

They could have targeted the Eagles.

It shook them, and further convinced Rose they couldn't shoot until they'd gotten close enough to take a look at the bandit to make sure.

"He could have shot me BVR," said Rose about the bandit, but "the last thing you want to do is shoot a friendly."

He approached from the rear and it turned out to be a MiG-23, low and fast. He shot a Sparrow that exploded "right in the center of the fuselage," causing a "pretty big fireball," which slammed the MiG into the dirt, killing the pilot.

"It's a tough business," he said of his thoughts about the dead Iraqi. "It's shoot or be shot. That's why war is not good."

Mongillo was having similar thoughts. On January 29, he wrote: "Tomorrow is more destruction and death for Iraq. We bomb the Republican Guard. I hope it saves American lives and brings the war to an end quickly. I still don't like the idea of it, but I have a job to do. God will judge us all when it's over. I long to see my family. Nightly, I stare at my daughter's pictures. I want to go home."

And on the night of January 31: "Today we flew a 17-Hornet strike to Kuwait. A massive gaggle with each aircraft holding 5 to 6 MK-83s [thousand-pound bombs]. We had a grid box to bomb. You could see the little shoebox-shaped patterns in the sand . . . with tanks or buildings. We bombed from a roll in at [35,000 feet], pickled [dropped] at [25,000]. What an ugly job. Who knows how much death and destruction we bestowed on them.

"Skirmishes have started on the front. Marines have died. It's only going to get worse. Whose parents in the states have heard the news and wonder if it's their son? What wife lost a husband? What child will be fatherless? . . . Man is the most destructive thing this earth has seen. He destroys everything. The Persian Gulf is one big oil slick. When will mankind learn other ways other than death and destruction? I don't have the answer. . . .

The other scare tonight is of chemical weapons. Awful weapons—but is any death machine or tool a good one?

"What kind of world will my children grow up in? Will there still be war? Will our earth be polluted? Will our species become extinct? Will crime and drugs become even a bigger part of our civilization? . . . I want to go home and be with my family. I want to be there to protect them from the harshness of this world. I want to be there because they are not as strong as me or as mean at times. The sound of jets are overhead as they land on the carrier. Another mission returning—how many more will there be?"

But by February 11, Mongillo, referring to himself and the other pilots as "a different breed," was again "welcoming the challenge" of flying in combat. At heart he was a warrior, and, later, would ask me to be sure and say he backed the war.

One of the pilots I'd interviewed at Nellis was Captain Todd Denning, a tall, big-boned instructor at the F-16 Fighter Weapons School. While he was unassuming and helpful sitting and talking with me, he said his wife calls him "borderline psychotic" because of an innate aggressiveness he said he'd always had.

"I will get mad and I will get irritated at small things," he said, "mainly because I like to feel I am in total control of my environment and I must be aggressive to do that. When someone tends to try and screw up my environment that makes me mad and it makes me focus more in trying to get control of my environment."

It's a trait common to fighter pilots. When chaos reigns, the good ones tend to steel, get calmer, and actually do better than had things remained placid.

This trait is probably the real origin of the phrase "Don't make him mad."

Being an F-16 driver, Denning, who had grown up in Dade County, Florida, where his father was an Eastern Airlines pilot, said he considered himself an "all-around fighter pilot with a mission primarily aimed at bombing enemy targets" as well as shooting MiGs. And he wanted very badly to test himself in combat.

In the first few days of February, he got his wish.

Attached to General Glosson's planning staff, he was sent on four spur-of-the-moment combat sorties, the third of which, around February 3 or 4, brought out that innate aggressiveness and answered at least some of the questions he had about how he would perform.

After refueling under rushed circumstances from an earlier mission, his four-ship flew north. Not mentioning exactly what the target was, he wrote in his journal that it was "evidently something the Republican Guard wanted to protect [because we] started seeing airbursts below us before the first roll in. . . . As I followed the lead . . . white 57mm airbursts started appearing at my right 1 o'clock for about 200–300 feet."

He hit afterburner and zoomed out, the triple-A bursting first above him and then below as the Iraqi gunners tried to adjust.

He got high enough to get away and then he got mad.

"I . . . drove to line up for an attack out of the sun," he wrote. "Now that I knew they were aiming at me, it only strengthened my resolve to put bombs on the target. Fear was not part of the equation at the moment. I made a pass on a AAA site that would make a Gunsmoker [bombing competition participant] proud but on recovery, came out of the sun and into a real hornet's nest."

He was in trouble again.

The briefed maneuver at that point was to turn left ninety degrees, which was how the others had exited. But the Iraqi gunners had seen the others do it and were already laying bursts where they anticipated he'd go.

Instead, he turned right, only to see "the scariest part of the sortie—air bursts following me and catching up. I put my training to work and checked left for 10 seconds then continued right. The airbursts broke off into a random pattern and then quit as I got above [20,000 feet]."

Below him was a smoking patch of sky that should have been his grave.

It wasn't until he was seventy miles away, he wrote, that "the adrenaline finally made me go a little stupid. The rest of the way home [415 miles] I thought about those tracers and how it might feel if one went whistling up your asshole. I reasoned after about thirty minutes that that would be a point of momentary interest and wasn't worth thinking about.

"I feel like today I earned that gold star."

Several more Bitburg pilots got kills, and then, on February 7, the 58th scored three more enemy planes.

It was up north of Baghdad again on a two-ship CAP to prevent Iraqis from escaping to Iran. Thirty-third Tactical Fighter Wing Commander Colonel Rick Parsons, a Vietnam veteran, and his wingman, Captain Tony Murphy, a twenty-nine-year-old 58th pilot from Grant's Pass, Oregon, chased down two groups of fleeing Iraqis, downing three supersonic Sukhoi-17s, Murphy getting credit for two of the Fitters and Parsons one.

Murphy's kills brought the Eglin squadron's total to sixteen confirmed—more than half of the thirty air-to-air kills of Iraqi fighters made by U.S. fighter pilots through the end of February, when the war ended. The final official Coalition air-to-air total was usually quoted as thirty-five kills to zero, sometimes thirty-nine to zero. But both those higher figures included relatively defenseless helicopter shootings, two kills by a Saudi fighter pilot, and did not include the apparent shootdown of Scott Speicher as the United States's only air-to-air loss.

But with or without one loss, thirty or higher victories to zero or one is a remarkable score and helps shed light on why Israeli kill ratios are often so one-sided. The Arabs, although flying some comparable airplanes, are not as well trained, or, it appears, imbued with the same fighting spirit as their Western counterparts.

One wonders when America's enemies are going to get the picture that training, knowledge of one's opponent as well as of one's own machine, and spirit—not just technology—are the crucial factors in determining who wins in aerial combat.

I hope it will be never, and America will continue to prevail.

Even as they were mounting victories, making other F-15 units in Saudi jealous and mad because of their seeming luck and prowess, members of the 58th were telephoning Paco Geisler in Iceland to thank him for what he'd taught them and telling him they wished he was there.

"The guys started calling me the first night," Paco told me when I found him at the air force war college in Montgomery, Alabama, where he was taking career courses after Iceland and the war. They told him they wished he was still their CO, he said. "I told them, I appreciate talking to you but . . . you need to quit whining. Just do your job. Make me proud."

He was still angry that a promotion and air force rotation had made him miss out on going to war, especially leading the 58th in its record-making, award-winning deployment. But "the thing that really impressed me," he said, "was one day I talked to the DO [deputy commander of operations] at Eglin [Tuna Hardy] . . . a MiG killer in Vietnam, old Aggressor buddy of mine. . . . He called me in Iceland and I said, What's the count? He said, Well, I think you got twelve. I said, Goddamn, that's really good. He goes, Yeah, your guys are doing good. Well, they're not my guys. He goes, Yeah, they are. You trained 'em. . . . That made me feel good."

The response to my question was no reflection on the new CO, it appeared to me, just Geisler's honest response to a roll of the dice that still hurt. And as reflected in the squadron's early successes, 58th members repeatedly complimented the new CO for being tactically smart in designating the younger but highly capable weapons officers to lead in the crucial first sweeps.

"It started with Paco Geisler," said Magill, echoing others about how they did so well. "He set the pace for not accepting anything less than highly trained tactical aviators. . . . If you have a strong tactical leader, then you're going to have strong, competent aviators. That was the key to success."

That, and a little luck.

When the 58th got back to the States and heard Geisler was back from Iceland, they arranged a party for him.

"They get in touch with me and they want me to come out to the squadron bar that first Friday night that I'm back," he said. "They're all excited to see me and that kind of stuff, and the wives are going to come out and everything."

But he didn't go.

"I said, That's in the past. It's not my squadron. If I go out there and sit around in the bar and throw glasses and drink and shit, that's what we used to do. It's just reliving the past. They need to go forward."

But they pressured him. So the second Friday night, he went and "we had a hell of a reunion. . . . I was able to say, It's over, guys. I'm leaving. It's over. And that was it."

But there was one more thing to do.

When he left the first time, he'd presented the squadron with a bottle of authentic Russian vodka. With it was a plaque with an inscription on the bottom, saying, "To the first Gorilla to kill a MiG."

All the MiG killers had had their glasses by the time they'd returned from Saudi, but there was still one shot left.

They'd saved it for Paco. Several of them were religious men, and not so unlike the fraternity at the Last Supper; he downed the last shot in what amounted to a ritual fighter pilot good-bye.

AFTERMATH

ONE DAY A FRIEND, knowing I was writing this book, passed to me an article quoting Vietnam War ace Bill Driscoll in the alumni magazine of Stonehill College, Driscoll's alma mater. Driscoll, an F-4 backseater, still lectures at Topgun. What he was quoted in the article as saying about fighter pilots and successful air fighting deserves paraphrasing:

Dogfighting is a mix of tension, fear, and unbearable pressure. All participants know that the loser is probably going to die in a fiery explosion. Preparation, confidence, steel nerves, and aggressiveness will enable the winner to capitalize on the loser's mistakes, which is usually the way the winner is determined.

The successful fighter pilot must *want* to engage the enemy in life-or-death combat—not just be a flier—and truly *believe* that he can win. Talent is nice, but hard work and commitment can elevate pilots of even average ability to ace status, which brought Driscoll, in the article, to the character of fighter pilots—the reason I like them in this era of so much crime, false heroes, and hypocritical self-serving agendas:

Naval aviators, especially those who make it to Topgun, are intensely motivated, disciplined, focused, and prepared. Most important, they have the cool and confidence to prevail over almost any problem they encounter.

We need such people in this society.

Ken Crandell, a Vietnam veteran, who, at the time I spoke to him, was CO of the F-14 RAG at Oceana and therefore had a chance to see new fighter pilots coming in as a group, said they'd changed over the years. "Not so much light-your-hair-on-fire types," he said, "more Yuppie." Their instructors, too, I had noticed, were more likely now to be driving BMWs than motorcycles or Corvettes, as they had in the 1960s or 1970s, and were sometimes more interested in tending to their financial portfolios than going to the club on Friday nights.

But in their essence, in my opinion, fighter pilots have not really changed. The good ones are still the dedicated, confident, goal-oriented, challenge-seeking individuals who have been flying fighters since World War I.

"Unadulterated overachievers," Driscoll calls them.

Sure, sometimes their egos and their selfishness destroy marriages and other relationships by subordinating everything in their lives to that great high of roaring off in a "whop-ass machine and whomping ass," as one of them described it. And some of them meet with unhappy endings, like Steve Tate, whom I was sorry to hear had left the air force shortly after returning from Desert Storm because he was accused by his superiors—falsely he says—of DUI and fraternizing with enlisted girls.

But the great majority of the good ones are like most of the men I met researching this book—talented, intelligent, pushing themselves to the brink to succeed, caring as much about their responsibilities as themselves, and loathing war while at the same time wanting it as their crucible. They are God-fearing and trusting in the sense that they feel that someone watches over them and that not everything they've encountered in their unique lives can be explained by a tangible fact, or their own prowess.

Who could not admire them, for they live daily with danger and through hard work, courage, and skill consistently prevail. And their purpose is high, however tainted it may be with the wish for personal glory or achievement.

They are protectors and explorers, men who challenge the darkness and dark forces for a cause, which most of them believe is righteous. And if they don't, they often challenge out of a sense of duty, which is a rare commodity in our country today.

And they have fun, which must give their lives a sense of fulfillment and satisfaction all of us strive for.

Fighter pilots—at least the good ones—are the inheritors of our country's Wild West tradition; the good gunslingers, the Wyatt Earps and Doc Holidays, of our modern era; men we depend on when trouble calls but forget about when trouble is gone.

The country is lucky to have them and, I hope, will enable them to stay strong and ready. Inevitably, as we move from war and clearly defined threats, we cut the very resources that keep fighter pilots at the edge of their game—the daily training and honing they need so badly. Technology, as so many instant pundits wrongly think, is not the most important ingredient in a successful air war, especially dogfights.

The training of the pilot is.

Already the air force has eliminated its Aggressor squadrons; the navy has eliminated its Adversaries. If the trend of cutting back on training continues, we are in for a rude awakening. As when the F-15 Eagles accidentally shot down two American helicopters over Iraq, we will gasp at the consequences.

There was a breakdown there, and I can't help thinking it was due to the cutbacks in training.

Perhaps the most impressive statistic that came out of Desert Storm was the fact that, despite the numerous chances for such fratricide in that war, there was not a single air-to-air shootdown of a friendly by U.S. fighter pilots.

As this book reveals, that was not an accident. It was the result of training and attitude. The fighter pilots in Desert Storm were about as good as fighter pilots can be—honed that way by their incessant training. They will remain that way only if they are allowed to continue the levels of training they maintained in the 1970s and 1980s.

But most probably, what will happen—as has always happened between wars—is that the good ones, given their hot machines, will just go off and fight on their own, regardless of resources or regulations, and then when their skills are needed—

when the next war comes along and we come hat in hand begging to be saved—they'll be the resource that turns it around.

We won't hear about it for a long time because it will be top-secret. But it'll happen.

I hope it won't be too late.

Check six.

GLOSSARY

A-6—Intruder. Two-seat, all-weather navy attack plane with distinct bubble canopy. Introduced in the Vietnam era. Variations of it have been used for refueling and electronic warfare. Electronic warfare version is called Prowler.

A-7—Single-seat attack bomber used by both the navy and air force. Entered service during the Vietnam War. Made by Vought and called Corsair II.

ACM—Air combat maneuvering, also called dogfighting.

AIM-ACE—Cryptic acronym for lengthy, secret air tests and battles staged in 1976 and 1977 to evaluate dogfighting weapons and tactics for the future. The full name of the tests and air wars, conducted by select navy and air force pilots, was Air Combat Evaluation and Air Intercept Missile Evaluation. Also called AIMVAL-ACEVAL.

AIM-7—See *Sparrow*.

AIM-9—See *Sidewinder*.

All-aspect—Type of missile that can home on a target from almost any direction, not just the rear.

Atoll—Soviet-made heat-seeking air-to-air missile generally considered a copy of and inferior to the American Sidewinder. Also called an AA-2. There are various upgraded versions.

AWACS—Airborne warning and control system, usually housed in an E-3 airplane. Used to spot enemy aircraft and generally be the eyes and ears for all aircraft in a battle area. Controllers mind the equipment and keep in touch with all airborne elements of the battle.

BFM—Basic fighter maneuvers used in dogfighting or ACM.

Bingo—Radio word used to signal that you have just enough fuel left to return to base.

Bogey—An unidentified airborne target that may be hostile, as opposed to a *bandit*, which is an identified enemy.

Bolter—Unsuccessful landing attempt on a carrier. Tailhook fails to engage arresting wires and the plane has to fly off for another try or landing elsewhere.

Break—A quick, maximum-G turn suddenly taken to avoid a missile or gun shot.

BVR—An acronym meaning beyond visual range and referring to the capability of an air-to-air missile. It can be shot at a target that cannot be seen by the shooter. Some BVR missiles can be shot one hundred miles from a target and still have a reasonable chance of hitting.

CAG—Carrier air group commander; World War II term still used, although carrier groups are now called wings.

CAP—Combat air patrol; a route or position in the air that enables fighters to do a specific job. There are several types of CAPs. A BARCAP positions fighters as a barrier between threats and an aircraft carrier. A MIGCAP gives them position from which to hunt and attack MiGs, and so on.

Check six—Fighter pilot lingo for "Watch your behind [the six o'clock position or rear of the airplane]."

Compartmentalization—Focusing only on the task at hand, especially in emergencies, when any loss of focus probably means panic and disaster.

Constant Peg—Secret U.S. Air Force program involving enemy aircraft.

F-8—Crusader, Vietnam-era single-seat fighter, also called the MiG Master.

FFARP—Fleet fighter ACM Readiness Program, mini-Topgun programs run by navy dogfight teaching units against operational squadrons in order to keep them up to speed.

Fitter—NATO designation for a Sukhoi-22.

Fox One—Code for having shot a radar missile, like a Sparrow.

Fox Two—Code for having shot a heat-seeking missile, like a Sidewinder.

Foxbat—NATO designation for a MiG-25 fighter-bomber. The plane itself is fast but not very maneuverable.

Foxhound—NATO designation for the high-speed, high-altitude MiG-31 interceptor.

FWS—Fighter Weapons School, the air force's elite school for fighter pilots.

G—A force of gravity exerted on the pilot or crewman of an airplane as it accelerates or turns. Although, at sea level, the force is literally 32.2 feet per second per second, it is roughly akin to body weight in the air. Thus three Gs is a force roughly three times a person's weight.

HARM—High-Speed Anti-Radar Missile, used by standoff aircraft to home in on radars being used against them.

HUD—Heads-up display of all the navigation and weapon information on the glass of the canopy in front of the pilot so he won't have to take his eyes off the target to find it.

IFF—Identification Friend or Foe; electronic system that broadcasts and receives special codes from aircraft identifying them as friendly. Conversely, if the aircraft in question is not responding with the proper code, it can be assumed to be foe.

IP—Instructor pilot; an air force term for a pilot who has reached a plateau in knowledge and ability in the airplane and can thus teach successful airfighting to others.

Jink—Erratic maneuvering in both the horizontal and vertical planes to present as unpredictable a target as possible.

JO—Junior officer.

Loose-deuce—Older term, used mostly in the navy, for two fighters flying together in mutual support. They fly roughly side by side with a maneuvering interval between. Either fighter can take lead depending on the position of the threat.

LSO—Landing signal officer. The officer-flier on the carrier deck who is directing the recovery.

Magic—French-made air-to-air heat-seeking missile with considerable capability. Many Third World countries have bought them for their jets.

MiG-25—See *Foxbat*.

Mirage—Nimble, French-built fighters designed by the Dassault-Breguet company. The most famous is the delta-winged Mirage III, which Israel used successfully in the 1967 war against Egypt. The later Mirage F1 did not have the delta wing, but the newest Mirage 2000, in service with many countries since 1983, does.

NAS—Naval air station.

Nugget—Junior aviator fresh out of training.

O'club—Officers' club.

Phoenix—Long-range radar missile first used by the F-14 Tomcat.

Pickle—Dropping bombs.

Pipper—The point on the gunsight put on the target in order to hit it.

RAG—Replacement air group, the navy's term for the unit that trains pilots in a certain aircraft.

Raghead—Derisive term for Arab person.

Red Flag—A multiday air war game at Nellis Air Force Base, Nevada, designed to show fighter and bomber crews what they will experience in a real war and how to deal with it. The exercises often involve many airplanes and include bombing targets and air-to-air fighting.

RIO—Radar intercept officer, one of two crewmen in a jet like an F-14 Tomcat. The RIO, also called the "backseater" in the navy, and "Wizzo" in the air force (for "weapons system officer"), usually works the radar while the pilot flies the plane.

ROE—Rules of engagement; predetermined by headquarters to govern a fighter pilot in a hostile encounter.

RTU—Replacement training unit; the squadron that trains pilots in the fighter they have been assigned just prior to their going to a squadron.

SA—Situational awareness; knowing what is going on around you in any piece of sky and being able to react successfully to it. Very critical in an air battle and needed in order to be good at dogfighting. Some of it can be learned but a lot of it is innate talent.

SAM—Surface-to-air missile, used to shoot down aircraft.

Sidewinder—Also called AIM-9; heat-seeking air-to-air missile of the Vietnam era that has been upgraded through many versions and is still used today, mostly in an all-aspect form. AIM stands for "air intercept missile."

Sparrow—Also called AIM-7; Vietnam-era air-to-air radar missile that has been upgraded and refined into a very reliable all-aspect weapon. Was used on most Gulf War air-to-air kills.

Strike U—Nickname for the navy's Strike Warfare Center at Fallon, Nevada, where fighter and bomber crews are taught how to conduct strikes in a coordinated or "integrated" manner. It is the latest of the service's air warfare schools and is similar to Red Flag at Nellis.

Sukhoi—Soviet aircraft designer-manufacturer, abbreviated SU, that made front-line fighters and bombers in the modern era, most notably the SU-17 Fitter, SU-24 Fencer, and the formidable SU-27 Flanker, which is considered by some to be even more deadly than the Russian-made MiG-29.

Trap—Landing on the carrier, derived from the fact that the aircraft tailhook "traps" a landing wire across the deck.

Topgun—Nickname for the navy's Fighter Weapons School, where fighter pilots and crews get graduate-level air-to-air training.

VF—Navy designation for a fighter squadron.

VID—"Visual identification," used mainly when referring to a pilot's ability to identify an enemy plane by eyesight.

Viper—Unofficial nickname most fighter pilots prefer for the F-16 Fighting Falcon.

XO—Executive officer; second in command of a squadron or other unit.

INDEX

313